Microsoft®

Windows 8 for the Over 50s

in Simple steps

Joli Ballew

Use your computer with confidence

Get to grips with practical computing tasks with minimal time, fuss and bother.

In Simple Steps guides guarantee immediate results. They tell you everything you need to know on a specific application; from the most essential tasks to master, to every activity you'll want to accomplish, through to solving the most common problems you'll encounter.

Helpful features

To build your confidence and help you to get the most out of your computer, practical hints, tips and shortcuts feature on every page:

ALERT: Explains and provides practical solutions to the most commonly encountered problems

HOT TIP: Time and effort saving shortcuts

SEE ALSO: Points you to other related tasks and information

DID YOU KNOW?
Additional features to explore

WHAT DOES THIS MEAN?
Jargon and technical terms explained in plain English

Practical. Simple. Fast.

Dedication:

For my over 50s friends, family and fans; I wrote this book especially for you!

Author's acknowledgements:

The older I get and the more books I write, the more people there are to thank and acknowledge. For this book specifically, that includes Steve Temblett, Robert Cottee and Melanie Carter, along with all the other people who worked behind the scenes to turn the words into pages, and the pages into books.

I would also like to thank my supportive family, including Jennifer, Andrew, Dad and Cosmo, as well as my extended family, including the mothers and grandmothers and step-grandmothers who all play a part. And finally, I'm thankful to my agent, Neil Salkind, who always encourages me, stands up for me and is my biggest fan. Everyone should have someone like that in their life.

Publisher's acknowledgements

We are grateful to the following for permission to reproduce copyright material:

All Twitter screenshots courtesy of Twitter, Inc.; all Facebook screenshots courtesy of Facebook, Inc.

In some cases we have been unable to trace the owners of copyright material, and we would appreciate any information that would enable us to do so.

in Simple steps

Contents at a glance

9 Stay in touch with others

10 View, navigate and share photos

11 View, manage and listen to music and media

12 Install hardware and software

13 Secure Windows 8

Top Ten Windows 8 Problems Solved

Contents

Top 10 Windows 8 Tips for the Over 50s

7 Surf the web with Internet Explorer

8 Set up and use Mail

9 Stay in touch with others

10 View, navigate and share photos

11 View, manage and listen to music and media

12 Install hardware and software

13 Secure Windows 8

Top 10 Windows 8 Problems Solved

Top 10 Windows 8 Tips for the Over 50s

Tip 1: Shut down your computer

Your Windows 8 computer will go to sleep after a specific amount of idle time. When this actually happens depends on several factors, including which power configuration you've selected and whether a tablet or laptop is plugged into the mains or is running on batteries. The sleep state is quite efficient and doesn't use much energy, so it's often okay to let the computer go to sleep instead of turning it off each time you're finished using it. However, there will be times when you want to turn the computer or tablet off completely.

1. Access the charms and click or tap Settings.
2. Click or tap Power.
3. Click or tap Shut down.

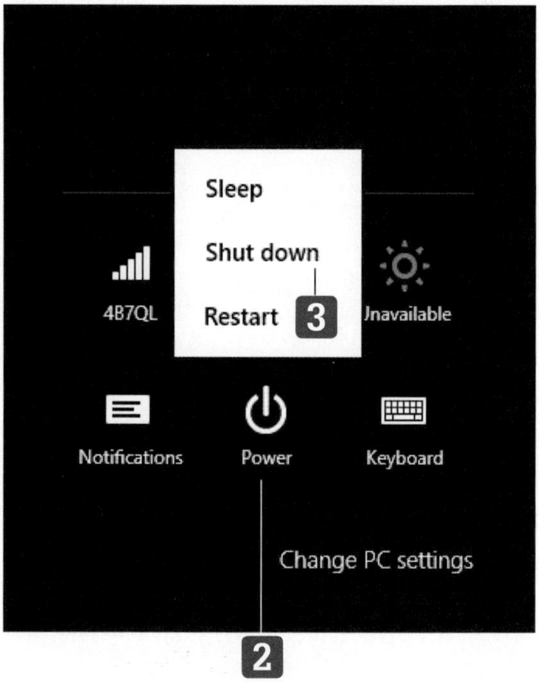

ALERT: During aeroplane takeoffs and landings, you'll be prompted to turn off all devices. You can't just let them go to sleep.

HOT TIP: If you are relocating a desktop computer, turn it off before you unplug it.

Tip 2: Turn live tiles off or on

Live tiles flip every second or two to show ever-changing information as it relates to the app. For example, the Photos tile will flip through your digital photos, and the Sports tile will show the latest sports headlines. If this is distracting, you can disable it for any or all live tiles.

1. At the Start screen, locate any live tile (you may not yet have any, and not all tiles are live).

2. Right-click the live tile if you want to enable or disable. Note that a tick appears by it.
3. Click Turn live tile off. (Alternatively, you can opt to turn a live tile on.)
4. Repeat as desired.

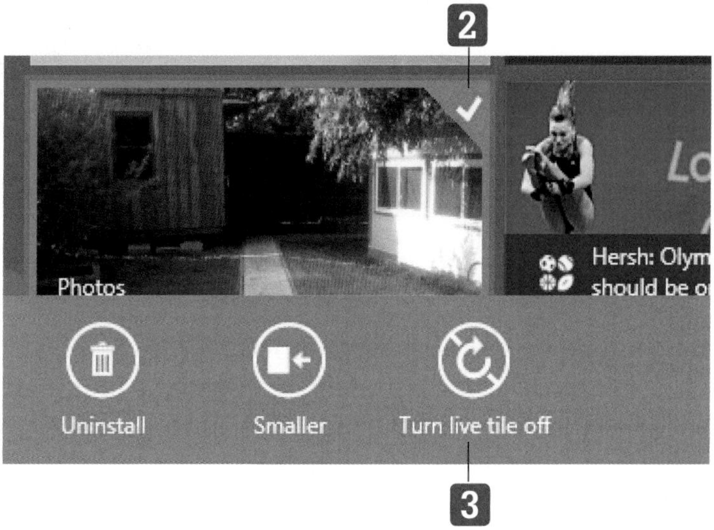

HOT TIP: To select a tile using touch only, tap, hold and drag the tile downwards.

HOT TIP: Check out the pink background!

Tip 3: Move among apps quickly

There are several ways to move among apps, including using a flicking motion inward from the left side of a touch screen to access the previously used app. You can also tap the Windows key or move the cursor to the bottom left corner of the screen and click once to access the Start screen, and thus the available list of apps. There are other ways to explore.

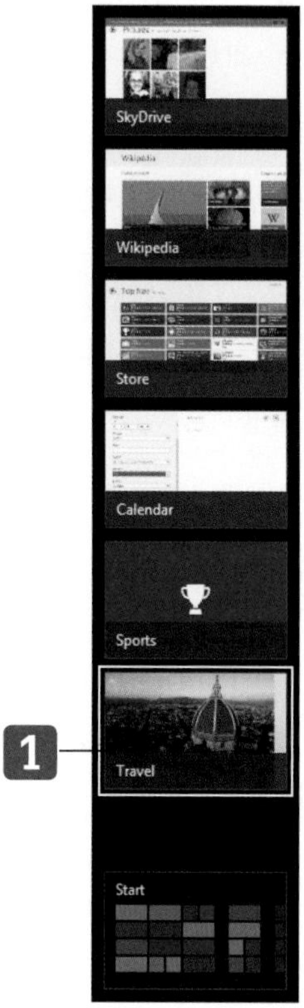

If you have a keyboard and mouse, try these techniques while on any screen or in any app:

1. Hold down the Windows key and press the Tab key to show small thumbnails of each open app. Press Tab repeatedly until you get to the app you want to use, then let go of both.
2. Hold down the Alt key and press the Tab key to show a row of open apps. Press Tab repeatedly until you get to the app you want to use, then let go.

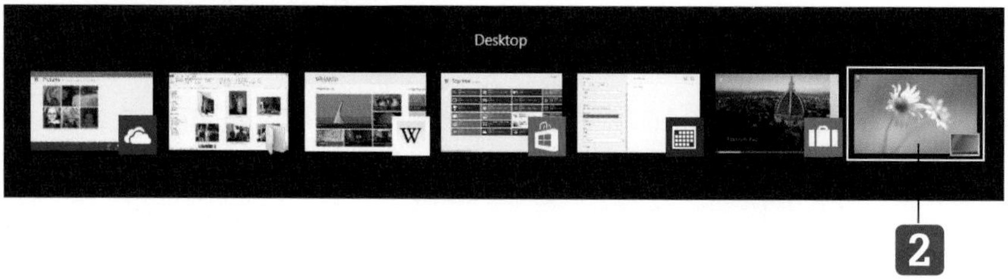

3. Position your mouse in the top left corner of the screen to view and click the last used app. Drag the mouse downwards slowly to view the other available apps.

DID YOU KNOW?
Some tablets offer USB ports. You may be able to connect a USB mouse. Likewise, if Bluetooth is an option, you may be able to connect a Bluetooth keyboard.

HOT TIP: The left to right flicking motion from the left edge of a touch screen is the best option for moving among open apps on a tablet.

Tip 4: Make icons easier to see in File Explorer

The items in a folder may be presented in a list, as icons or as tiles. When the items are set to Large icons or Extra large icons, they are easier to see.

1. Open File Explorer.
2. In the Navigation pane, click Pictures.
3. From the View tab, select a new layout. For Pictures, try Extra large icons.

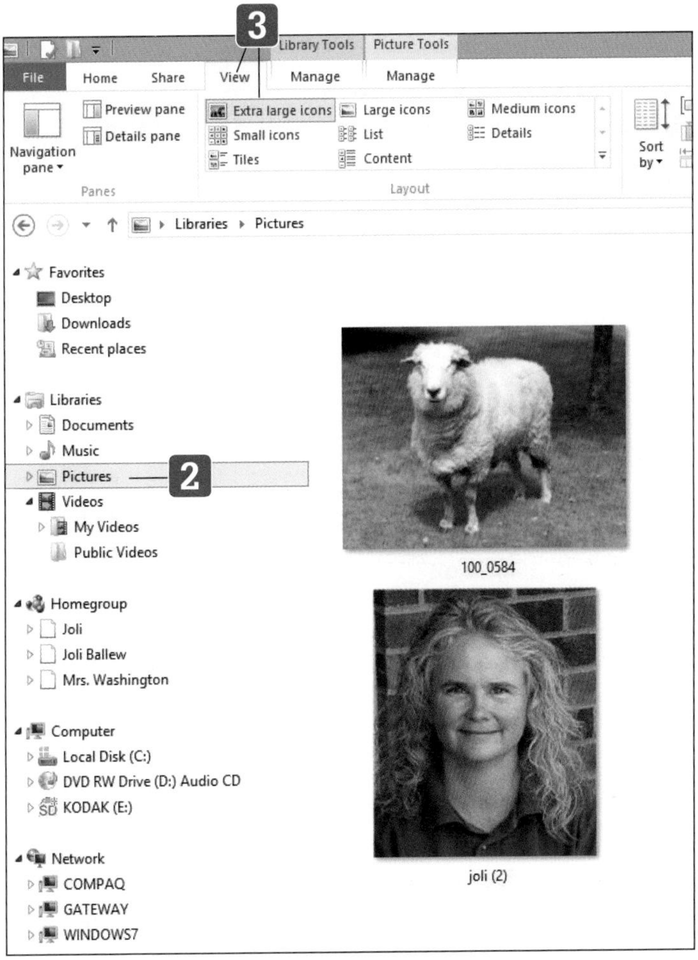

DID YOU KNOW?

You can opt to show the Preview pane or Details pane in any File Explorer window. These options are also on the View tab.

HOT TIP: To see information about the content in a folder, such as the date it was last modified, its size or type, choose List from the View pane.

Tip 5: Back up data quickly and easily

One way to back up your data is to copy it to an external drive. You can copy data to a DVD drive, a USB flash drive, a network drive or a larger external backup drive (among others). You copy the folder to the external drive the same way as you'd copy a folder to another area of your hard drive – you use the Copy command from the Home tab of any File Explorer window.

1. Using File Explorer, select the data to copy.
2. From the Home tab, click Copy to.
3. Click Choose Location.
4. Select the desired location.
5. Click Copy.

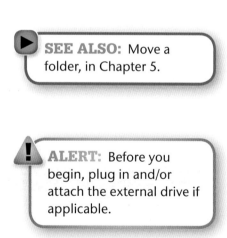

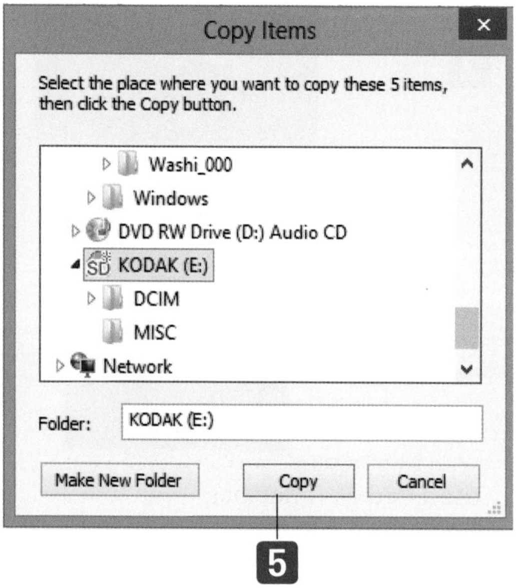

SEE ALSO: Move a folder, in Chapter 5.

ALERT: Before you begin, plug in and/or attach the external drive if applicable.

Tip 6: Connect to a free wireless hotspot

Wi-Fi hotspots are popping up all over the country in coffee shops, parks, libraries and more. Wi-Fi hotspots let you connect to the Internet without having to be tethered to an ethernet cable or tied down with a high monthly wireless bill. These are public networks.

1. Get within range of the public wireless network.
2. Use the keyboard shortcut Windows key + I to access the Settings charm, then click the Network icon.
3. Click the desired network.
4. Place a tick in the Connect automatically box if you plan to connect to this network again, and then click Connect.

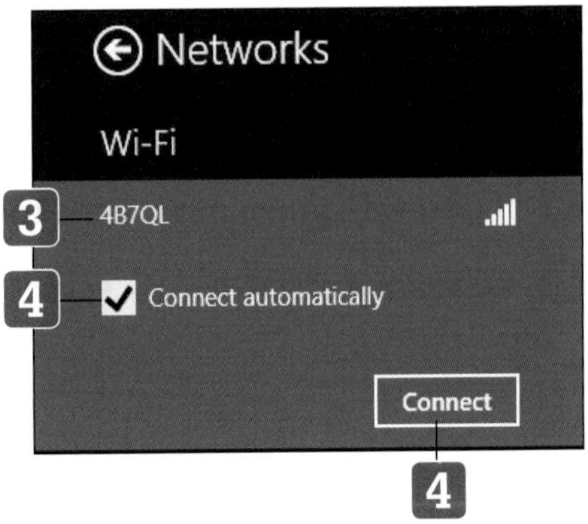

5. Click No, don't turn on sharing or connect to devices. This tells Windows you do not trust this network and want to consider it a public network (as opposed to a private one).

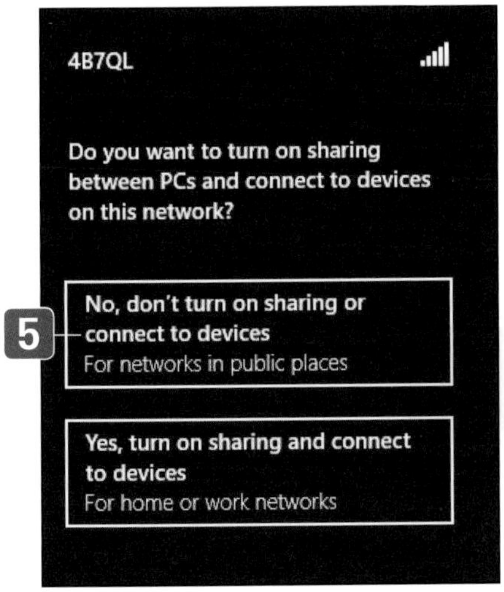

ALERT: You'll need a laptop or tablet with the required wireless hardware to use a free Wi-Fi hotspot.

HOT TIP: You'll be prompted for a security key if you're logging on to a secure network. You should not be prompted when logging on to a free, public Wi-Fi hotspot.

HOT TIP: To find a Wi-Fi hotspot close to you, go to http://maps.google.com and search for Wi-Fi hotspots.

Tip 9: Install a digital camera, webcam or smartphone

Most of the time, installing hardware is easy. You simply plug in the device and wait for it to be installed automatically. Once it's installed, you can set what you'd like to happen by default. Before you start, make sure the device is charged, plugged into a wall socket or has fresh batteries.

1. Read the directions that came with the device. If there are specific instructions for installing it, follow them. If not, continue here.
2. Connect the device.
3. If applicable, turn on the device. (You may have to set an older digital camera or camcorder to its playback position.)
4. Wait while the installation completes. When prompted, click or tap to choose what happens when you connect the device next time.
5. Choose what to do when you connect the device.

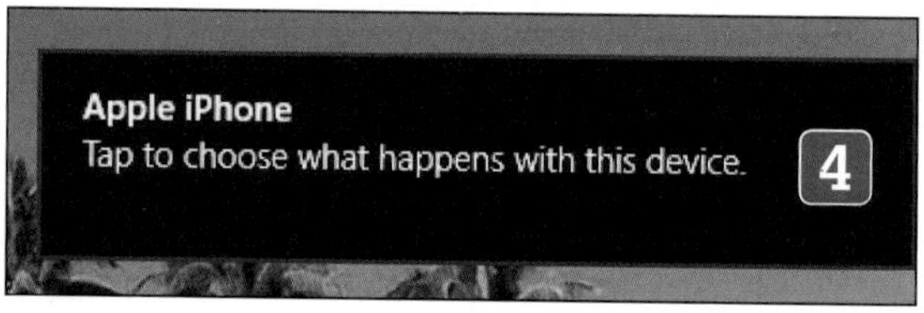

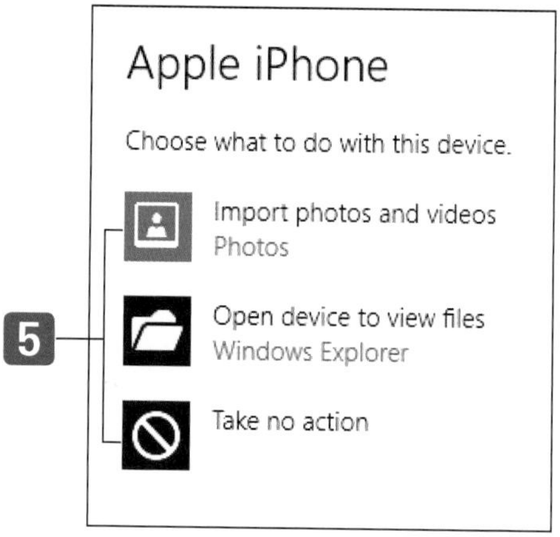

HOT TIP: If you missed the prompt to configure what to do when you connect the device and it's no longer available, don't worry. Just disconnect and reconnect it. It will appear again (at least until you set what you'd like to do all the time).

DID YOU KNOW?

Sometimes you'll receive a CD with a device. The hardware may work fine without it. If you want to keep unnecessary data and programs off your PC, see if the hardware will work without it first. You can always install the CD later if you need to.

Tip 10: Install anti-virus software

Windows 8 does not come with anti-virus software. You have to obtain and install this yourself. It's extremely important to do this if you haven't already; it will protect your computer from known threats, viruses, malware and so on.

1. You can purchase popular anti-virus software from well-known companies such as Kaspersky, Symantec, AVG and McAfee.
2. You can obtain free and reliable anti-virus software from Microsoft: Microsoft Security Essentials. Visit www.microsoft.com to learn more.
3. Once you've installed the software, configure the software to check for updates and install them daily.

HOT TIP: Consider purchasing a book to help you learn more about staying safe, such as *Staying Safe Online*, an *In Simple Steps* guide from Pearson Education also written by Joli Ballew.

DID YOU KNOW?

If a threat does get by your anti-virus software, theoretically it can do less damage if you're logged on with a standard user account than if you are logged on with an administrator account. Consider creating a standard user account for yourself if you often access websites that aren't 'mainstream', where these threats are more prolific.

1 Learn Windows 8 basics

Introduction

Congratulations on the acquisition of Windows 8! Whether you upgraded your existing system, purchased a new Windows 8 desktop computer or laptop, or purchased the new Microsoft Surface or other compatible tablet, you'll learn how to use it here.

If you have experience with Windows-based computers, you'll notice right away that Windows 8 is very different from what you're used to. In fact, Windows 8, initially at least, looks more like a large smartphone than a regular computer. It has apps like a smartphone, and you can get more from the Windows Store. These apps help you do things and get information quickly, and are less cumbersome and easier to use than more complicated applications. Don't worry though; the familiar desktop, where you'll find the Recycle Bin, taskbar and a place to work with the programs and accessories you're already familiar with is available. You'll learn how to access the desktop in this chapter.

First things first, though. You need to log in, explore the Start screen, learn a little about the new charms and other features, and understand something about apps. Additionally, you need to understand what kind of device you own – a tablet, laptop or desktop computer – and what, if any, limitations exist.

Know what kind of device you have

There are many different types of devices that can run Windows 8, including tablets, netbooks, laptops and desktop computers. It's important to know what kind of device you own so that you'll know which features of the Windows 8 operating system are available to you.

1. Simple tablet – Simple tablets run Windows 8 RT and offer access to the Start screen and the various apps, as well as access to many desktop features. You can connect to wireless networks, access and play media and games and more, though.
2. Desktop PC or laptop – Traditional computers generally run Windows 8 or Windows 8 Pro, and offer access to all of the features mentioned for tablets, plus everything you'd expect in a computer, including the ability to install hardware and install software, access the full desktop and perform any and all computing tasks.
3. High-end tablet – These tablets run some version of Windows 8 but you may or may not have access to a physical keyboard, USB ports and other desktop or laptop hardware.

ALERT: To get the most from Windows 8, you really need to have an always-on Internet connection.

HOT TIP: Some tablets offer only a touch screen and do not offer a physical keyboard. Desktop computers, laptops and high-end tablets may offer keyboard, mouse *and* touch.

Set up Windows 8

The first time you turn on Windows 8 you are prompted to make choices regarding how you'd like to set it up. The following list summarises these prompts.

1 Background Color – Use the slider to select the background colour of the Start screen.

2 Computer Name – Type a name for your computer, which must be unique if you have a personal network.

3 Network – Type the name, passcode and other attributes of your home network if applicable.

4 Settings – Select the default options. You can always change the settings later.

5 Microsoft Account or Local User Account – Choose how to log in to your computer. We suggest a Microsoft account, detailed in the next section.

6 Password – Type the password you'll enter to unlock your computer. If you input a Microsoft account during set-up, input the password already associated with that account.

7 Password hint – Type a few words that you type to remind you of what your password is, should you ever forget it.

1

HOT TIP: You can change any decision you make during set-up if you decide to later.

SEE ALSO: Consider a Microsoft account, next.

Consider a Microsoft account

You might not know the differences between using a local account and a Microsoft account. Here's a summary.

1. Microsoft account – A global account you use to log in to your Windows 8 computer. When you use this kind of account, Windows 8 will automatically configure certain apps with personalised information and your preferences and settings will be available no matter what Internet-enabled Windows 8 computer you log on to.
2. Local account – A personal account you use to log on to your Windows 8 computer that is associated only with that computer. Your account settings and preferences can't 'follow' you from one Windows 8 computer to another like a Microsoft account can.

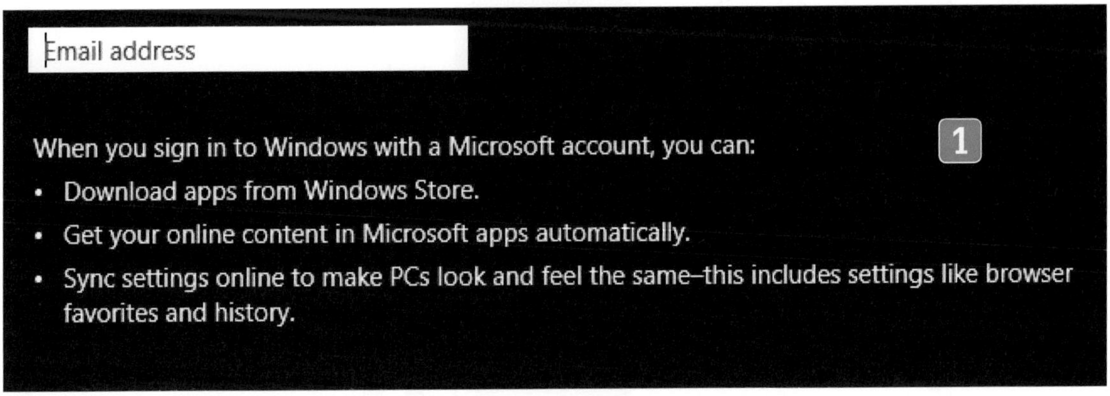

Email address
When you sign in to Windows with a Microsoft account, you can:
Download apps from Windows Store.
Get your online content in Microsoft apps automatically.
Sync settings online to make PCs look and feel the same–this includes settings like browser favorites and history.
1

ALERT: You must have a Microsoft account to use the Microsoft Store to get apps, movies, music and video.

HOT TIP: It's never too late to switch from a local account to a Microsoft account. Learn how later in this chapter.

Log in to Windows 8

The Lock screen appears when you turn on or wake up your Windows 8 computer. You must bypass the Lock screen before you can use your computer.

1 If you have a touch screen, use your finger to swipe upwards from the bottom.

2 If you have a physical keyboard do any of the following:

- Swipe upwards with the mouse.
- Tap any keyboard key.
- Click anywhere on the screen.

3 Type your password and tap Enter on the keyboard, or type your password and tap or click the right-facing arrow.

4 The Start screen appears.

5 To lock the computer, log out or to sign in as a different user, click your account name on the Start screen.

SEE ALSO: Refer to Chapter 2 to learn how to replace your password with a numeric PIN.

DID YOU KNOW?

You can tap or click the icon that looks like an eye that appears in the Password window after you've entered the password to see the actual characters (instead of the dots that appear by default).

Explore the Start screen

Once you gain access to the Start screen, your computer is ready to use. Note the items available there and understand that your Start screen might look different from the one shown here.

1. Read the names of each of the apps. Try to imagine what the app might offer.
2. Position your mouse at the bottom of the screen; if a scroll bar appears, there are additional apps or applications available. Scroll right to view them.
3. Click your user name in the top right corner to see the option to lock your computer.
4. Position your mouse in the bottom right corner to access the transparent 'charms'.

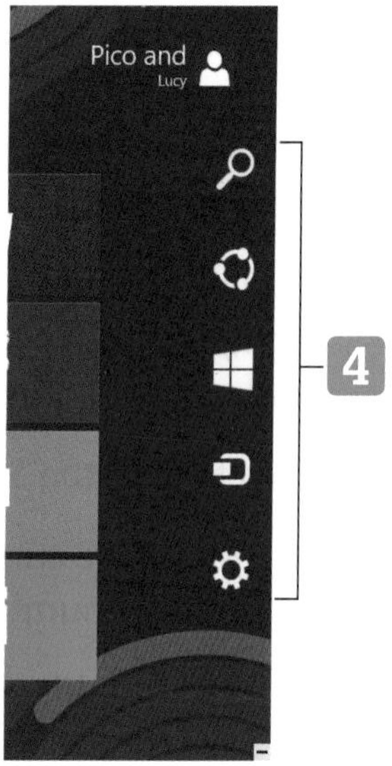

SEE ALSO: Access charms and Understand charms, later in this chapter.

HOT TIP: To view all of your apps and applications, right-click an empty area of the screen and click All apps. On a touch screen, flick up from the bottom, and then click All apps.

ALERT: If you use a simple tablet, you may have limited desktop resources.

Understand charms

There are five charms. What you see when you click any one of them may differ depending on what you're doing at the time. For instance, if you click the Share charm while on the Start screen, you'll be notified there's nothing available to share there. If you click the Share charm while in the Maps app, you can share the location or directions you've looked up with others via email or other options.

1. Search – To open the Search window where you can type what you're looking for. Note the categories: Apps, Settings, Files.
2. Share – To share something with others, such as a map to a location.
3. Start – To access the Start screen.
4. Devices – To access devices that can be used with the open app, window or program.
5. Settings – To access settings available with the open screen, app, program and so on. You'll use this charm to join networks, change the volume, shut down the computer, and more.

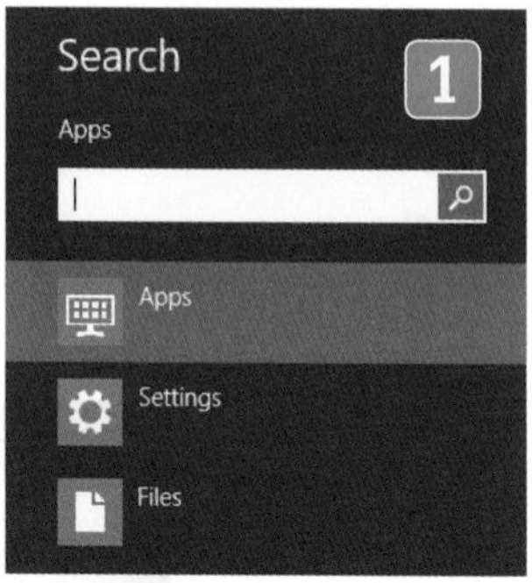

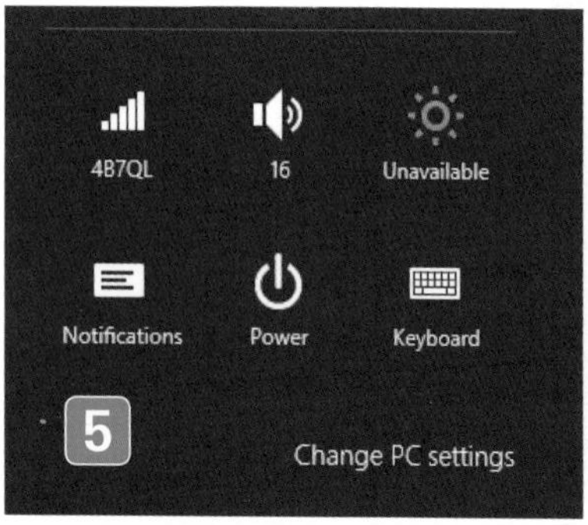

HOT TIP: If you can't seem to access the charms using one method (perhaps positioning your mouse in the bottom right corner), try another (such as Windows key + C).

HOT TIP: From the Settings charm, you can click or tap Change PC settings to access the PC Settings screen. You can make changes to your computer there, including creating a PIN, changing the Lock screen picture, adding users and so on.

DID YOU KNOW?
You can access charms from anywhere in Windows 8, even the desktop or while in an app.

Access the traditional desktop

The Start screen offers a Desktop tile. This is the tile you use to access the familiar, traditional computing environment you're used to (if you've used a computer before, that is).

1. Use any method to access the Start screen if you aren't already on it. (You can tap the Windows key on a keyboard.)
2. From the Start screen, click or tap Desktop.

Note the following desktop features:

3. The Recycle Bin.
4. The taskbar.
5. The Internet Explorer icon.
6. The File Explorer icon.
7. The Notification area.

? DID YOU KNOW?

Look for the keyboard icon in the Notification area. You can tap this icon to bring up the touch keyboard when you need it.

! ALERT: The Start button is no longer available on the taskbar. If you'd like to access something like it, press the Windows key + X key combination. Otherwise, locate the item you want to open on the Start screen or All Apps screen.

Explore File Explorer

File Explorer helps you locate the data on your hard drive. You can access your documents, music, pictures, videos and so on from one window. File Explorer also offers a 'ribbon' where you can perform tasks on data you select. For example, if you select a picture, the option to Print is available from the Share tab.

1. Tabs – Tap or click to access options related to the tab's title.
2. Tab commands – Tap or click the commands as desired. If a command is greyed out, it can't be used.
3. Show/Hide the ribbon – Tap or click to always show the ribbon or to hide it.
4. Libraries – Tap or click any library title to view the data you've stored there.
5. Favorites – Tap or click any item under Favorites to access data in the folder.
6. Search – Type keywords in the Search window to locate specific data in a folder.

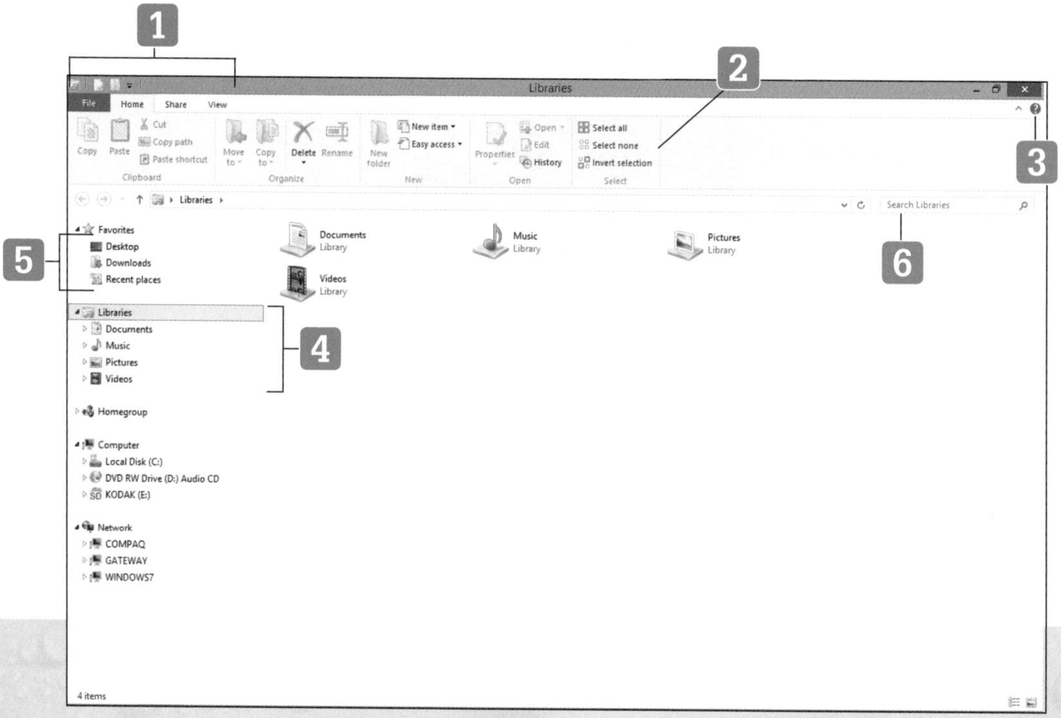

HOT TIP: When saving data, always save it to a related folder or library. Save pictures in the Pictures library, music in the Music library, and so on.

DID YOU KNOW?

File Explorer used to be called Windows Explorer.

Switch to a Microsoft account

You switch from a local account to a Microsoft account in PC settings. There are several ways to access the PC settings screen; one way is from the Settings charm.

1. Access the charms. (Windows key + C is one way.)
2. Click Settings.
3. From the Settings options click Change PC settings.
4. In the left pane, click Users; in the right, click Switch to a Microsoft account.
5. Type your current password.
6. Complete the process to sign in with a Microsoft account. After you do, you'll see the option to switch to a local account, as seen here.

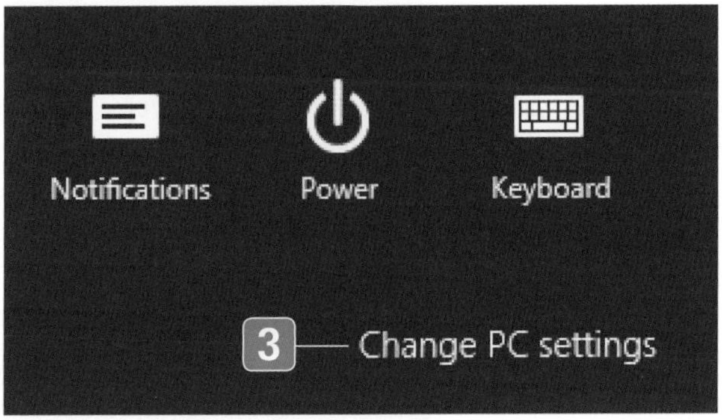

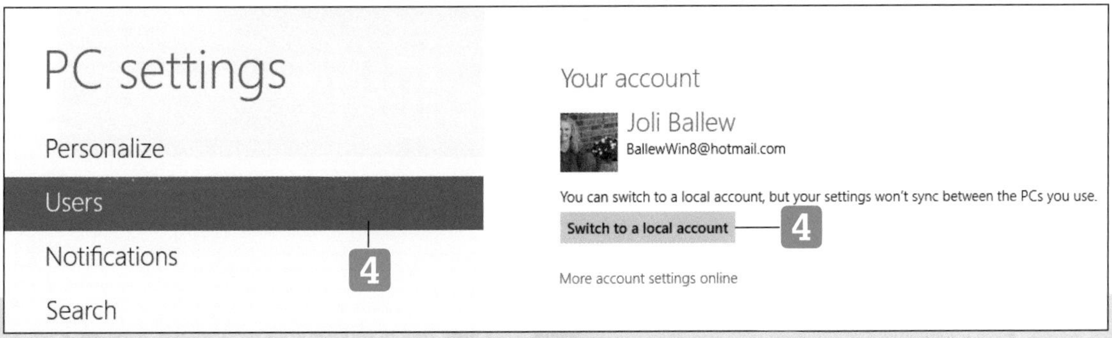

HOT TIP: If you don't have an email address or if you want a new one, you can get one during the sign in process.

HOT TIP: Use the keyboard shortcut Windows key + I to go directly to the Settings charm.

Shut down your computer

Your Windows 8 computer will go to sleep after a specific amount of idle time. When this actually happens depends on several factors, including which power configuration you've selected and whether a tablet or laptop is plugged into the mains or is running on batteries. The sleep state is quite efficient and doesn't use much energy, so it's often okay to let the computer go to sleep instead of turning it off each time you're finished using it. However, there will be times when you want to turn the computer or tablet off completely.

1. Access the charms and click or tap Settings.
2. Click or tap Power.
3. Click or tap Shut down.

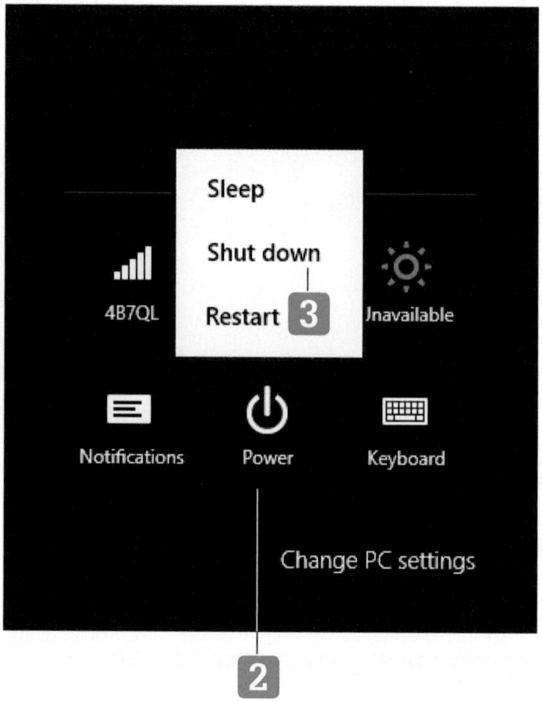

HOT TIP: If you are relocating a desktop computer, turn it off before you unplug it.

ALERT: During aeroplane takeoffs and landings, you'll be prompted to turn off all devices. You can't just let them go to sleep.

2 Make Windows 8 easier to use, see and navigate

Introduction

The best way to learn your way around Windows 8 is to explore and configure some of the features for personalising it. When you do, you learn a little more about navigating the Start screen, charms and the desktop, as well as menus, tabs and drop-down lists. At the same time, you make Windows 8 easier to use by configuring such settings as volume, screen resolution, the size of the Start screen tiles and even how long it takes to log in.

Change the volume

If you have a laptop or tablet there is probably a button on the outside of it for increasing or decreasing the volume. Likewise, if you have physical speakers connected to a desktop computer, they probably have some sort of volume control too. However, if your speakers are built into your computer or tablet and you don't see any external controls, you'll have to change the volume using Windows 8.

Using a keyboard:

1. Press the Windows key + I.
2. Click the Volume icon.
3. Use the slider that appears to change the volume.

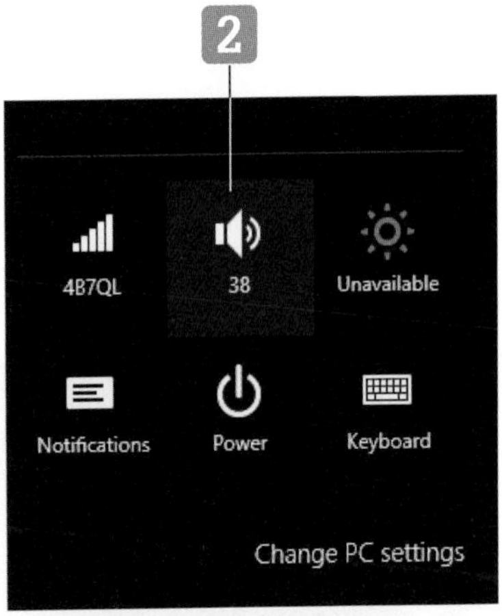

Using touch:

4. Swipe in from the middle of the right side of the screen.
5. Tap Settings, and tap the Volume icon.
6. Use your finger to increase or decrease the volume.

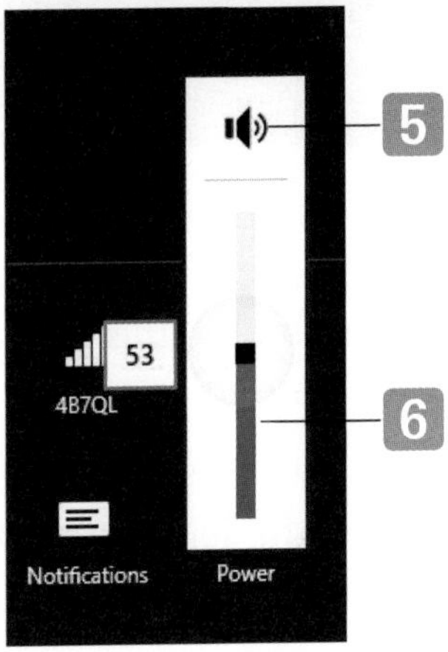

DID YOU KNOW?
Most all-in-one computers have speakers inside the unit itself and often no external volume control.

HOT TIP: To use a mouse or other pointer, position the cursor in the bottom right corner of the screen, click the Settings charm and then click the Volume icon.

Change the screen resolution

Screen resolution is determined by how many pixels (small squares of colour) appear on the screen. The resolution may be low (800 × 600 or 1024 × 768) or high (1920 × 1080 or higher). At a lower resolution, items on the screen appear larger. At a higher resolution, they appear smaller. You may want to change the resolution if you have trouble viewing what is on the screen.

1. Press the Windows key to access the Start screen.
2. Type resolution.
3. Click Settings.
4. Click Adjust screen resolution in the results.

DID YOU KNOW? Changing the screen resolution also affects the size of the tiles on the Start screen.

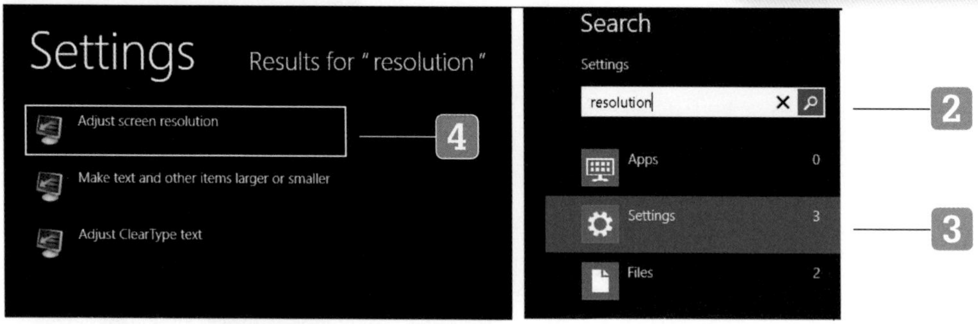

5. Click the arrow beside Resolution and select an option. You may see a warning like this one if you choose a low resolution.
6. When prompted, decide if you want to keep the selected resolution or choose a different one.
7. Click OK when finished.

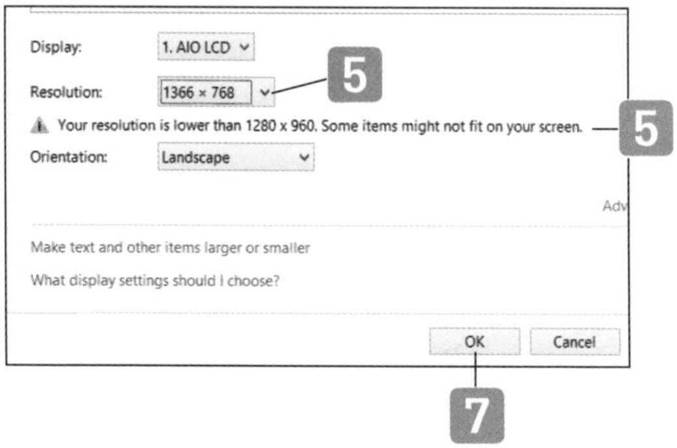

DID YOU KNOW? From the desktop, you can right-click and choose Screen Resolution to make changes.

HOT TIP: The screen resolution settings are available from the Control Panel. Feel free to explore additional Control Panel display options now.

Personalise the colour of the Start screen background

When you first set up your Windows 8 computer, you chose the colour of the Start screen background. You can change it from the PC settings hub. Changing the colour may help you better see the tiles on the Start screen.

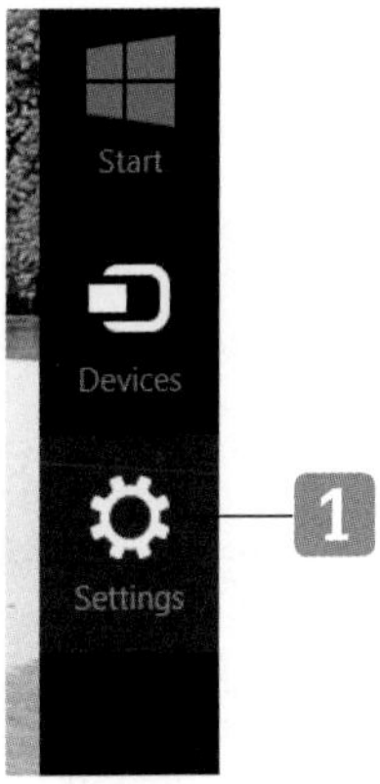

1. Bring up the charms and click Settings. (You can use the keyboard shortcut Windows key + C, flick in from the right side of the screen using your thumb, or position the cursor in the bottom right corner of the screen and move the cursor upwards.)
2. Click Change PC settings.
3. In the left pane click Personalize; in the right pane click Start screen.
4. Move the slider to the desired colour and click the desired design.

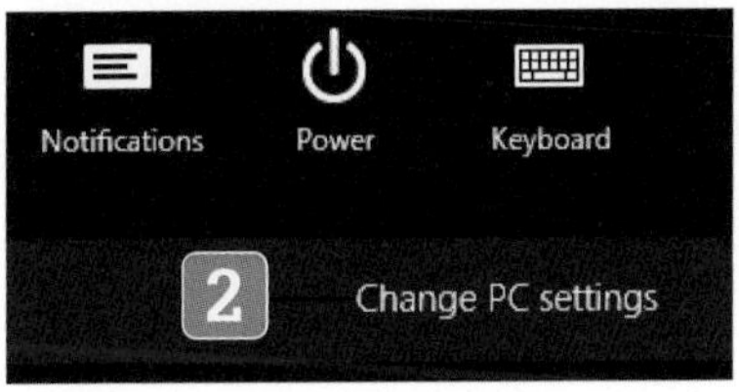

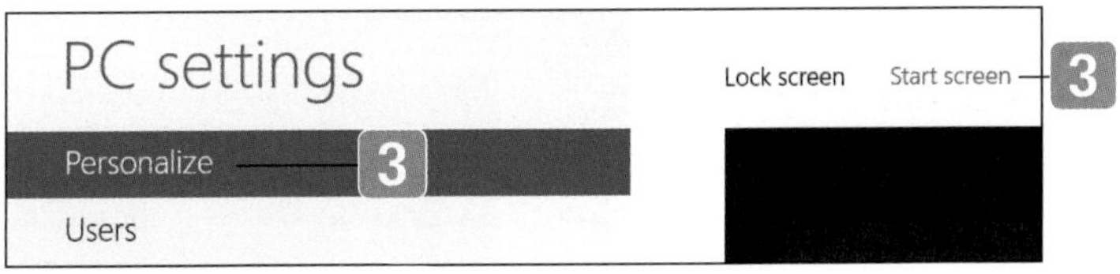

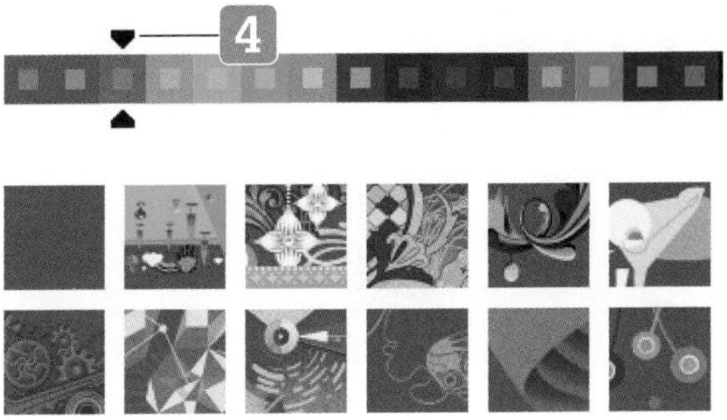

HOT TIP: Notice when you change the Start screen background the colour of the categories in the PC settings hub changes too.

DID YOU KNOW?

If you use a Microsoft account to log in to your Windows 8 computer and change the colour of the Start screen background, when you log on to any other Windows 8 computer with that same Microsoft account, you'll see the same colour there too.

Turn live tiles off or on

Live tiles flip every second or two to show ever-changing information as it relates to the app. For example, the Photos tile will flip through your digital photos, and the Sports tile will show the latest sports headlines. If this is distracting, you can disable it for any or all live tiles.

1. At the Start screen, locate any live tile (you may not yet have any, and not all tiles are live).

2. Right-click the live tile you want to enable or disable. Note that a tick appears by it.
3. Click Turn live tile off. (Alternatively, you can opt to turn a live tile on.)
4. Repeat as desired.

HOT TIP: To select a tile using touch only, tap, hold and drag the tile downwards.

HOT TIP: Check out the pink background!

Make app tiles larger or smaller

Some tiles are small and square, and others are larger and rectangular. Currently you can make any rectangular tile smaller (and then larger again). You cannot resize tiles that are natively square.

1. At the Start screen, right-click the Desktop tile. Note that a tick appears by it.
2. Click Smaller.
3. Repeat and click Larger.

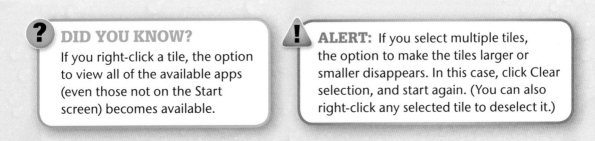

? DID YOU KNOW?
If you right-click a tile, the option to view all of the available apps (even those not on the Start screen) becomes available.

! ALERT: If you select multiple tiles, the option to make the tiles larger or smaller disappears. In this case, click Clear selection, and start again. (You can also right-click any selected tile to deselect it.)

Reposition apps on the Start screen

As you use your computer, over time you'll learn which apps you use most and which you use least. You may want to move the apps you use regularly to the left side of the Start screen and the apps you use less frequently to the right.

If you use a mouse:

1. Left-click the app to move and hold down the left mouse button.
2. Drag the app to its new location. (Here we're moving the Travel tile, which is live.)
3. Drop it there.

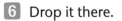

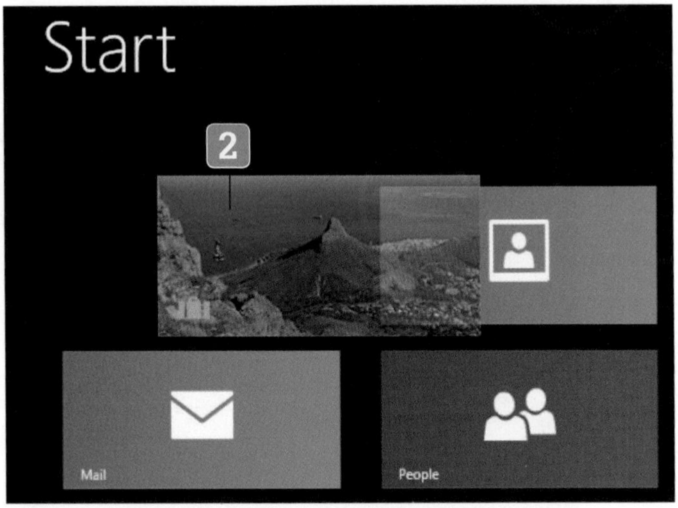

If you use your finger on a touch screen:

4. Tap and hold the app tile.
5. Drag it to its new location.
6. Drop it there.

DID YOU KNOW?
If a number appears on a tile on the Start screen, it means that there is new information or that the app needs your attention. For instance, a number on the Mail icon means you have unread mail.

ALERT: It may take some practice to learn how to reposition an app's tile with your finger. Sometimes it helps to tap, hold and drag *downwards* first (all in one fluid motion), and then drag the tile to the desired location *after* it's been moved downwards from its current position.

Add a tile to the Start screen

You can add more tiles to the Start screen. You can add tiles for File Explorer windows, websites and even desktop apps, to name a few. In this exercise you'll add the Calculator desktop app. (It's called a desktop app because it opens on the desktop and not in an app window.)

1. Right-click an empty area of the Start screen. On a touch screen, flick upwards from the bottom of the screen.
2. Click All apps.
3. Scroll to locate the Calculator app and right-click it.
4. From the bar that appears at the bottom of the page, click Pin to Start.
5. Return to the Start screen and locate the new tile. It will be located on the far right.

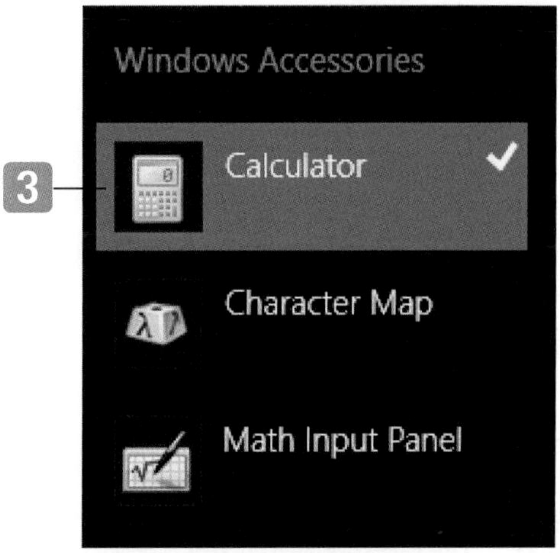

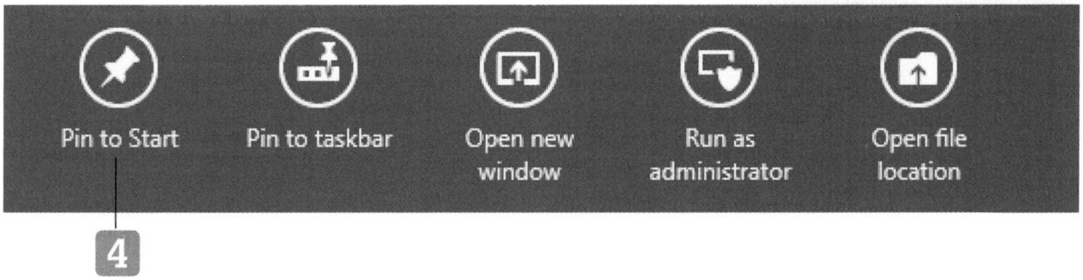

HOT TIP: If you have previous computer experience, you can add tiles for the desktop applications, system tools, windows and other items that you know you'll use often. You may want to add Control Panel if you're familiar with that feature already.

DID YOU KNOW?
You can open an app from the All apps screen by clicking it once.

Remove a tile from the Start screen

You can remove an unwanted tile from the Start screen by selecting it and then choosing Unpin from Start. If you wish, you can select multiple tiles to remove.

1. Right-click (or tap, hold and drag downwards on) any tile you'd like to remove.
2. Repeat as desired to select additional tiles.
3. Click or tap Unpin from Start.
4. You can deselect any selected tiles by clicking Clear selection.

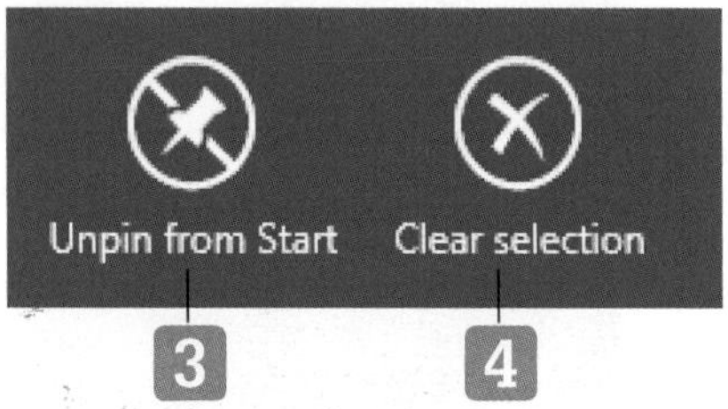

DID YOU KNOW?
When you remove a tile from the Start screen you don't uninstall it. You can always access it (and even add it back) from the All apps screen.

HOT TIP: After you've removed unwanted tiles, reposition what's left by dragging the remaining tiles to the desired positions.

Log in with fewer keystrokes

When you log in you probably have to type a password. This can become tiresome after a while, especially if you don't have a physical keyboard or if your password contains capital letters and lower case ones, numbers and special characters. You can change your login requirements so that you need only enter a numeric personal identification number (PIN) instead.

1. At the Start screen, type PIN. (If you don't have access to a physical keyboard, from the Settings charm, tap Keyboard.)
2. On the right side of the screen, click Settings.

3. Click Create or change PIN.
4. Click Create a PIN.
5. Type your current password, click OK, and then enter the desired PIN twice.
6. Click Finish.

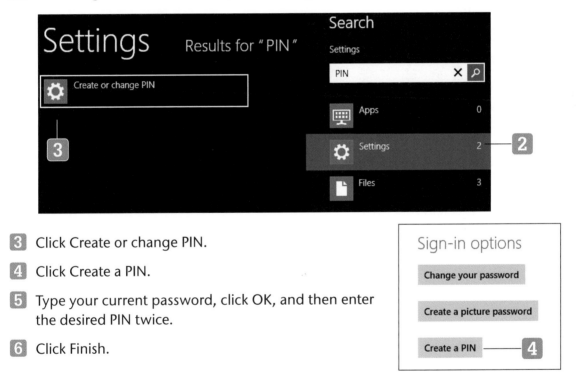

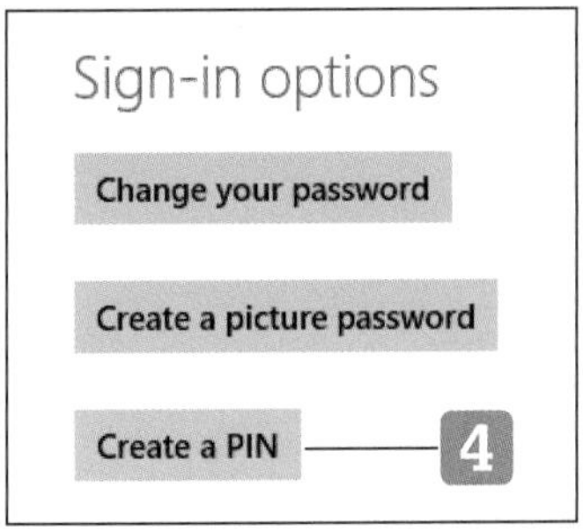

HOT TIP: When creating a PIN try to avoid things like 12345 or 9876. Avoid using your birthday too. (Make it at least a little difficult to guess!)

HOT TIP: Notice the option above Create a PIN, Create a picture password. This option enables you to select a picture and configure a touch pattern on it to unlock your computer.

Create shortcuts on the desktop

You can personalise the desktop just as you can personalise the Start screen. If you work at the desktop regularly you can create shortcuts there for items you use often. This makes it easier to open them when you need them.

1. From the Start screen, click the Desktop tile.
2. On the desktop, from the taskbar, click the Folder icon.

3. Locate an item you'd like to create a shortcut for. You might choose, say, the Documents library:
   - Right-click the item. (On a touch screen, use a long tap.)
   - Click Send to.
   - Click Desktop (create shortcut). Note the option to Pin to Start (that's the Start screen).
4. Repeat as desired.

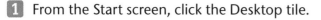

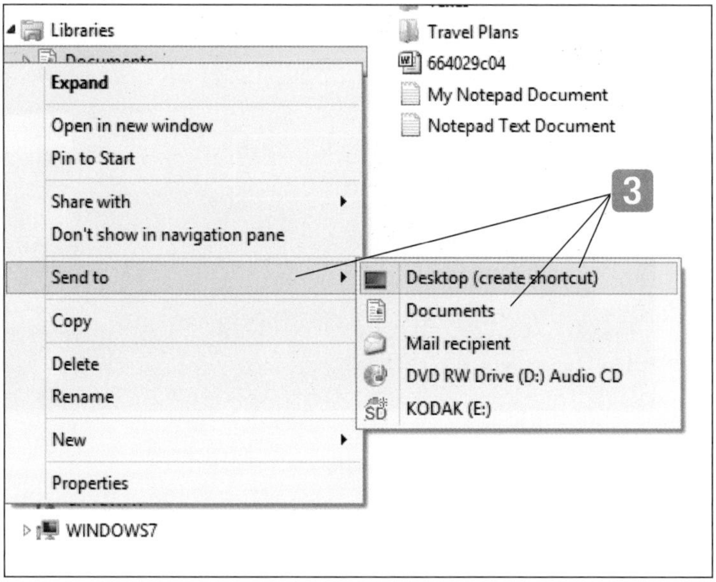

DID YOU KNOW?

To create a shortcut for your user folder, click Computer in the Navigation pane, double-click Users, and right-click your user folder.

DID YOU KNOW?

While on the desktop click the Windows key + X to quickly access the Control Panel, Device Manager, Power Options and other desktop applications. If you know this shortcut there's no need to create shortcuts for those features on the desktop.

Pin items to the taskbar

If you'd rather not clutter up your Desktop with shortcuts, you can opt to add icons for items to the taskbar. This is called 'pinning' an item. You already know you can choose Pin to Start to add tiles to the Start screen. Another option is Pin to taskbar.

1 From the Start screen (or the All apps screen), right-click an item you'd like to add to the taskbar.

2 Click Pin to taskbar. If you don't see this option, it can't be pinned.

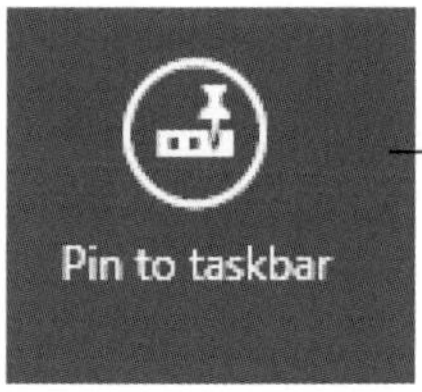

3 Repeat as desired, and then note the new items that are pinned.

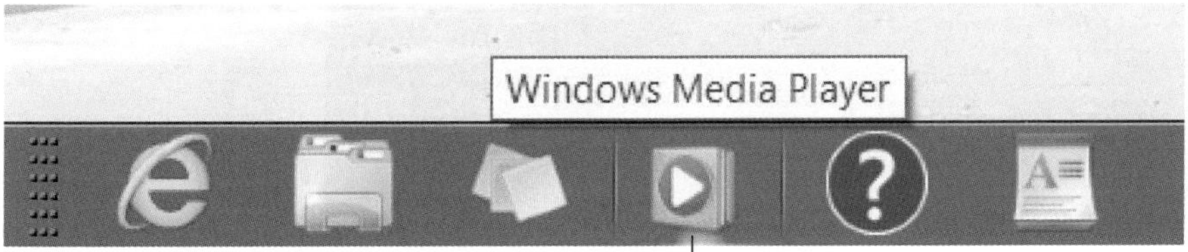

HOT TIP: You can configure icons on the taskbar to appear as large buttons or small ones. Right-click the taskbar and click Properties to access the options.

HOT TIP: Once an item is pinned to the taskbar, you only have to click or tap it once to open it.

Explore accessibility options

Accessibility options help you use the computer if you have a disability. If you have trouble viewing what is on the screen, reading the notifications that appear, using the keyboard or hearing alerts, you can enable certain accessibility options to make it easier.

1. From the Start screen type Accessibility.
2. Click Settings.
3. If you see the option you'd like to enable, click it. Otherwise, click Let Windows suggest Ease of Access settings.
4. Proceed through the process as prompted.

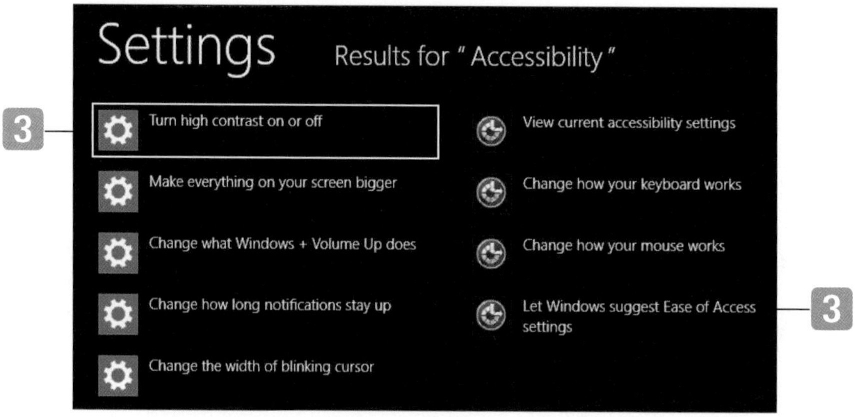

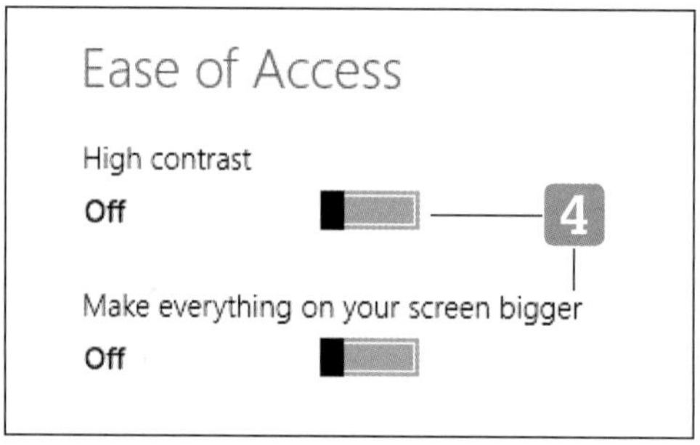

ALERT: What you see when you select an option depends on which option you select.

HOT TIP: If you aren't sure which options to enable, click Let Windows suggest Ease of Access settings. Work through the wizard and let Windows decide what's best for you.

Explore touch techniques

If your tablet does not have a physical keyboard, you'll rely on touch techniques to perform tasks, access data, type and so on. Although you'll learn more techniques as you work through this book, here are the more common ones.

1. Flick up from the bottom to access additional commands and features specific to the open app or window. Here's what you see when you flick upwards in Maps.
2. Flick from the middle of the left side of the screen inwards to move from one open app to another. When you do, one app slides in and the other slides out. (Multiple apps must be open.)
3. Flick from the middle of the right side of the screen inwards to access charms.

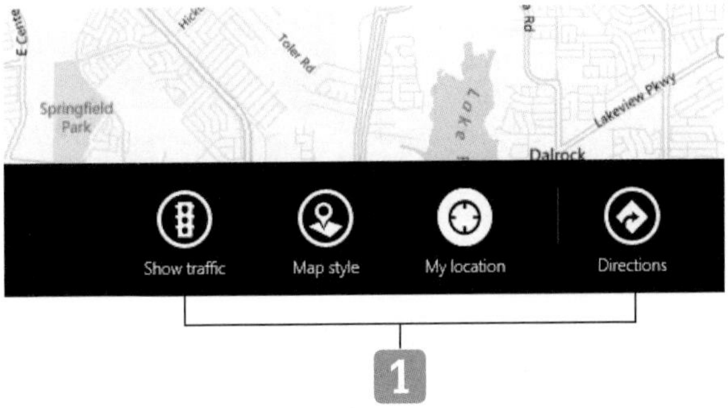

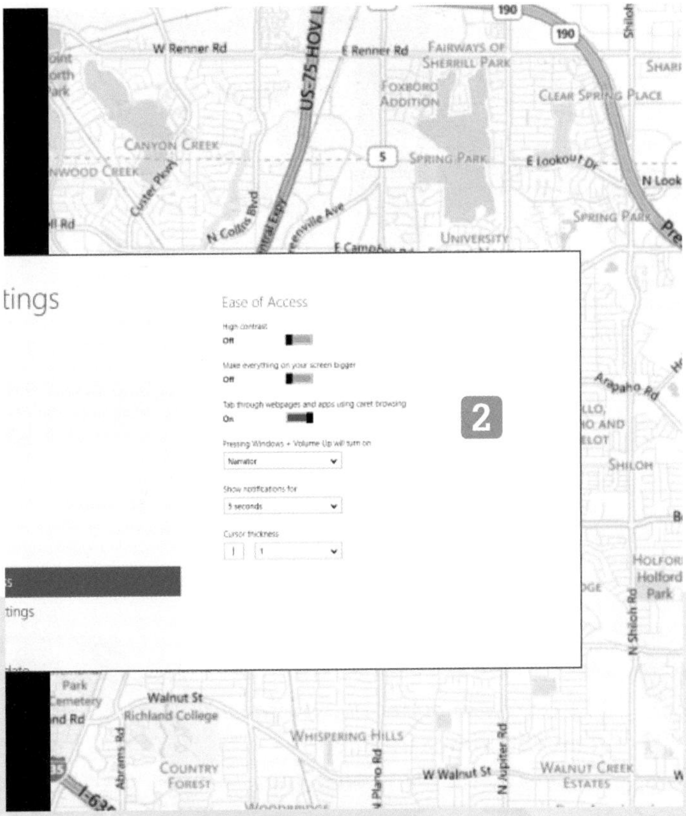

4 Tap any item to open it; tap and hold any item to select it; tap, hold and drag downwards a little to perform other tasks (such as to move an item).

5 Double-tap an item on the desktop to open it.

6 Tap and hold an icon on the desktop to access the contextual menu.

HOT TIP: A double-tap is like a double-click using a mouse.

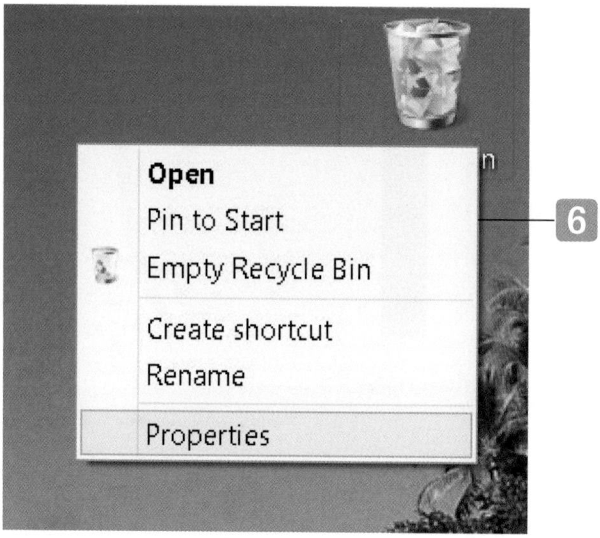

DID YOU KNOW?
A tap–hold–drag motion is similar to holding down the mouse button and dragging an item.

DID YOU KNOW?
The tap-and-hold technique often produces what a traditional right-click does.

3 Use apps to be more efficient

Throw away your physical maps

You can use the Maps app to locate a place or get directions from one place to another. No more fumbling with physical maps!

1. From the Start screen, click the Maps tile.
2. If prompted to let Maps discover your location, click Allow.
3. Right-click or swipe upwards from the bottom to access the available Maps charms.

4. Explore the following:
   - Show traffic – To view the current flow of traffic as green, yellow or red. Green means traffic is moving; red means it's extremely slow or stopped.
   - Map style – To switch from the default Road view to Aerial view.
   - My location – To have Maps place a diamond on the map to indicate where you are.
   - Directions – To get directions from one place to another.

ALERT: You will not be able to view traffic conditions if the traffic where you are is not monitored.

DID YOU KNOW?

By default, Maps will use your current location as the starting point, provided you allow it to access your position when prompted.

HOT TIP: Click My location, and then click Map style, Aerial view. Zoom in to view a picture of your own home, business or location as it appears from the sky!

Travel without leaving your home

The Travel app is one of the easiest to use, and is packed with information about places you may want to visit or read about. One of the most outstanding features is the ability to explore cities in 360 degree views.

1. From the Start screen, click the Travel tile.
2. Use the scroll bar on the screen or on your mouse to move through the information.
3. Click any item to view it; click the resulting Back button, located in the top left corner, to return.
4. Locate the Panoramas section; click any item with 360° on it.
5. Use your finger or mouse to drag on the image to move it around on the screen.

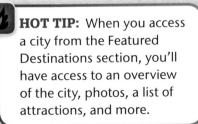

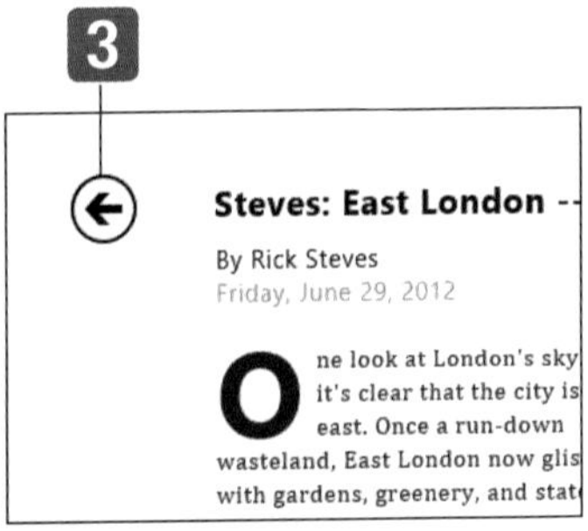
3
Steves: East London
By Rick Steves
Friday, June 29, 2012
One look at London's sky
it's clear that the city is
east. Once a run-down
wasteland, East London now glis
with gardens, greenery, and stat

Barcelona, Spain
360°
4
Rome, Italy
360°
4

HOT TIP: When you access a city from the Featured Destinations section, you'll have access to an overview of the city, photos, a list of attractions, and more.

DID YOU KNOW?
While in any app, such as Travel, you can access the previously used app by moving the mouse cursor to the top left corner and clicking. If you use touch only, flick inwards from the left middle edge.

Shop the Windows Store

So far you've been exploring apps that come with Windows 8. You can get additional apps from the Store, available from the Start screen. You'll need a Microsoft account to use the Store, even though many apps are free.

1. From the Start screen, click Store.
2. Scroll, browse, navigate and explore the items in the Store using techniques you've already learned, such as scrolling and clicking.
3. Click Top free under any category.

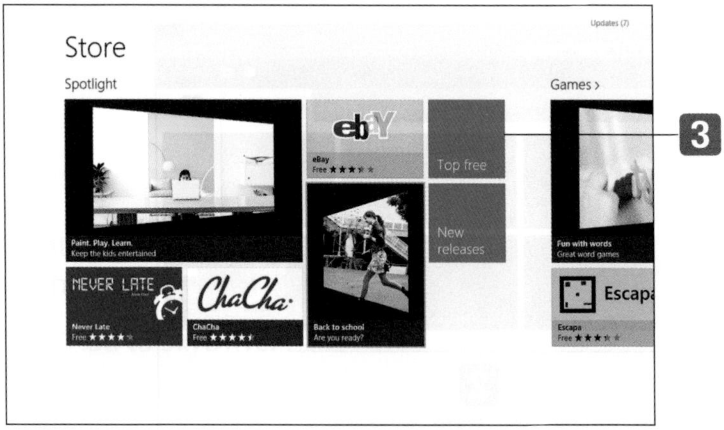

4. Locate an app you'd like to own. Click its tile.

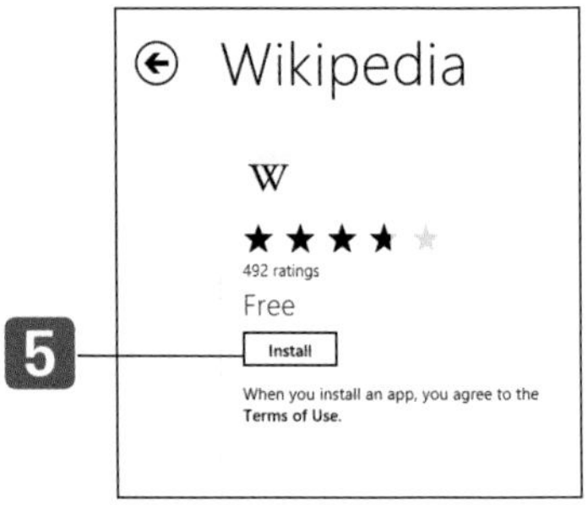

5. Read the information on the app's Details page, and if desired, click Install.

HOT TIP: You can continue shopping in the Store while an app downloads.

ALERT: Many apps are free, but many you'll have to pay for. If prompted to pay for an app, read the instructions for doing so, and set up the required payment account.

Use your free app

Once a new app is installed, you can find it on the Start screen. It will be on the far right side, although you can move it somewhere else if you'd like.

1 From the Start screen, locate the new app.

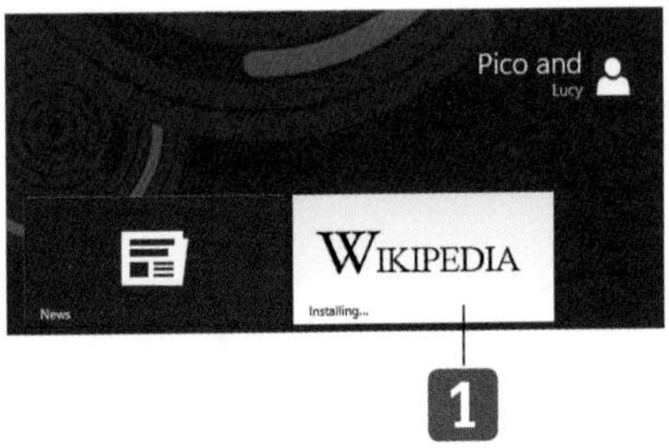

2 Click or tap the app tile to open it.

3 Read any directions, input required information and so on, if asked to do so.

4 Explore the app as desired.

DID YOU KNOW? When you leave an app to do something else, the app stops where it is; it 'pauses'. It does not continue to use system resources, and generally you don't have to 'start over' when you come back to the app, for instance when playing a game.

ALERT: Some apps offer in-app purchases. This means you can pay for more 'bombs', 'lives' and various additional features. Be careful; this can get expensive!

HOT TIP: You can unpin an app from the Start screen if you don't want it there, but if you know you won't use the app then opt to uninstall it instead. Right-click the app tile on the Start screen to access both of these options.

Move among apps quickly

So far you've learned several ways to move among apps, including using a flicking motion inwards from the left side of a touch screen to access the previously used app. You also know you can tap the Windows key or move the cursor to the bottom left corner of the screen and click once to access the Start screen, and thus the available list of apps. There are other ways to explore.

If you have a keyboard and mouse, try these techniques while on any screen or in any app:

1. Hold down the Windows key and press the Tab key to show small thumbnails of each open app. Press Tab repeatedly until you get to the app you want to use, then let go of both.
2. Hold down the Alt key and press the Tab key to show a row of open apps. Press Tab repeatedly until you get to the app you want to use, then let go.

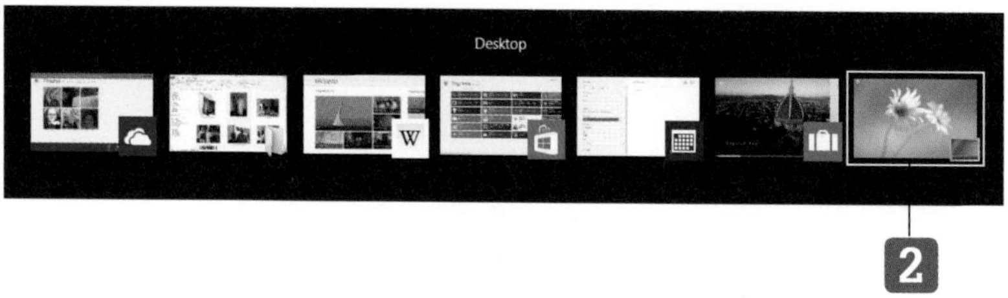

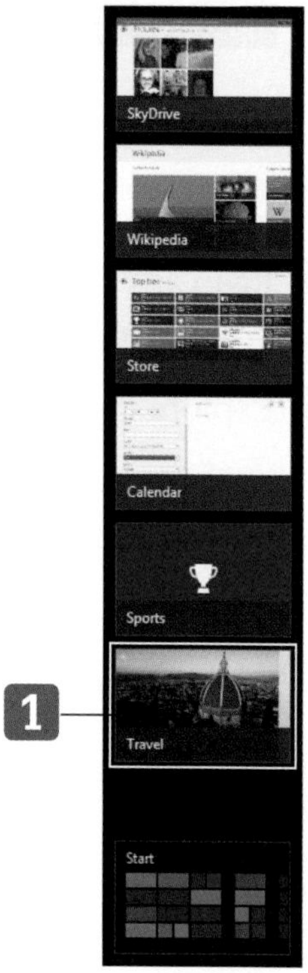

3. Position your mouse in the top left corner of the screen to view and click the last used app. Drag the mouse downwards slowly to view the other available apps.

HOT TIP: The left to right flicking motion from the left edge of a touch screen is the best option for moving among open apps on a tablet.

DID YOU KNOW?
Some tablets offer USB ports. You may be able to connect a USB mouse. Likewise, if Bluetooth is an option, you may be able to connect a Bluetooth keyboard.

4 Use desktop applications

Introduction

In the previous chapter you learned about 'Start screen' apps. These apps look, feel and act like apps you might use on any smartphone, iPad or Android tablet. Start screen apps have charms that enable you to navigate and use them. Each have somewhat limited features, and are not nearly as robust as the applications and programs you may already be used to.

In this chapter you'll learn about a different kind of app: the desktop app. Desktop apps open on the desktop, the traditional computing environment. These desktop applications can be programs you install, like Adobe Photoshop Elements, or less complex applications that come with new printers, cameras or scanners. They can be Windows accessories too, like the Calculator, Notepad, the Snipping Tool and Sound Recorder. Windows Media Player is a desktop application, and Control Panel opens on the desktop too, as does File Explorer. There are lots of programs and Windows features that need access to the desktop to run.

In this chapter you'll learn how to locate the desktop apps from the Start screen, and how to use a few of them. From then on, whenever an application opens on the desktop, you'll understand how to use it and why it's a desktop app.

Find the desktop applications

The Start screen offers access to the applications, programs, accessories and features available on your computer, including the desktop apps. If they aren't available on the Start screen, you can find them from the All apps screen.

2

1. Access the Start screen. You can press the Windows key to get there.
2. Scroll through what's shown. Almost everything that's there by default is a Start screen app tile.
3. Right-click an empty area of the screen and click All apps.
4. Scroll right and look at the available desktop apps. A few are shown here.

4

? DID YOU KNOW?

An app is a desktop app if it opens on the desktop.

WHAT DOES THIS MEAN?

Desktop: this is the traditional computing environment; it offers the taskbar, the Recycle Bin, the Notification area and so on.

Write a letter with Notepad

If you need to create and print a simple document like a shopping list or to-do list, or need to put together a weekly newsletter that you send via email, you can use Notepad. Notepad is a desktop app and it is one of the easiest to use.

1. From the Start screen, type notepad. Click Notepad from the results.
2. Click Format, and then Font.
3. From the Font dialogue box, under Size, click 20. Click OK.
4. Type your note, list or letter.

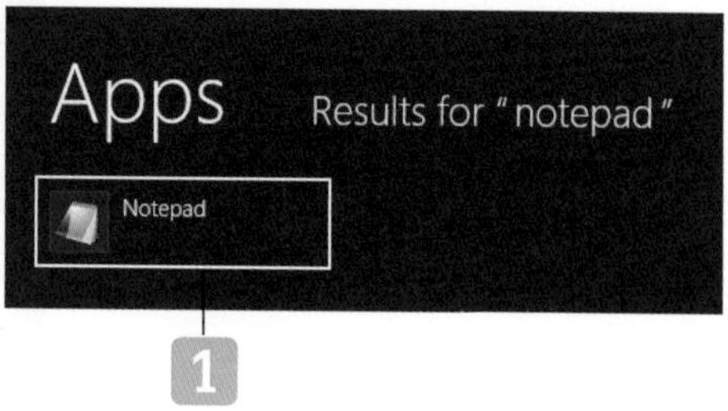

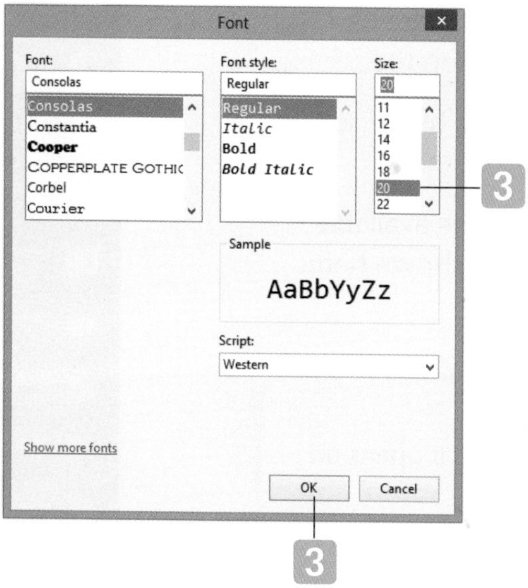

HOT TIP: Notepad has five menus: File, Edit, Format, View and Help. After you become familiar with these menus, what you learn will carry over to almost any other program you'll use.

ALERT: If you close Notepad before saving the file, your work will be lost.

Save a letter with Notepad

If you want to save a letter you've written in Notepad so you can work with it later, you have to click File and then click Save (or Save As). This will allow you to name the file and save it to your hard drive. The next time you want to view the file, you can click File and then click Open, if Notepad is already open, or you can search for the file from the Start screen by searching for the file name.

1. With Notepad open and a few words typed, click File.
2. Click Save As.
3. Type a unique name for the file. (Notice that the default folder for saving a Notepad document is Documents library.)
4. Click Save.

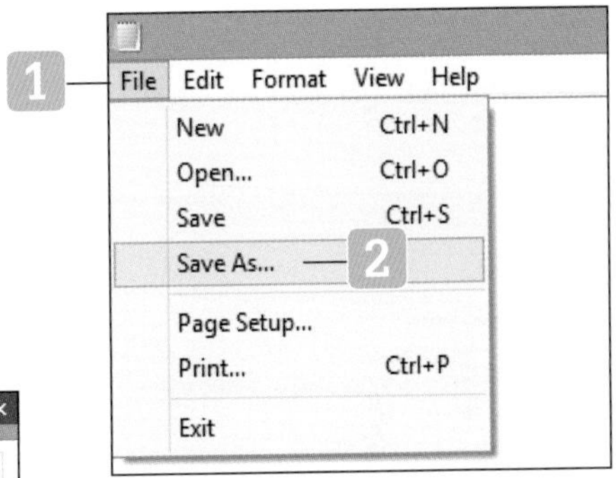

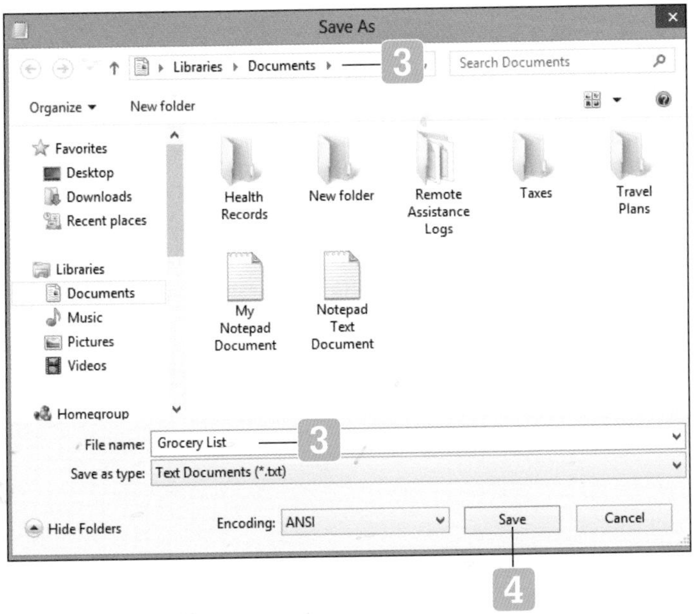

HOT TIP: You can reopen a saved file and make changes to it, and then click the Save icon. Your changes will be saved to the file.

HOT TIP: You can change the folder you save to by selecting another one from the left pane of the Save As window. This is called the Navigation pane. You could choose Desktop if you want the file to be saved directly to the desktop, for instance.

DID YOU KNOW?

If you only want to type something and print it, there's no reason to save it to your computer.

Print a letter with Notepad

Sometimes you'll need to print a letter so you can mail it, print a shopping list to take with you, or print a list of steps to complete a task. You can access the Print command from Notepad's File menu.

1. With the document open in Notepad, click File.
2. Click Print.
3. Select a printer (if more than one exists).
4. Set Preferences as desired; click Print.

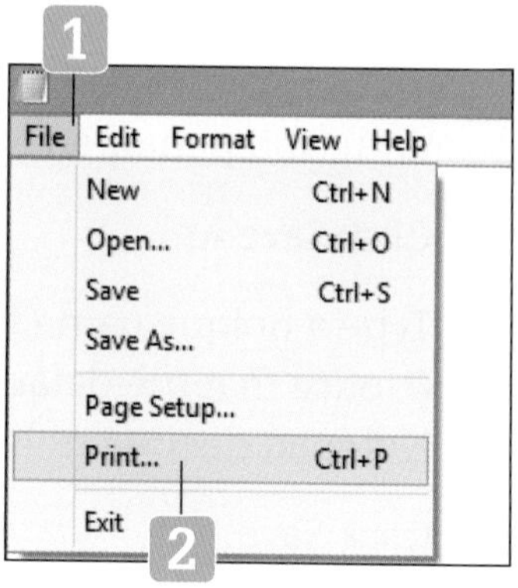

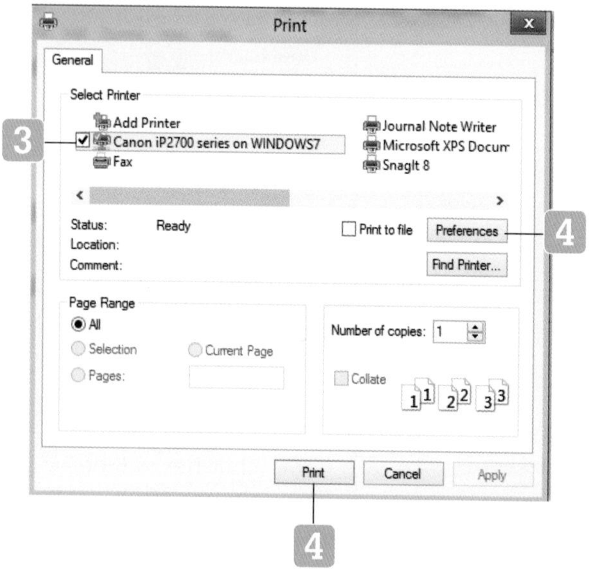

HOT TIP: You have to have a printer installed, plugged in and turned on to print. Additionally, the Print dialogue box must show that the printer is 'Ready' before you can print to it.

WHAT DOES THIS MEAN?

Printer Preferences: lets you select the page orientation, print order and the type of paper you'll be printing on, among other features.

Page Range: lets you select which pages to print.

Use the calculator

You've used a calculator before, and using the Windows 8 calculator is not much different from a hand-held one, except that you input numbers with a mouse click, keyboard, a number pad, or your finger. There are four calculators available, and Standard is the default. Calculator is available from the All apps screen.

1. From the Start screen, right-click and then click All apps.
2. Scroll right, and under Windows Accessories, click Calculator.
3. Input numbers and operations using any applicable method.
4. This is the Standard calculator. Click the View menu to see other calculator options. Note the other options.
5. Close Calculator by clicking the X in the top right corner of it.

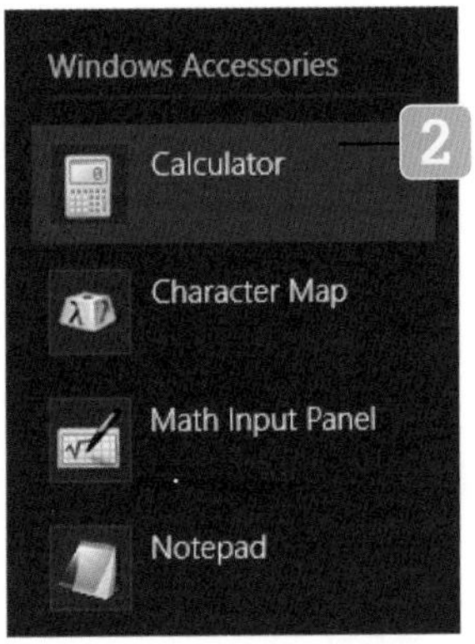

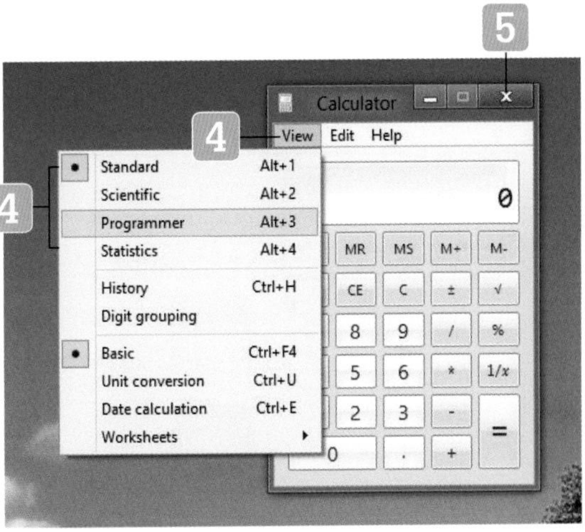

HOT TIP: Explore each menu option and the available features there. Make sure to look at View > Worksheets > Mortgage, to see how worksheets function.

HOT TIP: If you have trouble using the mouse to click the numbers on the calculator, use the keypad on your keyboard.

Take a picture of what's on the screen

Sometimes you'll see something on your screen you want to capture to keep or share. It may be part of a webpage (like a great news story or a fabulous place to go on holiday), or an error message you want to show your grandchild (who can probably resolve it). You can capture the screen using the Snipping Tool, another desktop app.

1. From the Start screen, type Snip.
2. In the results, click Snipping Tool.
3. Click New.
4. Drag your mouse across any part of the screen.
   When you let go of the mouse, the snip will appear in the Snipping Tool window.
5. Explore each menu: File, Edit, Tools and Help, and the options on the toolbar.
   Refer to the next task for more information.

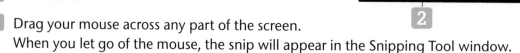

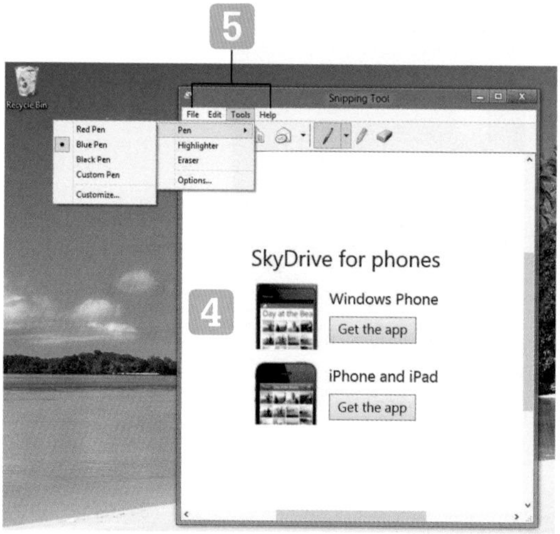

HOT TIP: Editing tools will become available after creating a snip. You can write on a clip with a red, blue, black or customised pen or a highlighter, and if you mess up, you can use the eraser.

DID YOU KNOW?
You can open the Snipping Tool from the Start screen's All apps page.

Share a screenshot

You can use the Snipping Tool to take a picture of your screen as detailed in the previous section. You can even write on it with a 'pen' or 'highlighter'. You can also email that screenshot if you'd like to share it with someone. You can save it too.

1. Take a screenshot with the Snipping Tool.
2. If desired, use the pen, highlighter and other tools to write on the image.
3. Click File, and click Send To.
4. Click Email Recipient.
5. Insert the recipients' names, change the subject if desired, type a message if desired, and click Send.

HOT TIP: If you think you'll use the Snipping Tool often, pin it to the Start screen or the taskbar on the desktop.

ALERT: If you select Email Recipient, this will insert the snip inside an email. Note that you can also send the snip as an attachment.

SEE ALSO: For more information on sending an email, refer to Chapter 8.

Record and save a sound clip

Sometimes the spoken word is best. With the Sound Recorder, you can record a quick note to yourself or others instead of writing a letter or sending an email. Sound Recorder is a simple tool with only three options, Start Recording, Stop Recording and Resume Recording. To record, click Start Recording; to stop, click Stop Recording; to continue, click Resume Recording. You save your recording as a Windows Media Audio File, which will play in the Music app and in Windows Media Player.

1. From the Start screen, type Sound Recorder.
2. Select Sound Recorder in the results.
3. Click Start Recording, speak into your microphone to record your message, then click Stop Recording. If prompted to save the file, click Cancel.
4. Click Resume Recording and speak some more.
5. Click Stop Recording to complete the recording.
6. In the Save As dialogue box (and notice this sound clip will save to the Documents library), type a name for your recording and click Save.
7. Click the X in the Sound Recorder to close it.

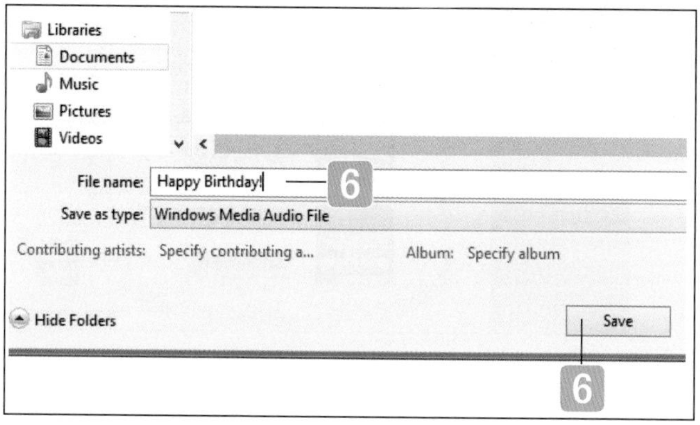

HOT TIP: You can use your saved recording in other Windows-related programs, email the clip, and you can save and play the clip on almost any media player.

ALERT: You can't record anything without a microphone.

Play a sound clip

You must locate the sound clip to play it. If you know it's in the Documents library and you know how to use File Explorer to get there, you can locate it yourself. If you aren't sure where it's saved or even what the Documents library is, you can let Windows 8 find it for you. We'll do the latter here.

1. From the Start screen, type the name of the file.
2. Click Files in the right pane.
3. Click your file in the left pane.
4. If you are prompted to fill out information, accept Express settings or perform other tasks, do so. You will only have to do this once.
5. Click the Play icon.

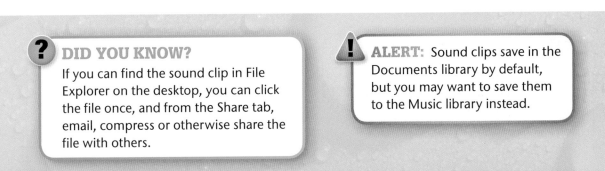

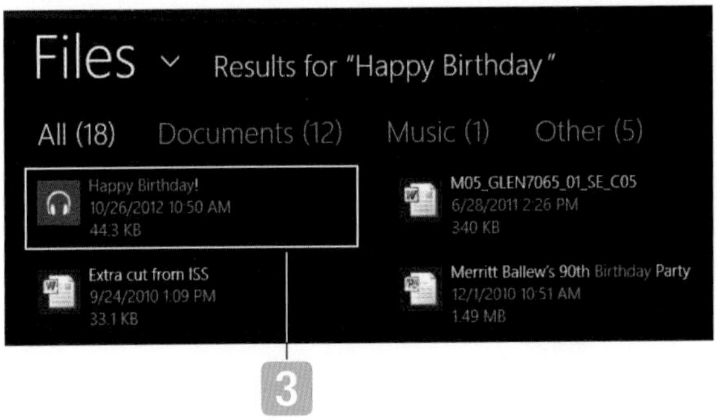

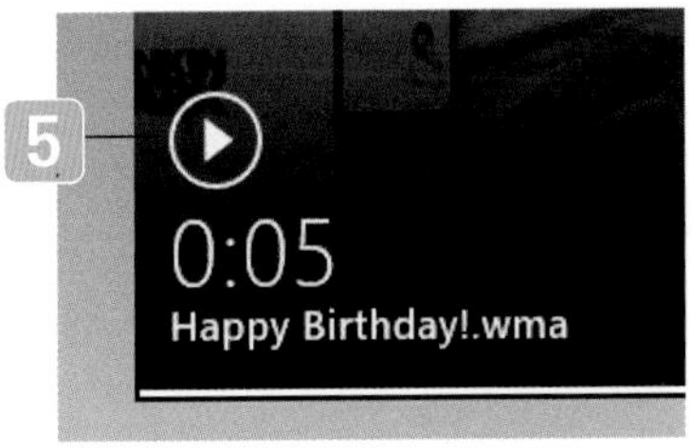

DID YOU KNOW?
If you can find the sound clip in File Explorer on the desktop, you can click the file once, and from the Share tab, email, compress or otherwise share the file with others.

ALERT: Sound clips save in the Documents library by default, but you may want to save them to the Music library instead.

Explore other desktop apps

There are many more desktop apps available besides those that have been introduced here. All are available from the All apps screen, or you can simply start typing their name at the Start screen to locate them. Here are a few to try before moving on.

1. Math Input Panel – Write an equation with your finger, stylus or pen and this application will type it for you. You can then copy and paste the equation anywhere that accepts text.
2. Paint – Create flyers, signs, flowcharts and other artwork.
3. Sticky Notes – Create your own digital notes.
4. WordPad – Create more complex documents than is possible with Notepad.
5. Windows Fax and Scan – To create faxes and send them. You must connect a phone line to your computer to get started.

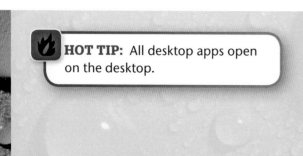

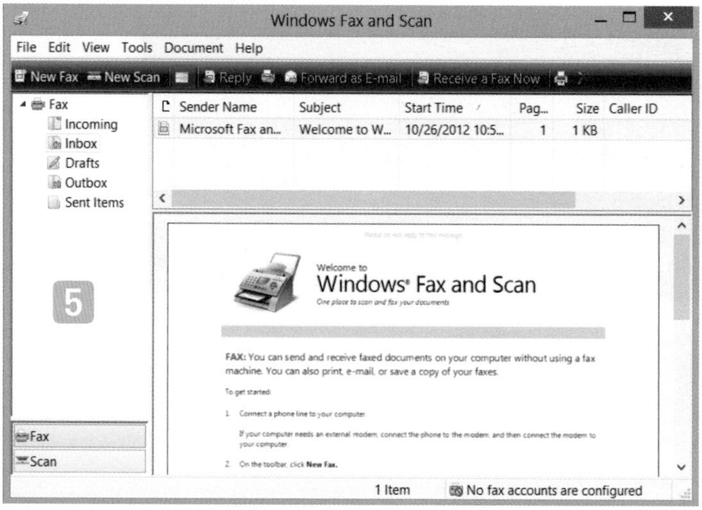

HOT TIP: All desktop apps open on the desktop.

5 Locate and manage the data you keep and acquire

Introduction

Data is the stuff you save to your computer. Data might be letters you write in Notepad, pictures you upload from your digital camera, music you copy from your CD collection, or movies you purchase from the Internet. Data can also consist of lists of email addresses, installation files you download, or your favourite websites in Internet Explorer.

Each time you manually opt to save data, you'll be prompted to tell Windows 8 *where* you want to save that data. For the most part though, Windows 8 will *tell you* where it thinks you should save the data. Documents go in the My Documents folder, Music in the My Music folder, Pictures in the My Pictures folder and so on. To get the most from Windows 8, you need to understand the file structure already in place.

In this chapter you'll learn where files are saved by default and how to create your own folders and subfolders for organising the data already in them. You'll learn how to copy, move and delete files and folders, how to share data, and how to view data in different ways. You'll also learn how to create a basic backup. All of this happens on the desktop, using File Explorer.

Explore your libraries

There are four libraries already available to you for saving and storing data: Documents, Music, Pictures and Videos. You'll find them in File Explorer, a window that opens only on the desktop. The first step in understanding how Windows 8 organises the data you keep and where to save data you create or acquire in the future is to understand these libraries.

1. Access the Desktop. (You can use the Windows key + D key combination or click the Desktop tile on the Start screen.)
2. Click the Folder icon on the taskbar.

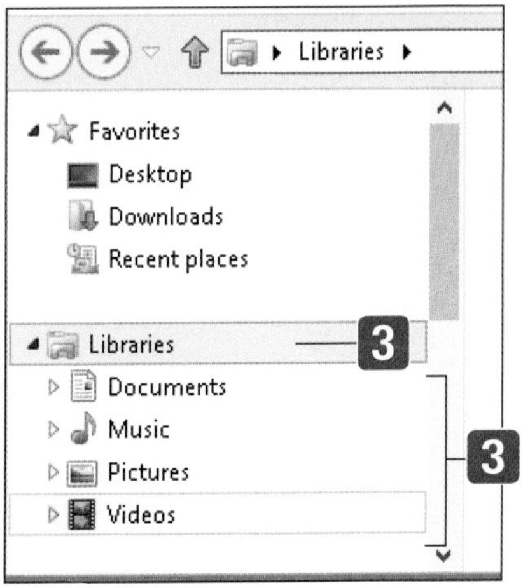

3. Position the cursor over Libraries, and if you do not see a down-facing arrow as shown here, click Libraries to show it (and the libraries underneath).

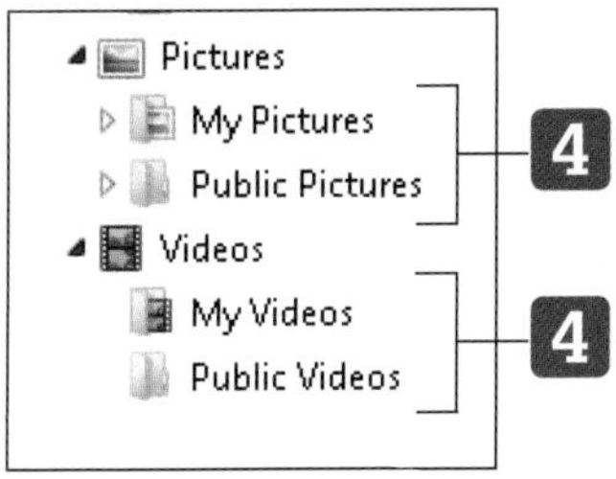

4. Click the right-facing arrow by each library entry so that it becomes a down-facing arrow. Note the folders that appear underneath. You store data here.

HOT TIP: You will see more folders than the personal and public folders if they are available, if you have purposely created or included them, or if you have permission to access them via shared folders on a network.

DID YOU KNOW?

If you click a library in the Navigation pane, you'll see what's in both the personal and the public folders; if you click only one of those, the data will be separated appropriately.

WHAT DOES THIS MEAN?

Library: a virtual storage area that makes it possible for you to access data that is stored in a personal folder (like My Documents) and the related public folder (like Public Documents), and any other folders or libraries you've created or specifically made available there.

Save data to a library

You must be adept at saving data to the proper library or folder. Sometimes you will save data using a desktop app's File menu. Other times you will use a download dialogue box. And in other cases, you may use a graphic like the one you see when using an app like SkyDrive. You may even use something completely proprietary, such as a menu or option in a software program you use with a digital camera or scanner. In all of these cases, you must know how to navigate the folder hierarchy already provided for you.

1. In a Start screen app, click the arrow beside Files to choose the desired library or folder.
2. In any Save or Save As dialogue box, locate the desired library in the Navigation pane.

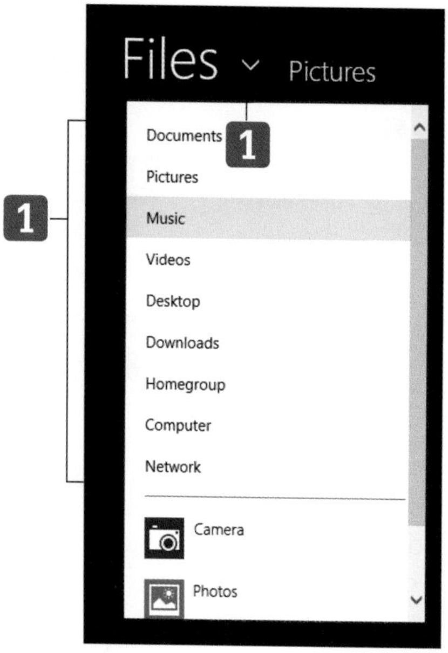

HOT TIP: When you save a file to a library, it is really saved to the related 'My' folder, such as My Documents or My Pictures. If you want to save the data to the related public folder instead, click the arrow beside the desired library and select the public folder underneath it.

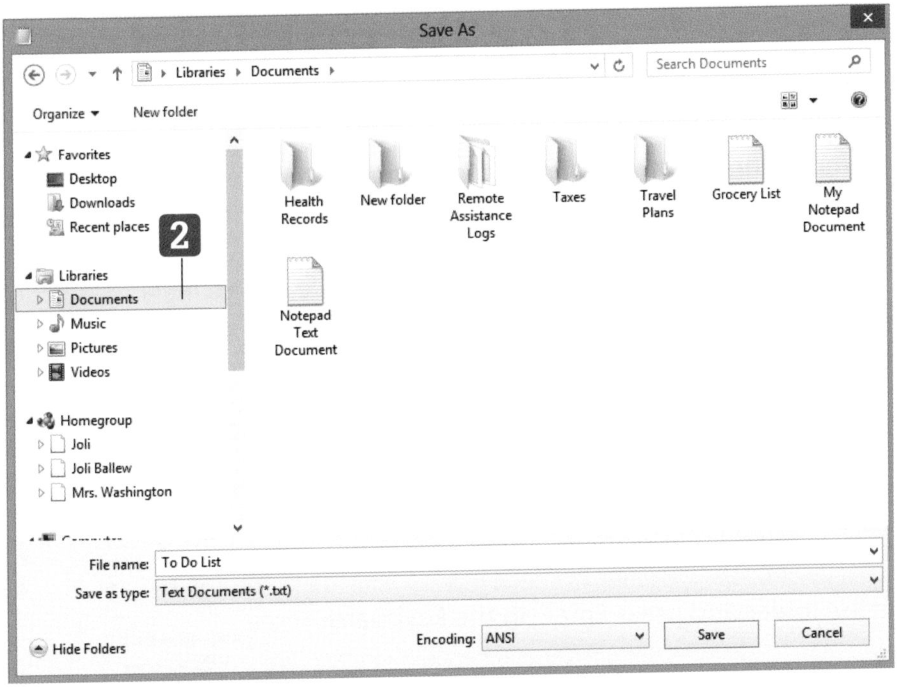

3 In Internet Explorer, click the arrow beside Save and click Save as. You may opt for the Downloads folder.

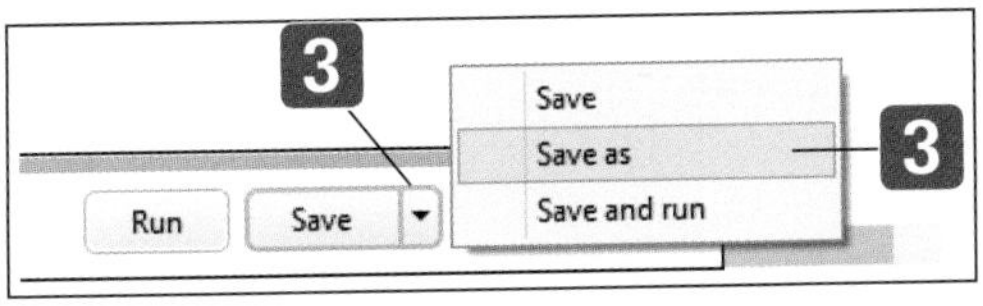

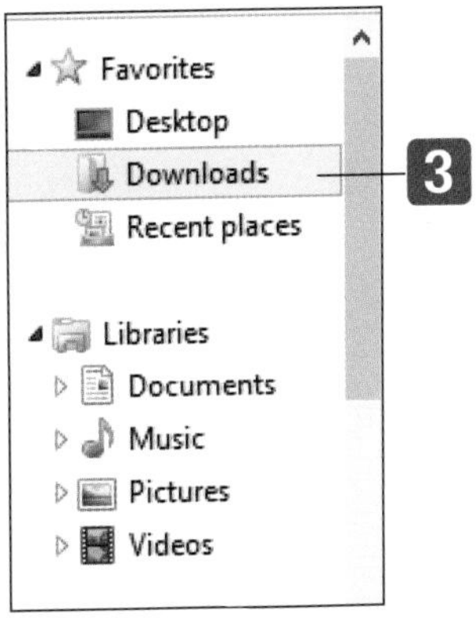

DID YOU KNOW?

You can save the file to a different computer on your network or a different drive on your computer from the Network and Computer options, respectively.

Create a folder or subfolder

For a while at least, it'll be just fine to save all of your pictures to the Pictures library and all of your documents to the Documents library. But after a while, those folders may become overrun with data. When this happens (or before), you should create subfolders and move related data into them.

1. At the desktop, use the Windows key + E keyboard combination to open File Explorer.
2. In the Navigation pane, expand any library and select a folder in it. (We've chosen My Videos.)
3. From the Home tab, click New folder.
4. Name the folder and press Enter on the keyboard.

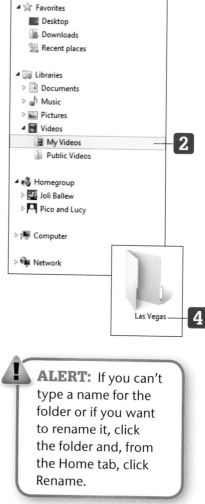

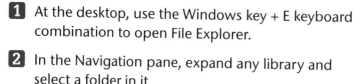

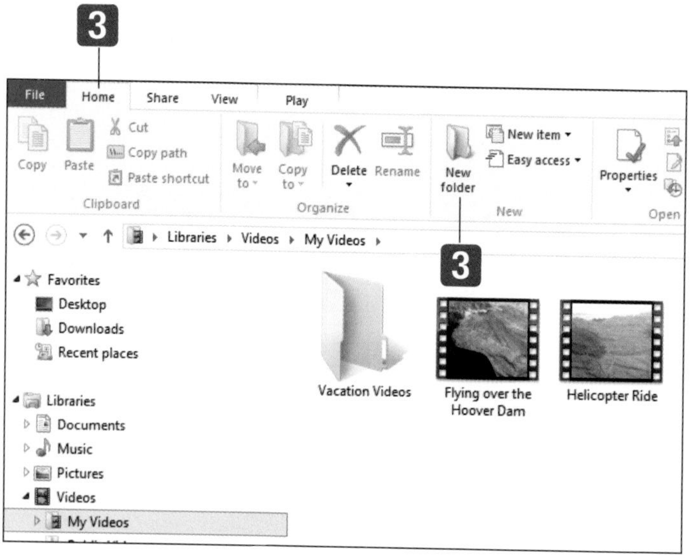

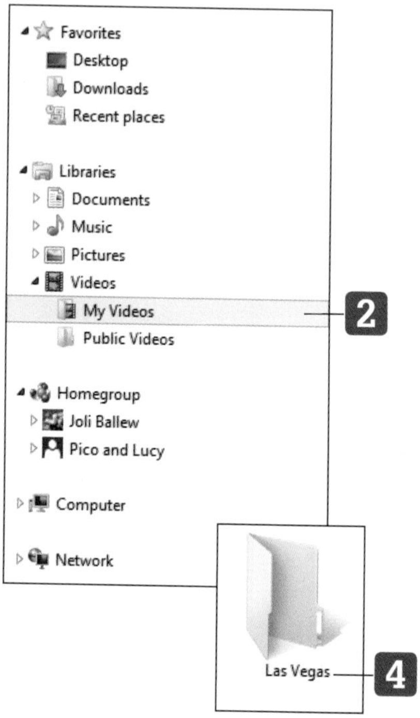

ALERT: If you can't type a name for the folder or if you want to rename it, click the folder and, from the Home tab, click Rename.

HOT TIP: Consider creating subfolders inside My Pictures named Children, Pets, Holidays and Friends, and then move related photos into them. Likewise, you could create subfolders inside My Documents named Taxes, Health, Resumes and Letters.

DID YOU KNOW?
You can right-click the desktop or inside any folder, point to New and then click Folder to create a new folder there.

Copy or move a file or folder

Folders are supposed to contain files. Files can be documents, pictures, music, videos and more. Sometimes you'll need to copy a file to another location. Perhaps you want to copy files to an external drive, memory card or USB thumb drive for the purpose of backing them up. In other instances, moving a file is a better option, such as when you create a subfolder to organise data in a folder.

1. In File Explorer, locate a file to copy or move; click it once to select it.
2. From the Home tab, click either Move to or Copy to.

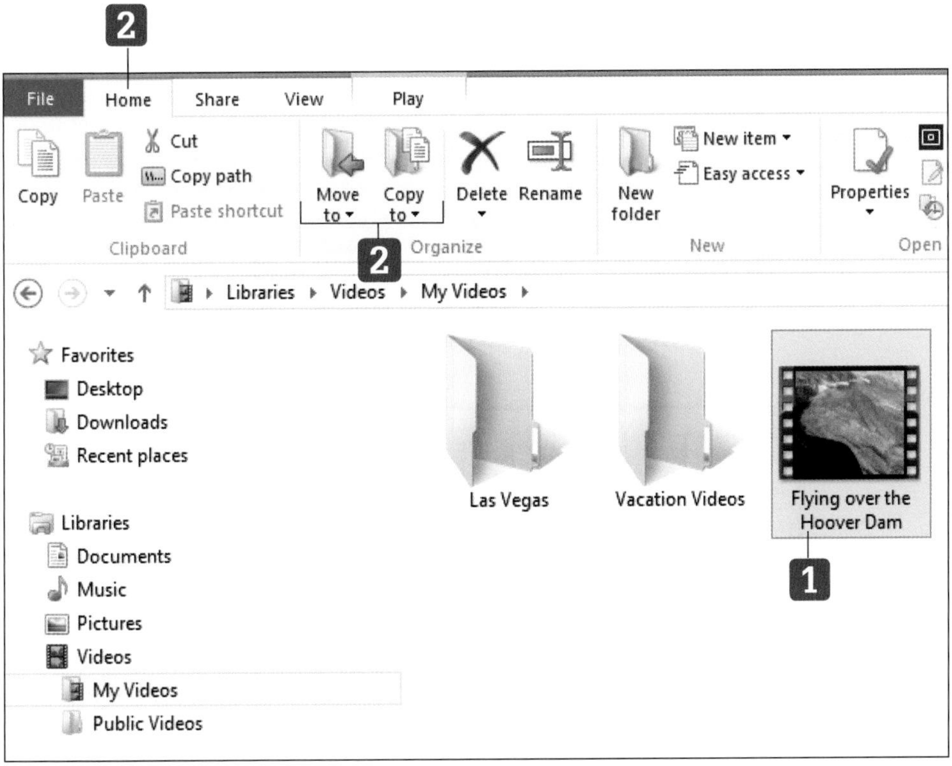

? DID YOU KNOW?

When you copy something, an exact duplicate is made. The original copy of the data remains where it is and a copy of it is placed somewhere else. For the most part, this is not what you want to do when organising data. When organising data, you generally want to move the data.

3 Choose the desired location from the list. If you don't see it, click Choose location.

4 In the Move Items or Copy Items dialogue box that appears, locate the desired folder.

5 Click the folder and then click Move or Copy.

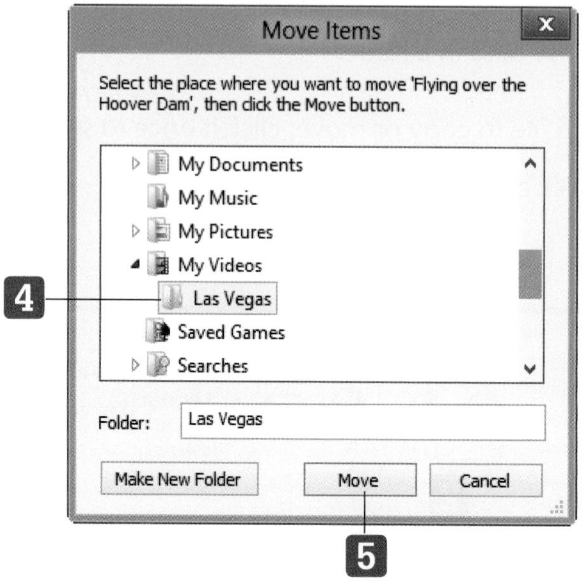

HOT TIP: Hold down the Ctrl key to select non-contiguous files, or the Shift key to select contiguous ones. Then, you can perform tasks on multiple files at once.

Delete a file or folder

When you are sure you no longer need a particular file or folder, you can delete it. Deleting it sends the file or the entire folder (contents and all) to the Recycle Bin on the desktop. This data can be 'restored' if you decide you need it later, provided you have not emptied the Recycle Bin since deleting the file.

1. Locate a file or folder to delete.
2. Either:
   - Right-click the item and click Delete, or
   - Click the file once and, from the Home tab, click Delete.

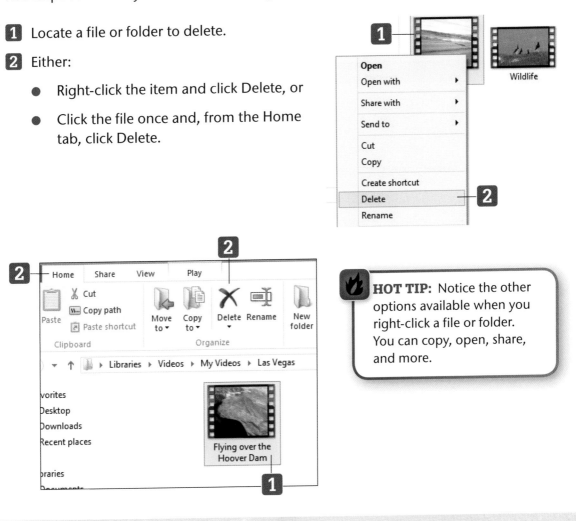

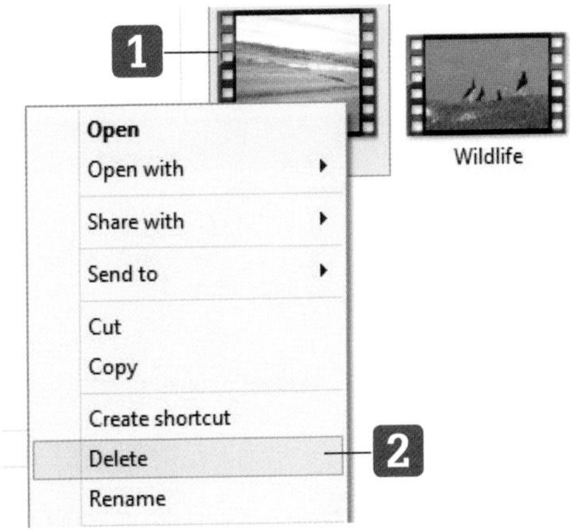

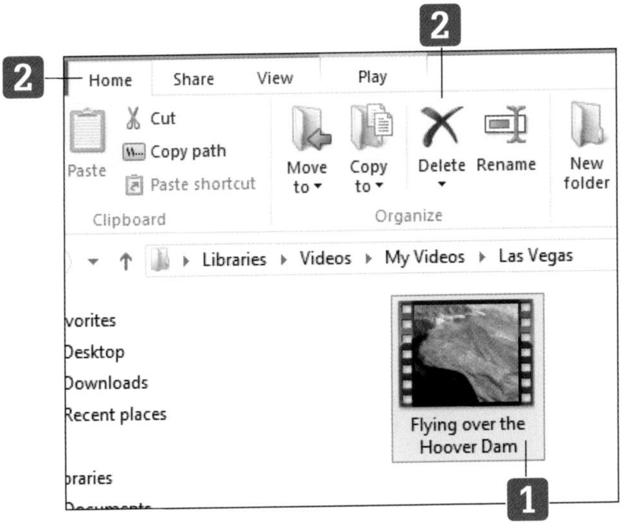

HOT TIP: Notice the other options available when you right-click a file or folder. You can copy, open, share, and more.

DID YOU KNOW?
It's best to keep unwanted or unnecessary data off your hard drive. That means you should delete data you don't need regularly, including items in the Recycle Bin.

Explore your personal folders

The libraries and the subfolders you create are not the only places to which you can save data; you have a personal user folder with additional folders, although you probably won't access them nearly as often as you do libraries. To access these folders, you must know how to navigate there.

1 Open File Explorer.

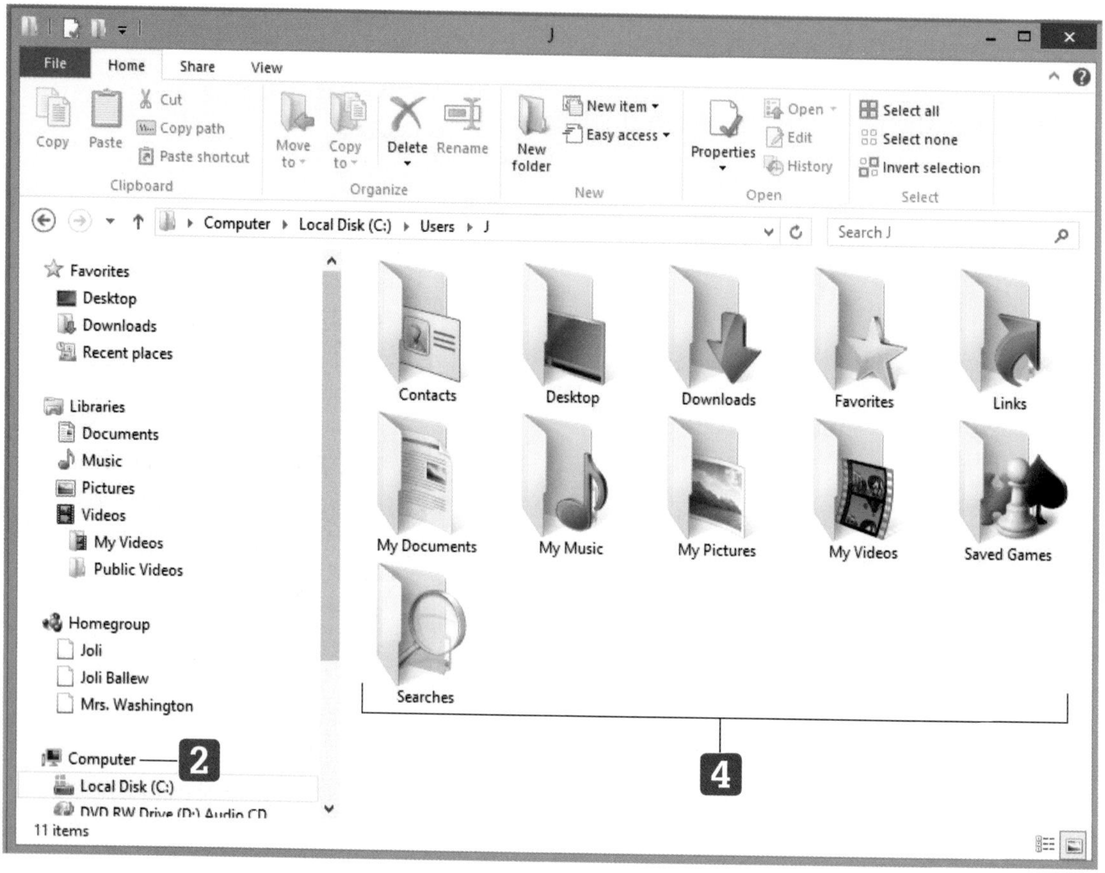

HOT TIP: Note the tabs at the top of the File Explorer window. We've changed the 'view' to 'medium icons' so they are easier to see.

HOT TIP: Right-click your user name while in the Users folder to create a shortcut for it on the desktop.

2. In the Navigation pane, click Computer.
3. In the Content pane, double-click Local Disk, then double-click Users, and then double-click your user name. The 'path' appears in the File Explorer window.
4. Explore these additional personal folders. Note that My Documents, My Music, My Pictures and My Videos are the same folders as you find in the related libraries.

WHAT DOES THIS MEAN?

Your personal folder contains the following folders, which in turn contain data you've saved:

Contacts: this folder might contain information about the contacts you keep, such as email addresses, phone numbers, home and business addresses and more.

Desktop: this folder contains links to items on your desktop.

Downloads: this folder does not contain anything by default. It does offer a place to which to save items you download from the Internet, such as drivers and third-party programs.

Favorites: this folder contains the items in Internet Explorer's Favorites list.

Links: this folder contains shortcuts to the Desktop and Recent places, among others.

My Documents: this folder holds documents you save and subfolders you create.

My Music: this folder contains music you save.

My Pictures: this folder contains pictures you save.

My Videos: this folder contains videos you save.

Saved Games: this folder contains information about the games you play.

Searches: this folder contains information about searches you've performed.

Search for a file

All of your data is likely saved to your hard drive. It's stored in libraries, folders and subfolders. You learned how to search for a file from the Start screen in the last chapter (you just type the file name and click Files to view the results). You can also navigate to a file using File Explorer and double-click it to open it.

1. Open the desktop and then open File Explorer.
2. In the navigation pane click Documents, Music, Pictures or Videos.
3. Note the files in there.
4. Double-click any file to open it, view it or play it.

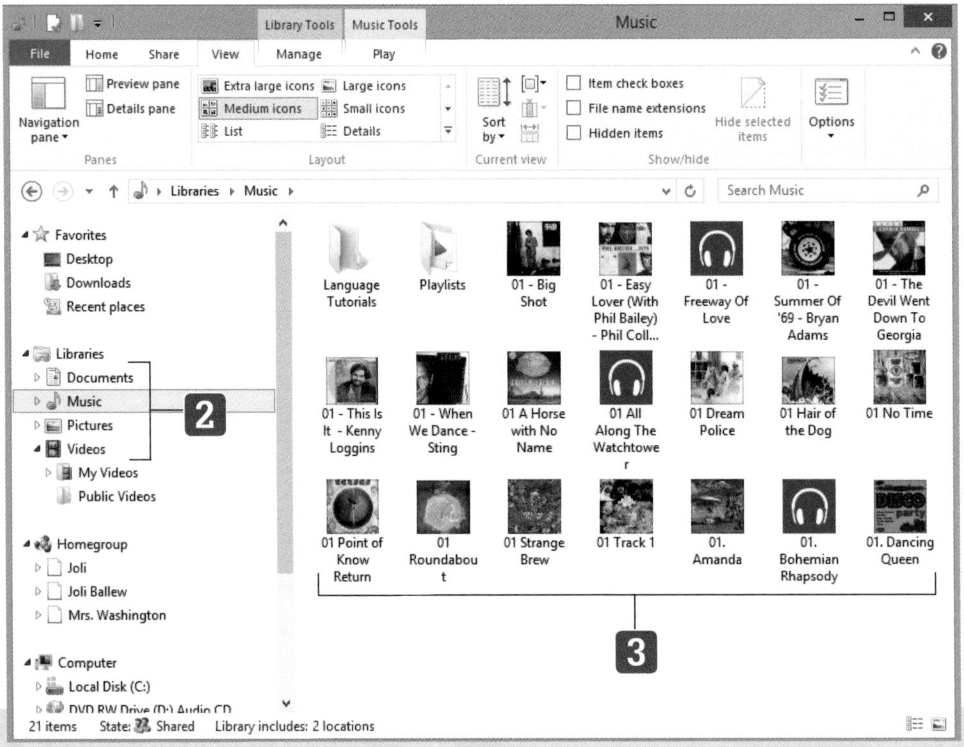

SEE ALSO: Browse for a file from a desktop app, next.

Browse for a file from a desktop app

You can open a file from inside a desktop application. Most offer a File menu with various options to locate and open files.

1. Open Notepad.
2. Click File, and then click Open.
3. Using techniques you've already learned in this chapter, locate the file to open. Double-click it.

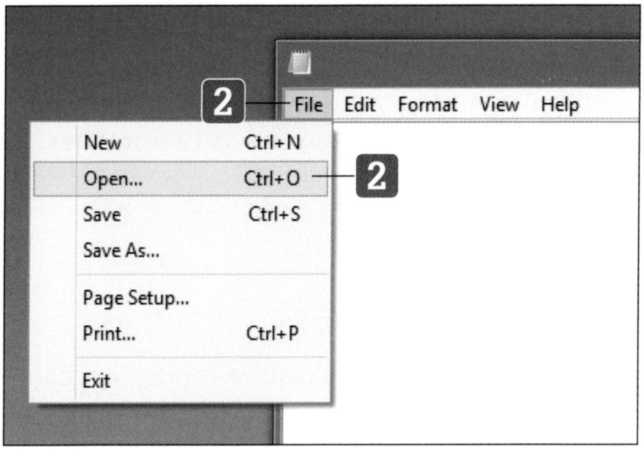

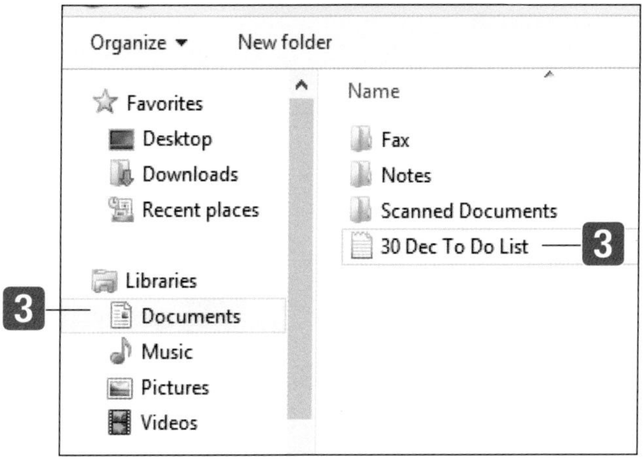

HOT TIP: If you always save pictures to the Pictures library, documents to the Documents library and so on, you'll never have trouble finding your files.

DID YOU KNOW?
Many desktop apps, including WordPad, offer a list of files (from the File tab) that you've recently opened or edited.

Change the size of an open window

A window can be minimised (on the taskbar), maximised (filling the entire desktop), or in restore mode (not maximised or minimised, but showing on the desktop). When in restore mode, you can drag from any corner or edge to resize it.

1. A maximised window is as large as it can be and takes up the entire screen. You can maximise a window that is on the desktop by clicking the square in the top right corner. If the icon shows two squares, it's already maximised.

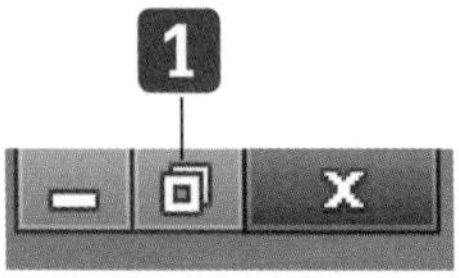

2. When a window is in restore mode, you can resize the window by dragging from any corner or edge. An icon is in restore mode if there is a single square in the top right corner. You can access this mode from the maximised position by dragging from the title bar downwards.
3. When a window is minimised, it does not appear on the screen, and instead is relegated to the taskbar. You cannot resize the window while on the taskbar.

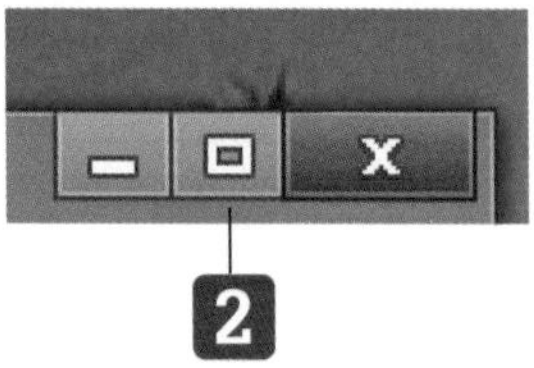

HOT TIP: To bring any window to the front of the others, click its title bar. This makes it the active window.

DID YOU KNOW?
Hold down the Alt key and press the Tab key repeatedly to move through open windows on the desktop. When you stop, the selected window will become the active window.

HOT TIP: You can quickly maximise a window by dragging its title bar upwards.

Use Snap, Peek and Shake

When working on the desktop with multiple open windows, sometimes minimising, maximising and restoring or resizing isn't exactly what you want to do. Perhaps you want to make two windows share the screen equally; see what is behind the open windows, perhaps to see information on the desktop; or minimise all of the open windows except one quickly. You can do this with Snap, Peek and Shake.

1. Snap – To position two open windows so that each takes up half of the screen, using their title bars, drag one quickly to the left and the other quickly to the right. Each will 'snap' into place.
2. Peek – To view what's on the desktop, position your mouse in the bottom right corner of the desktop. The windows will become transparent and you can see behind them.
3. Shake – To minimise all but one window, click, hold and quickly move your mouse left and right on the window to keep. This 'shaking' motion will make the others fall to the taskbar.

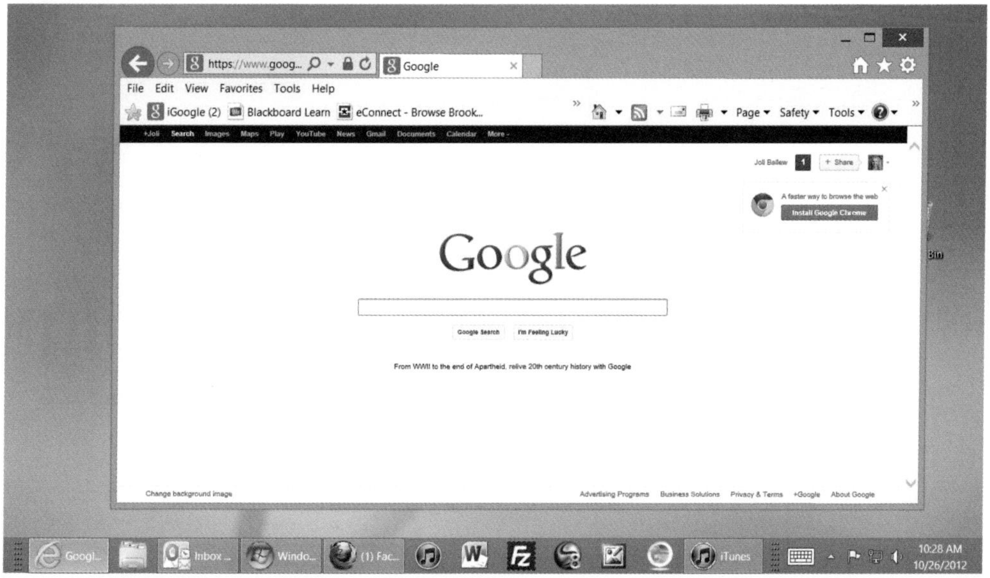

HOT TIP: Close desktop apps when you aren't using them. They will use resources in the background and could theoretically hamper performance.

DID YOU KNOW?
You can't do any of these things with Start screen apps.

Make icons easier to see

The items in a folder may be presented in a list, as icons or as tiles. When the items are set to Large icons or Extra large icons, they are easier to see.

1. Open File Explorer.
2. In the Navigation pane, click Pictures.
3. From the View tab, select a new layout. For Pictures, try Extra large icons.

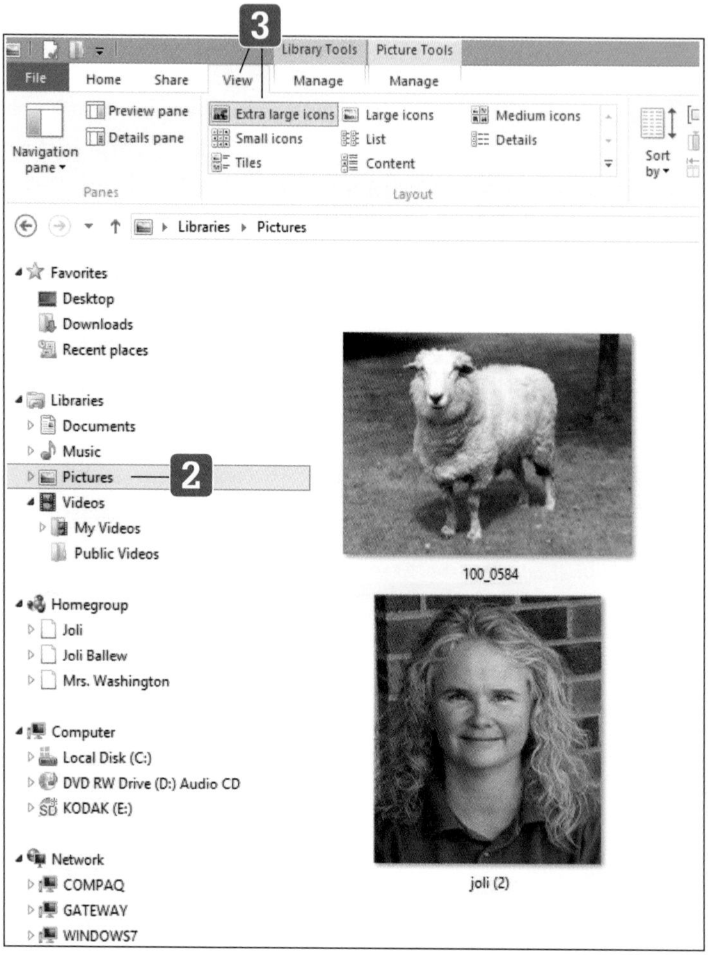

HOT TIP: To see information about the content in a folder, such as the date it was last modified, its size or type, choose List from the View pane.

DID YOU KNOW?

You can opt to show the Preview pane or Details pane in any File Explorer window. These options are also on the View tab.

Move data to public folders

If you want to share data with others on your network or with people who have user accounts on your computer, you can put the data in the related public folder. It's often best, for instance, to put all of the music you own in the Public Music folder; you can then access that music from anywhere on your network.

1. Locate the folder that contains the data to move. (It may be on a networked computer.)
2. Select the data. You can hold down the Shift or Ctrl key while selecting to select multiple files or folders.
3. From the Home tab, click Move to, and then Choose location.
4. Select the folder to move the data to.
5. Click Move.

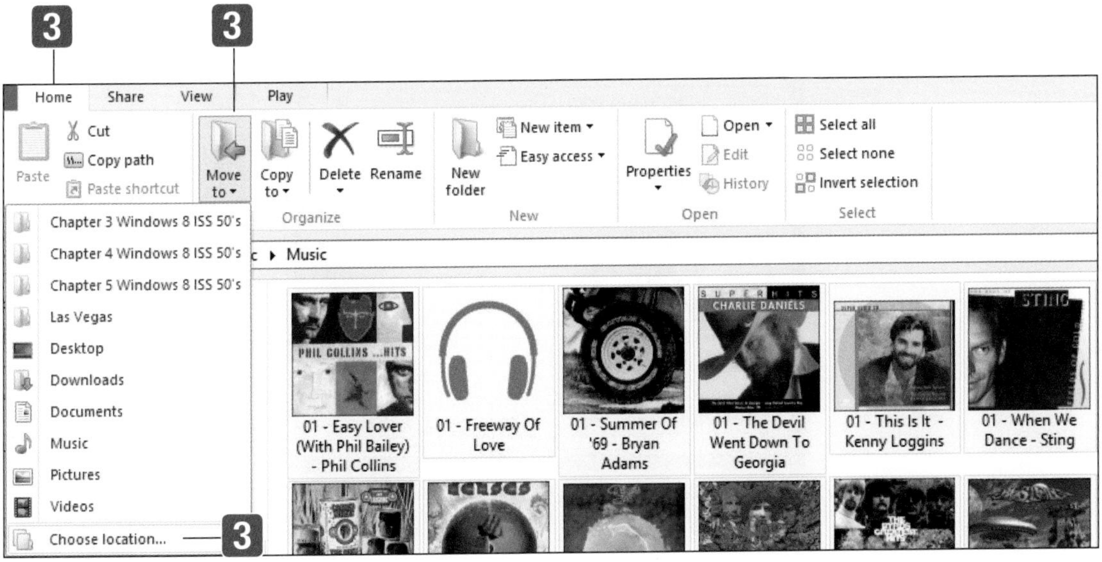

HOT TIP: Often, your new Windows 8 computer will have more hard drive space and a faster processor than any other (older) computer on your network. Thus, it may be best to move data you share to it, such as music, pictures and videos.

SEE ALSO: If you don't want to move data to public folders, you can share your personal folders instead. Refer to Chapter 6 to learn how.

Back up data quickly and easily

One way to back up your data is to copy it to an external drive. You can copy data to a DVD drive, a USB flash drive, a network drive or a larger external backup drive (among others). You copy the folder to the external drive the same way as you'd copy a folder to another area of your hard drive – you use the Copy command from the Home tab of any File Explorer window.

1. Using File Explorer, select the data to copy.
2. From the Home tab, click Copy to.
3. Click Choose Location.
4. Select the desired location.
5. Click Copy.

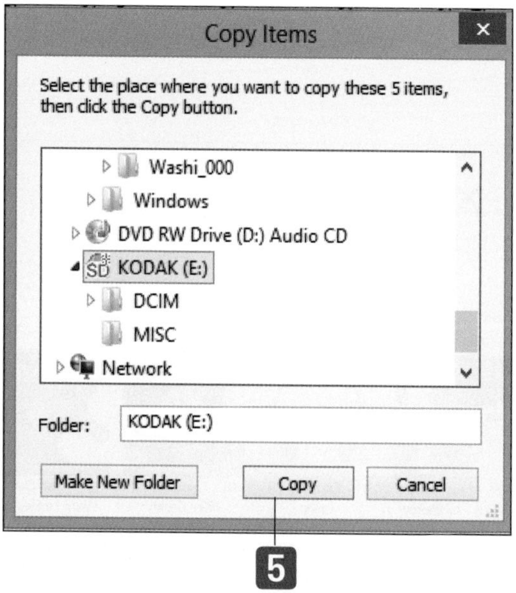

ALERT: Before you begin, plug in and/or attach the external drive if applicable.

SEE ALSO: Move a folder, earlier in this chapter.

6 Join networks and connect to the Internet

Introduction

A home network consists of two or more computers connected together for the purpose of sharing things like music, photos, printers and a connection to the Internet. There's often a modem that connects to the Internet, a router for connecting those computers together and a password for joining the network. If you have something like this at your house, you'll want to connect to it. Home networks are private and secure.

A free Wi-Fi hotspot is a different kind of network. This is generally offered by an establishment such as a library, pub, hotel or coffee shop and enables you and others to connect to the Internet for free while there. These networks also have a modem and router, and you connect wirelessly. This kind of network is public and is not secure.

In this chapter you'll learn how to join these two types of networks. You'll also learn how to enhance your home network with a homegroup, user accounts and strong passwords. Once your network is in good form, you can share personal data, enable a guest account and more.

Join your home network

You may have joined your own home network when you set up Windows 8. If you didn't, here are the guidelines for joining. If you don't have a home network, this won't apply to you.

1. Connect physically to a wired network using an ethernet cable or, if you have a wireless device, get within range of your wireless network.
2. Use the keyboard shortcut Windows key + I to access the Settings charm, then click the Network icon shown here (it should show that networks are 'Available').
3. Click the desired network in the resulting list.
4. Place a tick in the Connect automatically box if you plan to connect to this network again, and then click Connect.
5. Type the required passcode, passphrase or other credentials as prompted. Click Next.
6. Click Yes, turn on sharing and connect to devices. This tells Windows 8 you trust this network and want to consider it a private network (as opposed to a public one).

WHAT DOES THIS MEAN?

Private: this is a network you trust (such as a network at a friend's house, at your house or at work). This connection type lets your computer *discover* other computers, printers and devices on the network, and they can discover you. This is why you select Yes, turn on sharing and connect to devices. You want this to happen.

Public: this is a network that is not secure and that you cannot trust, such as networks in coffee shops, airports and libraries. Choose No, don't turn on sharing or connect to devices, before connecting to these kinds of networks. You do not want to share anything here.

ALERT: Almost all laptops and tablets have a button, switch or a key combination to enable or disable the Wi-Fi feature. If you have trouble connecting to a Wi-Fi network, make sure this is enabled.

DID YOU KNOW?

The network name and the password or passcode are created when you or a technician installs a modem or router.

Connect to a free wireless hotspot

Wi-Fi hotspots are popping up all over the country in coffee shops, parks, libraries and more. Wi-Fi hotspots let you connect to the Internet without having to be tethered to an ethernet cable or tied down with a high monthly wireless bill. These are public networks.

1. Get within range of the public wireless network.
2. Use the keyboard shortcut Windows key + I to access the Settings charm, then click the Network icon shown in the previous section.
3. Click the desired network.
4. Place a tick in the Connect automatically box if you plan to connect to this network again, and then click Connect.

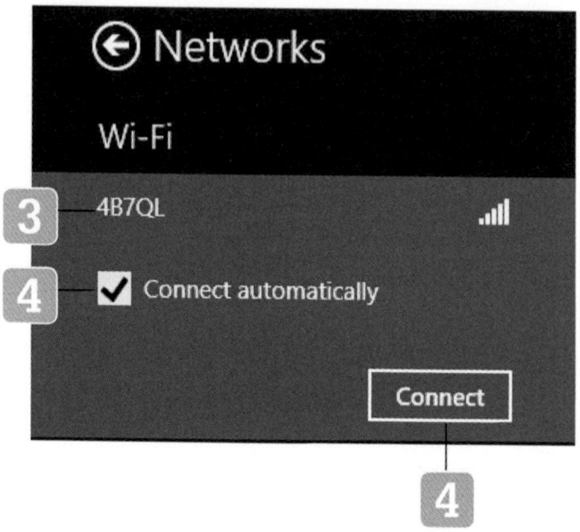

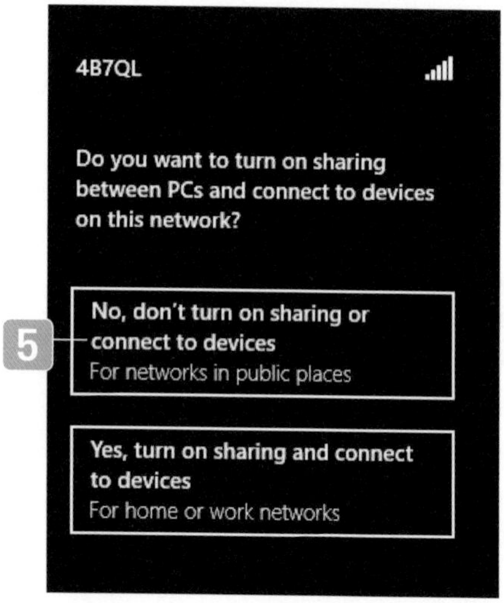

5. Click No, don't turn on sharing or connect to devices. This tells Windows you do not trust this network and want to consider it a public network (as opposed to a private one).

ALERT: You'll need a laptop or tablet with the required wireless hardware to use a free Wi-Fi hotspot.

HOT TIP: You'll be prompted for a security key if you're logging on to a secure network. You should not be prompted when logging on to a free, public Wi-Fi hotspot.

HOT TIP: To find a Wi-Fi hotspot close to you, go to http://maps.google.com and search for Wi-Fi hotspots.

Change the network type

If you made the wrong choice when deciding whether or not to turn on sharing and connect to devices the first time you connected to a network, you can change the setting. It's hidden away though, and is difficult to find if you don't know the trick.

1. From the Settings charm, click the Network icon.
2. Right-click the network you're connected to.
3. Choose Turn sharing on or off. Note the other options.
4. Select the proper setting:
   - No, don't turn on sharing or connect to devices – for public networks.
   - Yes, turn on sharing and connect to devices – for private networks.

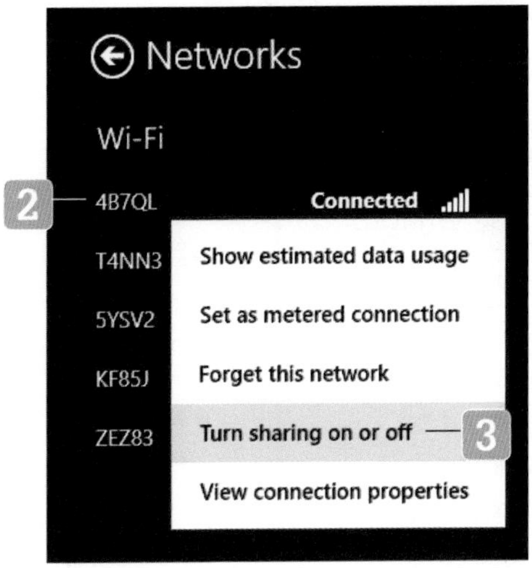

DID YOU KNOW?

You can right-click a network connection and choose View connection properties to retype the passcode or change settings related to the network such as security and encryption type.

HOT TIP: You can stop automatically connecting to a network by right-clicking it and choosing Forget this network.

Set up a homegroup

If you have a home network, if you want to share data among the computers that are connected to it, and if you have more than one computer on that network running either Windows 7 or Windows 8, you should create a homegroup. When you set up a homegroup, sharing is enabled for you, automatically.

1. Access the desktop. The Windows key + D is one way.
2. Right-click the Network icon on the taskbar, then click Open Network and Sharing Center.
3. If a homegroup exists on the network already, you'll see Available to join. Otherwise, you'll see Ready to create. Click the option you see.

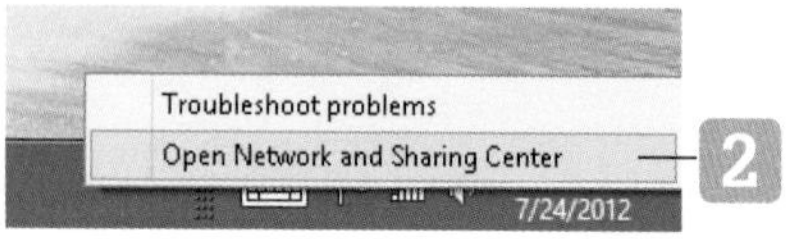

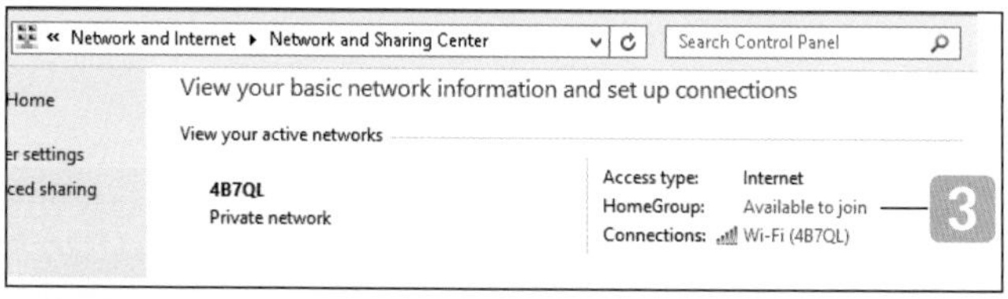

4. Click Create a homegroup or Join now, as applicable.
5. Click Next, and choose what to share.
6. If you created a new homegroup, write down the password – you'll need it to allow other computers to join. If you're joining an existing group, locate the password on another computer.

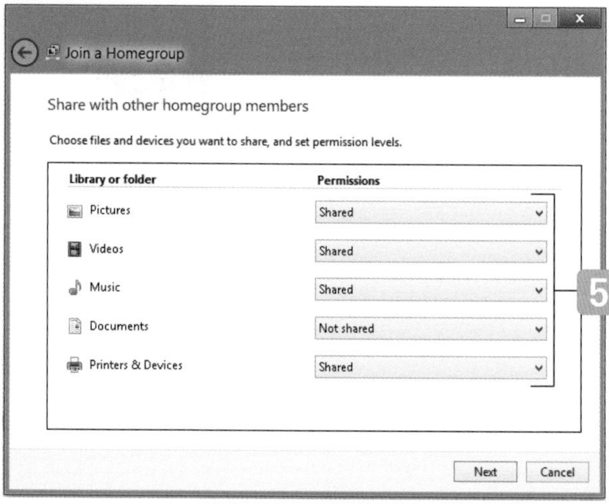

SEE ALSO: Locate the homegroup password, next.

HOT TIP: Even though only computers running Windows 7 or Windows 8 can participate in the homegroup, you can still create one even if you also have computers that run Vista or Windows XP. You can still share data using the public folders quite easily.

Locate the homegroup password

A homegroup password secures your homegroup. You'll need to know that password to connect another Windows 7 or Windows 8 computer to it.

1. In the Network and Sharing Center, click Joined beside HomeGroup.
2. Click View or print the homegroup password.

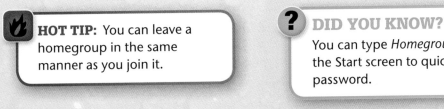

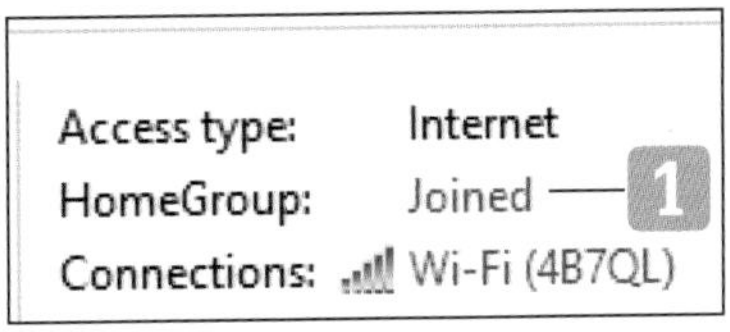

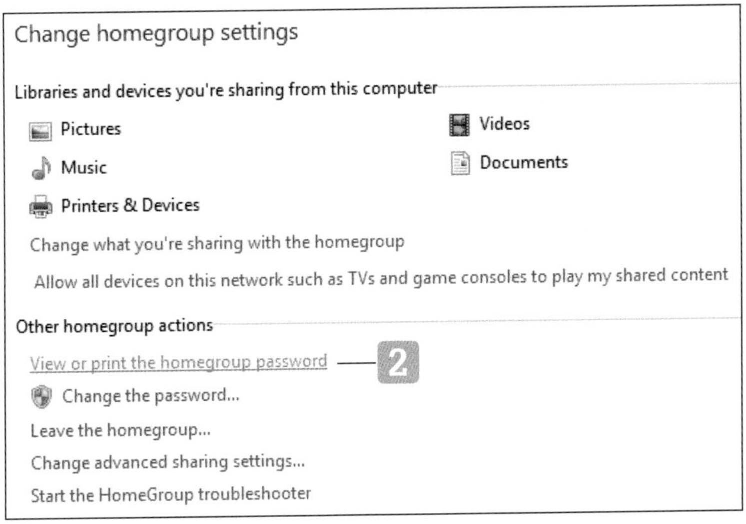

HOT TIP: You can leave a homegroup in the same manner as you join it.

DID YOU KNOW?
You can type *Homegroup password* at the Start screen to quickly locate the password.

Create a new user account

You created your user account when you first turned on your new Windows 8 computer. Your user account is what defines your personal folders and holds your settings for desktop background, screen saver and other items. If you share the computer with someone, they should have their own user account too. If every person who accesses your computer has their own standard user account and password, and if every person logs on using that account and then logs off when they're finished, you'll never have to worry about anyone accessing anyone else's personal data.

1. Click the Settings charm.
2. Click Change PC settings.

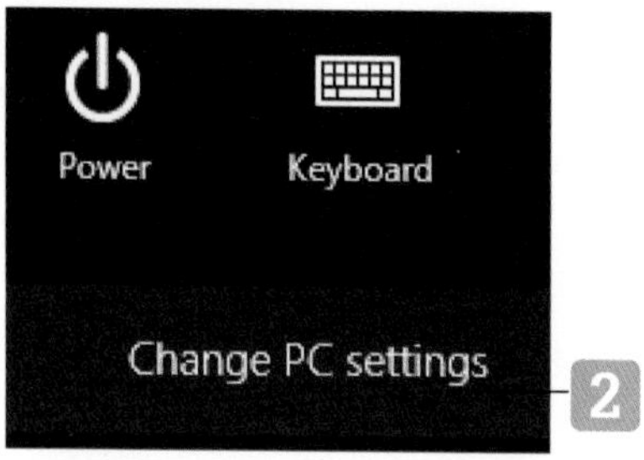

3. If applicable, click Users in the left pane. Then, select Add a user in the right pane.
4. Work through the process to add a new user. It's the same process as you worked through when you set up Windows 8.

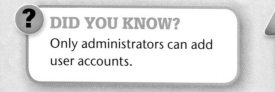

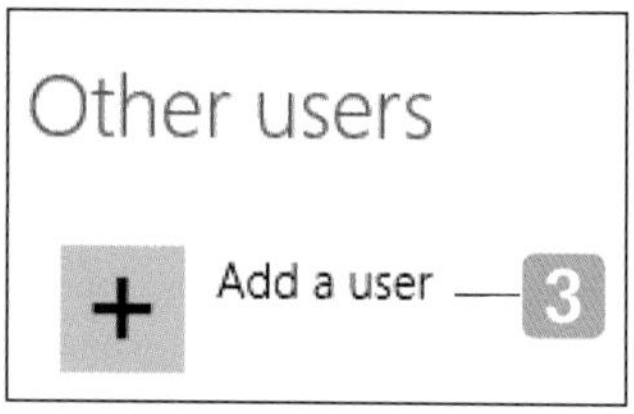

DID YOU KNOW?
Only administrators can add user accounts.

ALERT: All accounts should have a password applied to them. Refer to the next section, Require passwords.

Require passwords

All user accounts should be password-protected. If you logged in with a Microsoft account, a password is already configured. If you use a local account though, or created one for another person, you may have opted not to apply a password. Whatever the case, every account should have a complex password applied to it. This protects the PC from unauthorised access. To see if accounts exist that do not have passwords applied to them, view the users in the Manage Accounts window.

1. From the Start screen type Users.
2. Click Settings, and from the results choose Make changes to accounts.

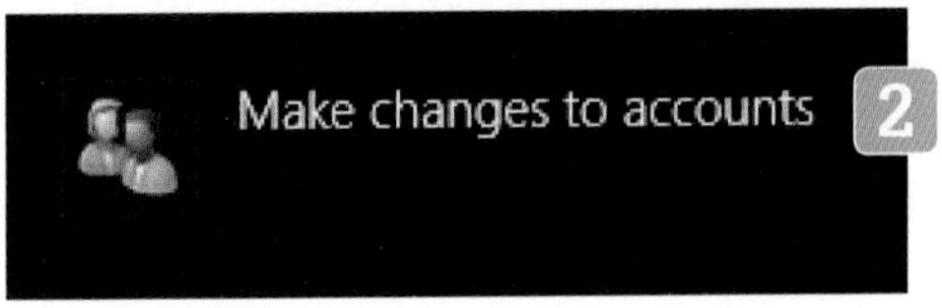

3. Verify each user account is password-protected (and that the Guest account is off).
4. If you find there is a user without a password, take the necessary steps to apply one.

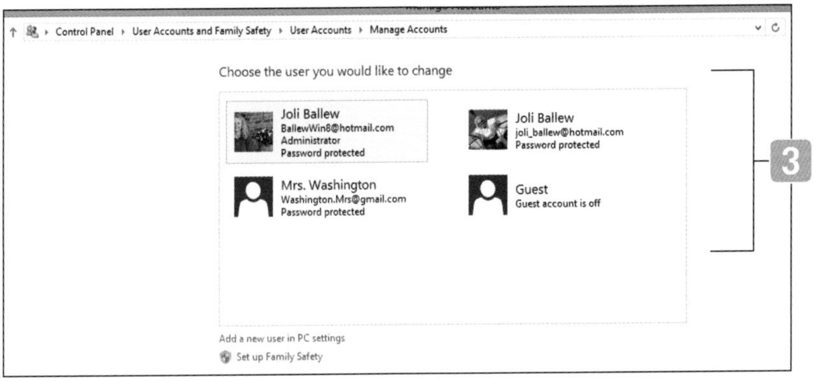

? DID YOU KNOW?
When you need to make a system-wide change, you have to be logged on as an administrator or type an administrator's user name and password.

! ALERT: Make sure your password contains upper and lower case letters and a few numbers. This is a stronger password than, say, your dog's name. Write the password down and keep it somewhere safe and out of sight.

Enable the guest account

If guests visit your home and bring their own laptop, you can give them the credentials required to access your network and connect to the Internet through it. If they don't bring their own computer and need to use yours, you can enable the guest account.

1. At the Start screen, type Guest.
2. Click Settings.
3. Click Turn guest account on or off.
4. If prompted, type your administrator password.
5. Click the Guest account and click Turn On.

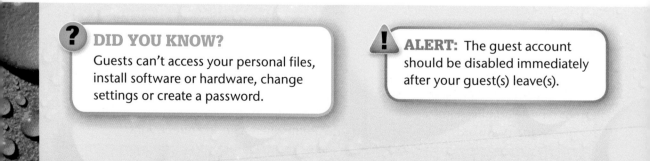

Settings
Results for "Guest"
Turn guest account on or off
3

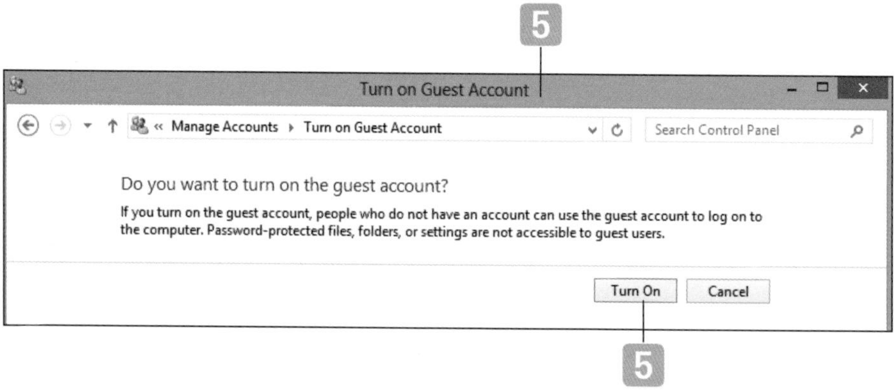
5
Turn on Guest Account
Manage Accounts
Turn on Guest Account
Search Control Panel
Do you want to turn on the guest account?
If you turn on the guest account, people who do not have an account can use the guest account to log on to the computer. Password-protected files, folders, or settings are not accessible to guest users.
Turn On
Cancel
5

DID YOU KNOW?
Guests can't access your personal files, install software or hardware, change settings or create a password.

ALERT: The guest account should be disabled immediately after your guest(s) leave(s).

Share a personal folder

Sometimes you won't want to save, move or copy data into public folders. Instead, you'll want to share data directly from a personal folder. When you do, you can hand pick who can view or edit the data.

1. From File Explorer, locate the folder to share.
2. Right-click the folder, and click Share with.
3. If you want to share with your homegroup or another user, select the appropriate option from the list. Follow any prompts to complete the process.
4. If you want to share with specific people who are not in a homegroup, choose Specific people, then:

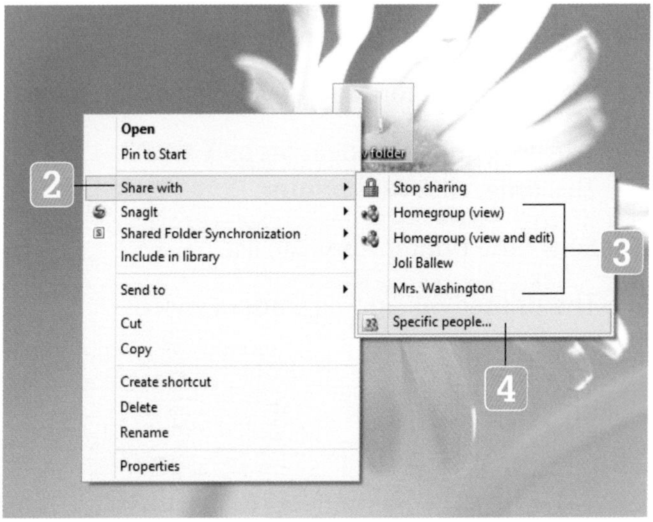

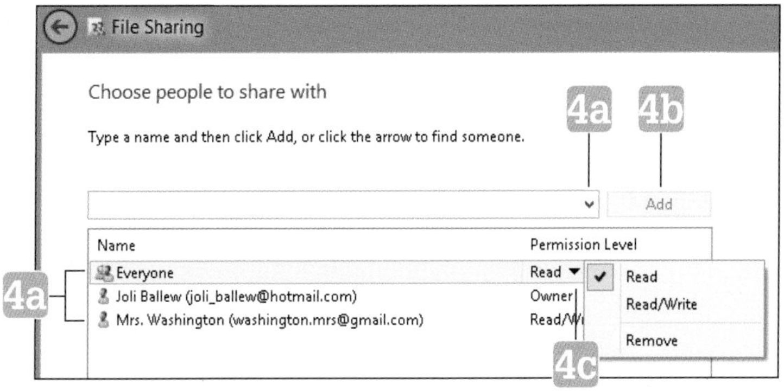

a) Click the arrow and choose with whom to share. (Everyone is an option.)

b) Click Add.

c) Click the arrow to set the permissions for the user.

d) Click Share.

HOT TIP: If you use a specific desktop folder often, right-click it and click Pin to Start. A tile for the folder will be added to the Start screen.

HOT TIP: Create and then share a folder on the desktop to set up a place to collaborate and share ideas.

Share a printer

If you have a printer connected to your computer, you can share it. Likewise, you can access shared printers connected to other computers.

1. At the Start screen, type Printers. Click Settings.
2. In the results, click Share printers.
3. Verify that Printers and devices is set to Shared.
4. To add a printer, repeat Steps 1 and 2. This time, click Add printer.
5. Select the printer from the list.
6. The printer will appear under Devices.

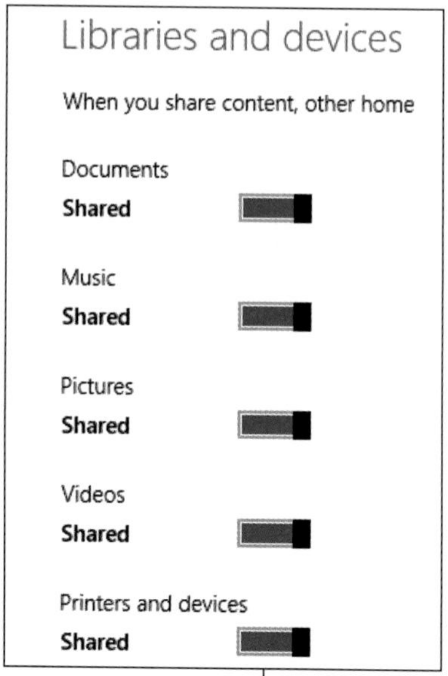

3

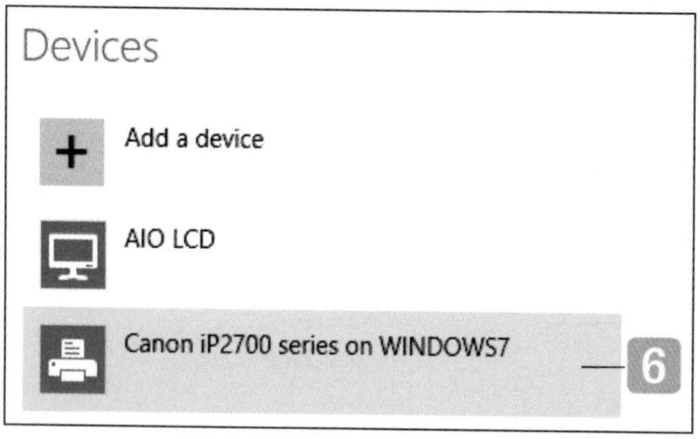

HOT TIP: To manually share a printer, open Control Panel and navigate to Devices and Printers. Right-click the printer to share and then choose Printer Properties. From the Sharing tab, select Share this printer.

ALERT: When others on your network access the printer for the first time, they may be prompted to install a driver for it. This is OK and will be managed by the PC.

Diagnose connection problems

If you are having trouble connecting to the Internet through a public or private network, you can diagnose Internet problems using the Network and Sharing Center.

1. At the Desktop, right-click the Network icon on the taskbar.
2. Click Troubleshoot problems.
3. Work through the troubleshooter to resolve the problem.

Troubleshoot problems
2
Open Network and Sharing Center
7/24/2012

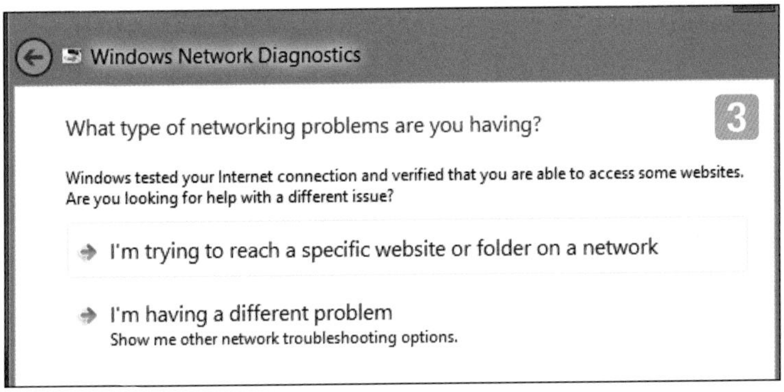
Windows Network Diagnostics
What type of networking problems are you having?
3
Windows tested your Internet connection and verified that you are able to access some websites. Are you looking for help with a different issue?
I'm trying to reach a specific website or folder on a network
I'm having a different problem
Show me other network troubleshooting options.

DID YOU KNOW?
There are additional troubleshooting tips in the Help and Support pages. From the Start screen, type Help and Support. Select Help and Support from the results.

ALERT: If you are prompted to restart your network, turn everything off first. Then, start the modem that connects your network to the Internet, wait two minutes, then turn on the router. Wait another minute and then turn on each of the computers.

7 Surf the web with Internet Explorer

Explore the Internet Explorer app

You open the Internet Explorer app by clicking or tapping its tile on the Start screen. When the app opens, look for the features listed here. You must right-click or flick upwards from the bottom of a touch screen to access these features. By default, nothing shows on the screen but the website itself.

1. Address bar – Here we've navigated to https://twitter.com.
2. Back – Use this to return to the previously visited webpage.
3. Refresh – Use to reload the webpage.
4. Pin to Start – Click to create a tile for the webpage on the Start screen.
5. Page Tools – Click to find something on a page, view the website in the desktop app and more.
6. Forward – Click to move to a previously visited page. This is available only after clicking the Back button.
7. Tabs – Click any thumbnail to return to a previously tabbed website. Note the option to remove the thumbnail (X), and the options to open and close tabs (+ and ···).
8. Content – This is the webpage content.

HOT TIP: Click anywhere on the webpage to hide the features shown here.

DID YOU KNOW?
If you position your cursor in the middle of the left or right side of the page, transparent Back and Forward arrows appear.

Visit a website

There are several ways to visit a website, including clicking links on other webpages, in emails and in messages. You can also navigate to a website by typing its name in the address bar.

1. From the Start screen, click the Internet Explorer tile.
2. Click once in the address bar. (Right-click if it's not visible.)
3. Type the desired web address.
4. If you've visited the page before, it will appear above the address bar and you can click it. If not, simply press Enter on the keyboard or click the right-facing arrow.

DID YOU KNOW?
After you've used the IE app for a while, the app will determine what websites you visit most. Then, when you click inside the address bar, thumbnails will be available to quickly access those sites.

HOT TIP: Navigate to a second and third website using the address bar, and then practise using the Back and Forward buttons and arrows.

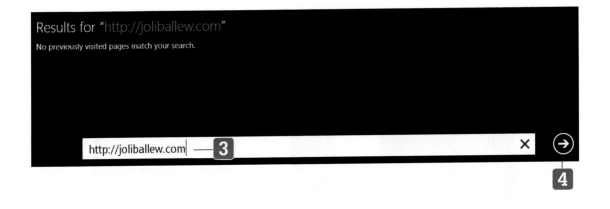

Manage tabs with the hidden toolbar

You saw the tabs and IE app features on the hidden toolbars on previous pages. You use these features to manage open websites and to open and close tabs. Before you start here, navigate to several websites from the address bar or using any other method.

1. Right-click the screen.
2. Click the X by any tab to close it.
3. Click the + sign (shown earlier) to open a new, blank page, and type the desired address or choose from the thumbnails that appear.
4. Right-click again. Click the three dots (also shown earlier). Note the options and explore as desired.

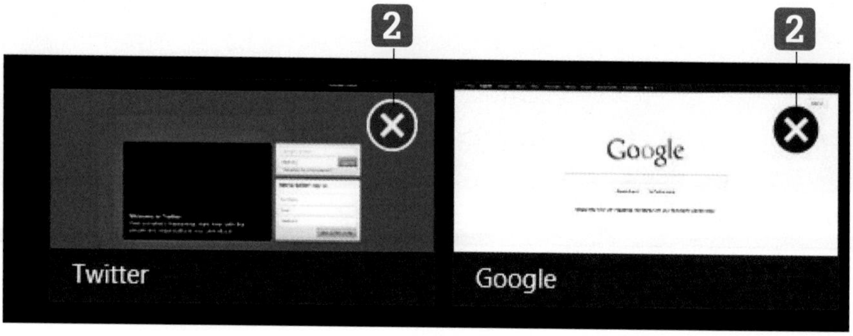

HOT TIP: To close all of your open tabs quickly, right-click, click the Tab tools icon (···), and click Close Tabs.

DID YOU KNOW?

If you opt to open a new tab using the InPrivate option (available from the Tab tools), IE won't remember the website in its History list, and won't save anything else related to your visit either.

Pin a website to the Start screen

If there's a website you visit often you can pin it to the Start screen. Then you can simply click the tile to open the IE app and go directly to it.

1. Use the IE app to navigate to a website.
2. Right-click if applicable to show the toolbars.
3. Click the Pin site charm. It looks like a drawing pin.
4. If desired, type a new name for the website.
5. Click Pin to Start.

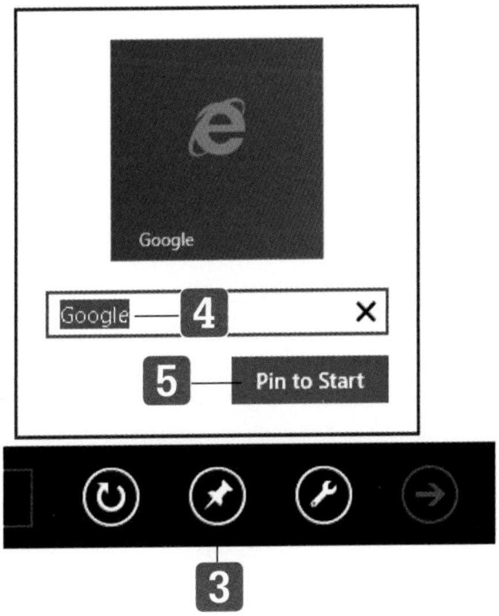

? DID YOU KNOW?
If you use a Microsoft account to log in to Windows 8, when you log in to another Windows 8 machine your Start screen configuration will be available there too.

HOT TIP: The newly pinned website will appear on the Start screen in the farthest right position.

Explore Settings

You can configure settings for IE from the Settings charm. These include the ability to delete your browsing history, enable a website to ask (or disable it from asking) for permission to ask for your physical location and more.

1. Open the IE app and, using any method, bring up the charms.
2. Click Settings.
3. Click Internet Options.
4. Explore the options.

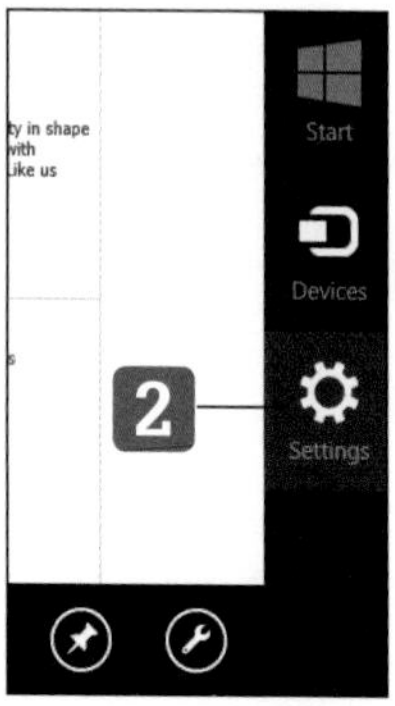

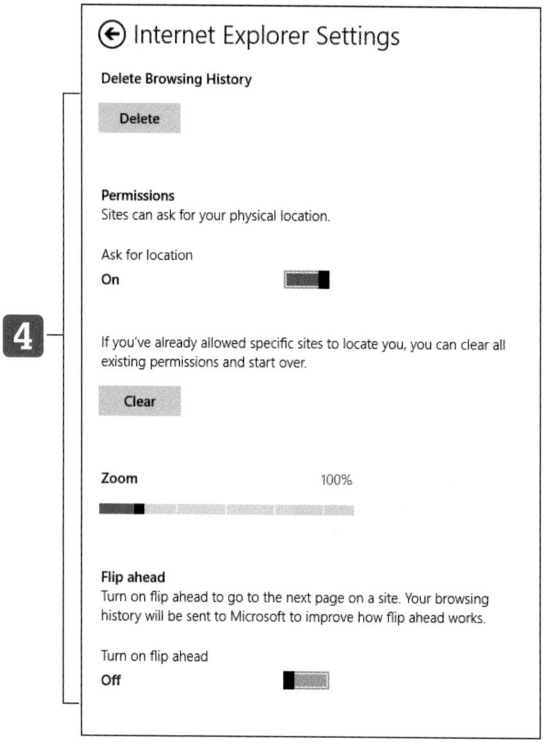

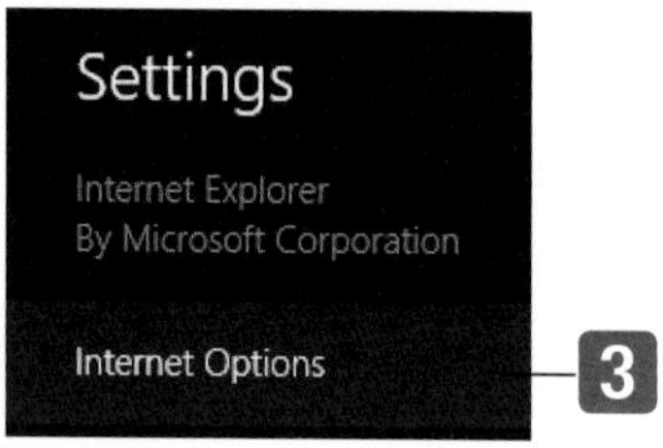

DID YOU KNOW?

Permissions is another option from the Settings charm while in the IE app. Here you can enable or disable notifications.

HOT TIP: You can change the language settings from Internet Options.

Explore the Internet Explorer desktop app

As you know, Windows 8 comes with another version of IE, the desktop version. To get started, first access the desktop, and once there, click the big blue e on the taskbar, which represents Internet Explorer.

1. In the IE desktop app, to go to a website you want to visit, type the name of the website in the window at the top of the page. This is called the address bar.
2. Press Enter on the keyboard.

Explore these features:

3. Tabs – Click any tab to access the related webpage. Click the blank tab to open a new, blank page.
4. Home – Click to access your configured home page(s).
5. Favorites, Feed and History – Click to view favourites or to add a webpage as a favourite.
6. Tools – Click to access all of the available settings.

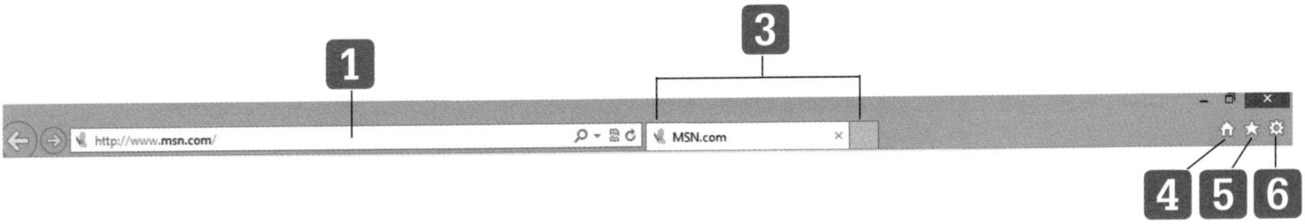

HOT TIP: If you've ever used Internet Explorer on another computer, the IE you'll find on the desktop is quite similar.

HOT TIP: Click the Tools icon and then Internet Options to configure IE. You can configure home pages, security options, privacy settings, family safety settings and more.

Use tabs

You can open more than one website at a time in Internet Explorer. To do this, click the tab that appears to the right of the open webpage. Then type the name of the website you'd like to visit.

1. Open Internet Explorer on the desktop.
2. Click an empty tab.
3. Type the name of the website you'd like to visit in the address bar.
4. Press Enter on the keyboard.

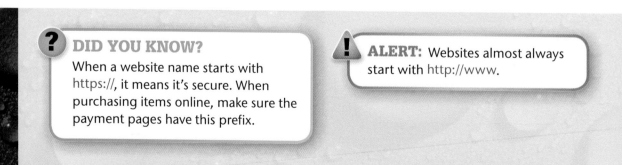

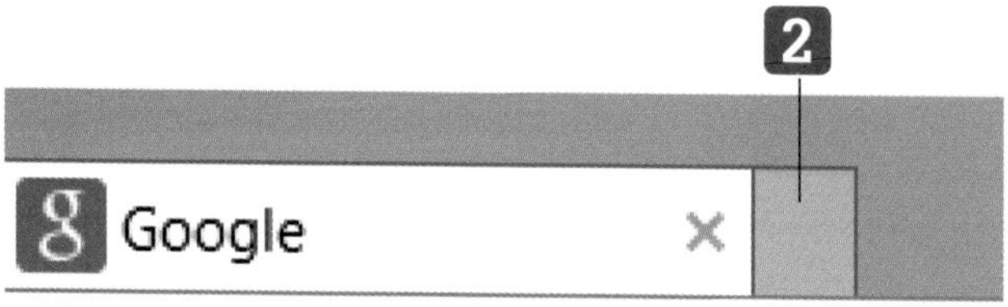

DID YOU KNOW?
When a website name starts with https://, it means it's secure. When purchasing items online, make sure the payment pages have this prefix.

ALERT: Websites almost always start with http://www.

Set a home page

You can select a single webpage or multiple webpages to be displayed each time you open Internet Explorer. In fact, there are three options for configuring home pages:

- Use this webpage as your only home page – select this option if you only want one page to serve as your home page.
- Add this webpage to your home pages tabs – select this option if you want this page to be one of several home pages.
- Use the current tab set as your home page – select this option if you've opened multiple tabs and you want all of them to be home pages.

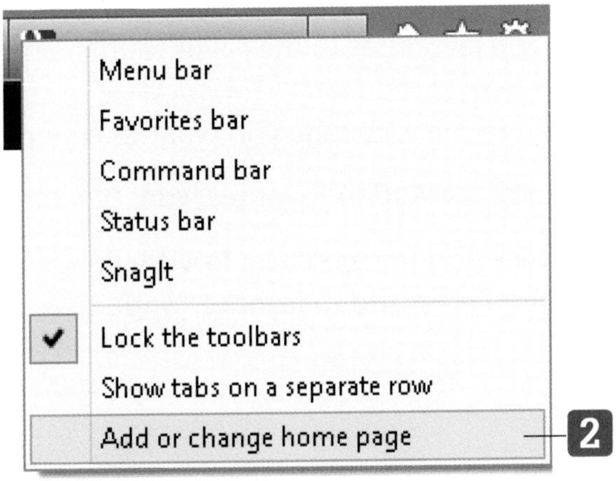

1 From the IE desktop app, use the address bar to locate a webpage (and use the empty Tab button to open additional webpages).

2 Right-click the Home icon and click Add or change home page. (Note you have additional choices, including showing various toolbars.)

3 Make a selection using the information provided regarding each option.

4 Click Yes.

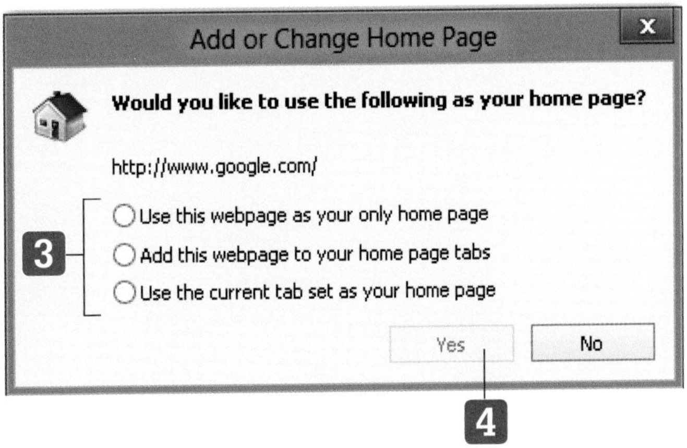

ALERT: You have to locate the webpage before you can assign it as a home page.

HOT TIP: To open your home pages, click the Home icon.

SEE ALSO: Visit a website, earlier in this chapter.

Mark a favourite

Favourites are websites you save links to so that you can access them easily at a later date. They differ from home pages because by default they do not open when you start Internet Explorer. The favourites you save appear in the Favorites Center. You can also save favourites to the Favorites bar, an optional toolbar you can enable in IE.

1. Go to the webpage you want to configure as a favourite.
2. Click the Add to Favorites icon. (It's the star.)
3. Click Add to favorites. (To add the website to the Favorites bar, click the arrow beside the Add to favorites option.)

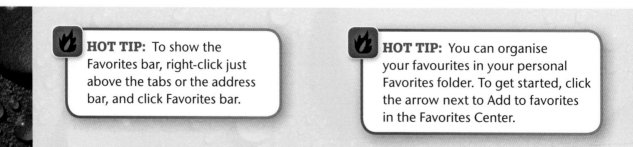

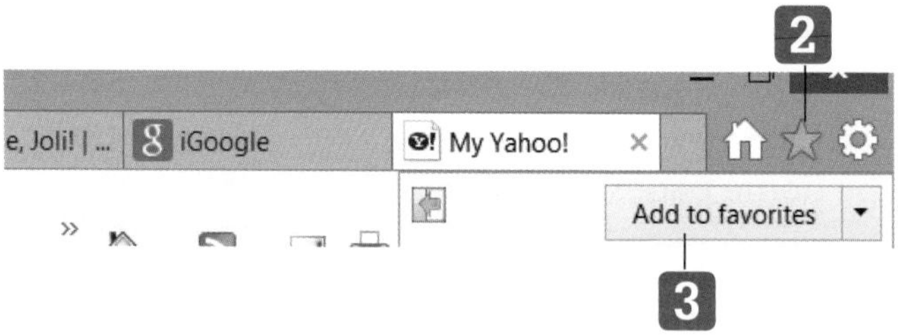

HOT TIP: To show the Favorites bar, right-click just above the tabs or the address bar, and click Favorites bar.

HOT TIP: You can organise your favourites in your personal Favorites folder. To get started, click the arrow next to Add to favorites in the Favorites Center.

Zoom in or out

If you have trouble reading what's on a webpage because the text is too small, use the Page Zoom feature. Page Zoom preserves the fundamental design of the webpage you're viewing. This means that Page Zoom intelligently zooms in on the entire page, which maintains the page's integrity, layout and look.

1. Open Internet Explorer and browse to a webpage.
2. If you have a physical keyboard, use the Ctrl + = and the Ctrl + – combinations to zoom in and out. (The = key also has a + sign on it.)
3. If you have a touch screen, pinch in and out with two or more fingers.
4. Alternatively you can:
   - Right-click the area above the tabs and address bar and place a tick by Status bar, and then
   - Click the arrow on the right end of the status bar to zoom to a specific amount.

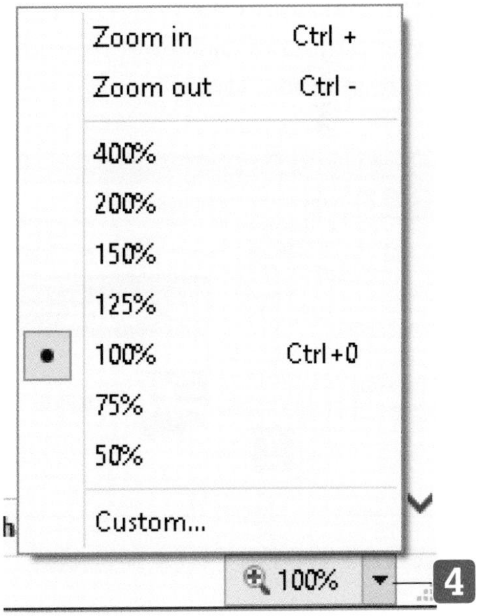

DID YOU KNOW?

The term *browse* is used to describe both locating a file on your hard drive and locating something on the Internet.

DID YOU KNOW?

The Page Zoom options are located under the Page icon on the command bar (which you'll have to enable), under Zoom, but it's much easier to use the link at the bottom right of the browser window, on the status bar.

Print a webpage

You can print a webpage in several ways. When you do though, remember that the pictures and adverts will be printed too, so you may want to copy the text and paste it into a Word document first.

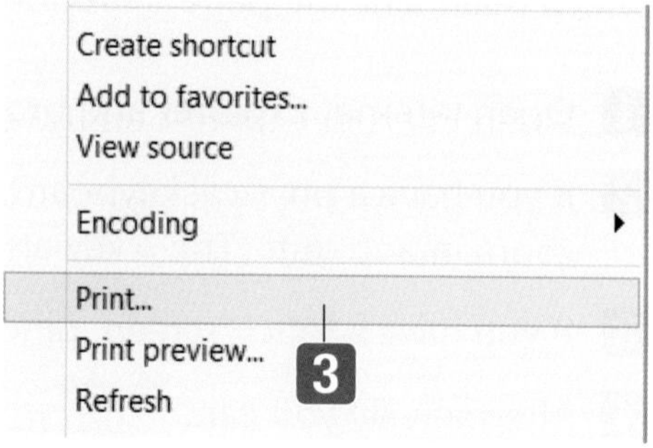

1. The Print icon is available from the command bar. To show the command bar, right-click just above the tabs and address bar and place a tick by it. The command bar and the Print option are shown here.
2. The key combination Ctrl + P will bring up the Print dialogue box.
3. You can right-click on an empty area of the webpage and click Print from the resulting contextual menu. A long tap on a touch screen works too.

? DID YOU KNOW?

You can search from the address bar. Simply type your keywords there and press Enter on the keyboard.

WHAT DOES THIS MEAN?

There are three menu options under the Print icon:

Print: clicking Print opens the Print dialogue box where you can configure the page range, select a printer, change page orientation, change print order and choose a paper type. Additional options include print quality, output bins and more. Of course, the choices depend on what your printer offers. If your printer can print only at 300 × 300 dots per inch, you can't configure it to print at a higher quality.

Print preview: clicking Print preview opens a window where you can see before you print what the printout will actually look like. You can switch between portrait and landscape views, access the Page setup dialogue box and more.

Page setup: clicking Page setup opens the Page setup dialogue box. Here you can select a paper size, source, and create headers and footers. You can also change orientation and margins, all of which is dependent on what features your printer supports.

Clear history

If you don't want people to be able to snoop around on your computer and find out what sites you've been visiting you'll need to delete your browsing history. Deleting your browsing history lets you remove the information stored on your computer related to your Internet activities.

1 Open Internet Explorer on the desktop.

2 Click the Alt key on the keyboard if you do not see the menu shown here.

3 Click Tools.

4 Click Delete browsing history.

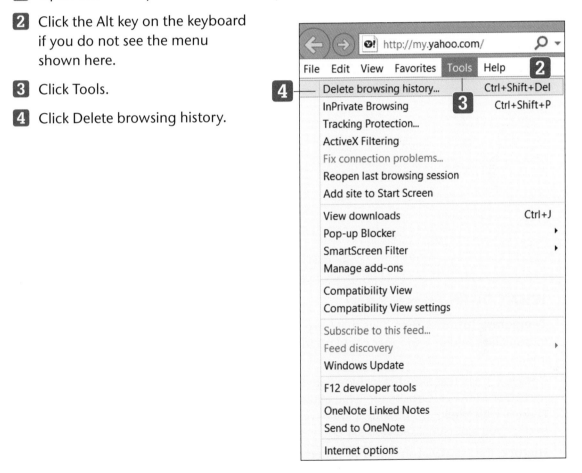

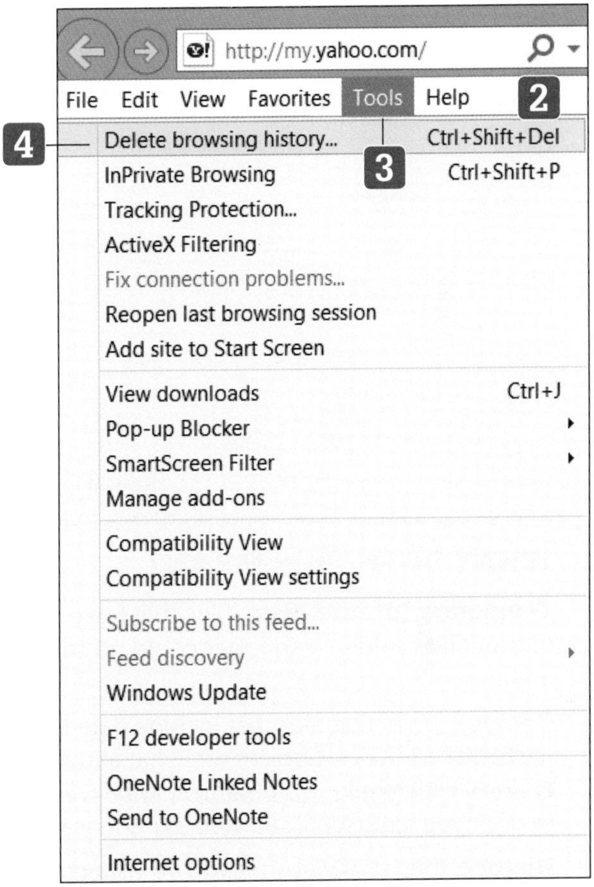

HOT TIP: Clicking the Alt key on the keyboard is what causes the menu bar to appear.

DID YOU KNOW?
You can also click the Tools icon, Internet Options, and from the General tab, opt to delete your browsing history.

5 Select what to delete, and click Delete. (You may want to keep Preserve Favorites website data selected.)

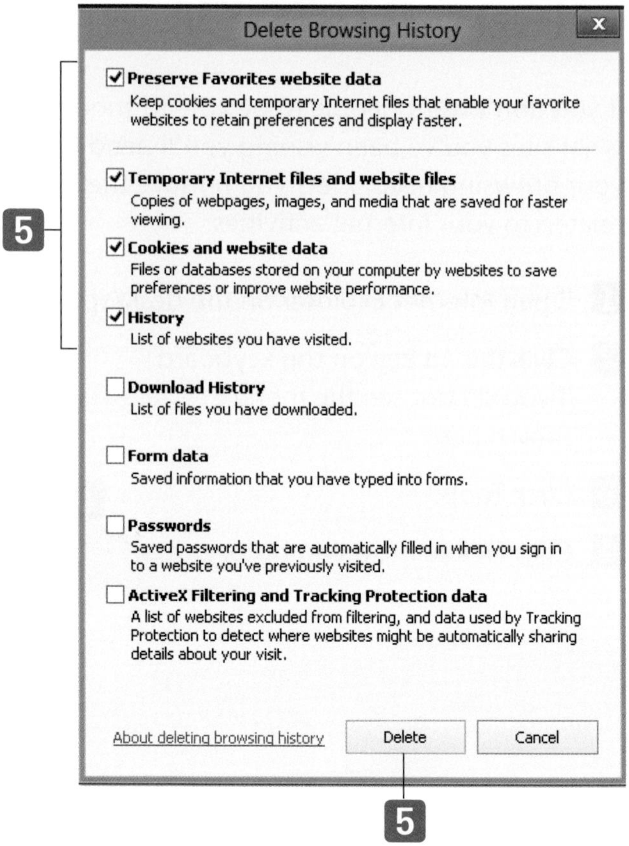
Delete Browsing History
Preserve Favorites website data
Keep cookies and temporary Internet files that enable your favorite websites to retain preferences and display faster.
Temporary Internet files and website files
Copies of webpages, images, and media that are saved for faster viewing.
Cookies and website data
Files or databases stored on your computer by websites to save preferences or improve website performance.
History
List of websites you have visited.
Download History
List of files you have downloaded.
Form data
Saved information that you have typed into forms.
Passwords
Saved passwords that are automatically filled in when you sign in to a website you've previously visited.
ActiveX Filtering and Tracking Protection data
A list of websites excluded from filtering, and data used by Tracking Protection to detect where websites might be automatically sharing details about your visit.
About deleting browsing history
Delete
Cancel
5
5

WHAT DOES THIS MEAN?

Temporary Internet files: files that have been downloaded and saved in your Temporary Internet files folder. A snooper could go through these files to see what you've been doing online.

Cookies: small text files that include data that identifies your preferences when you visit particular websites. Cookies are what allow you to visit, say, www.amazon.com and be greeted with 'Hello <your name>, We have recommendations for you!' Cookies help a site to offer you a personalised web experience.

History: the list of websites you've visited and any web addresses you've typed. Anyone can look at your History list to see where you've been.

Form data: information that's been saved using Internet Explorer's autocomplete form data functionality. If you don't want forms to be filled out automatically by you or someone else who has access to your PC and user account, delete this.

Passwords: passwords that were saved using Internet Explorer autocomplete password prompts.

InPrivate Blocking data: data that was saved by InPrivate Blocking to detect where websites may be automatically sharing details about your visit.

Stay safe on the Internet

Later on, you'll learn how to use Windows Firewall, Windows Defender and other security features (see Chapter 13). However, much of staying secure when online and surfing the Internet has more to do with common sense. When you're online, make sure you follow the guidelines listed below.

1. If you are connecting to a public network, make sure you opt not to share data when prompted.
2. Always keep your PCs secure with anti-virus software.
3. Limit the amount of confidential information you store on the Internet.
4. When making credit card purchases, logging into websites, or paying for travel reservations, always make sure the website address starts with https:// and use a secure site.

5. Always sign out of any secure website you enter.

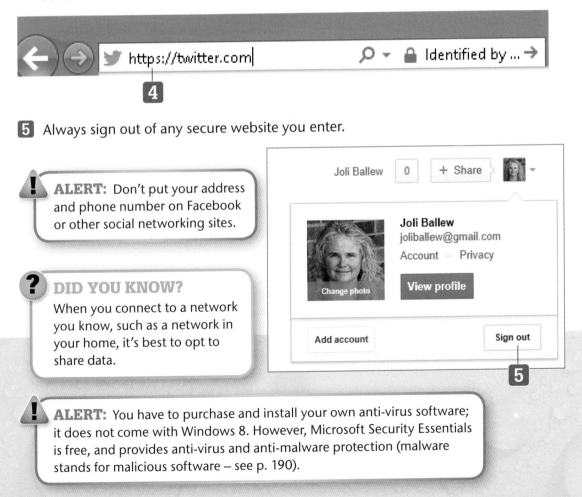

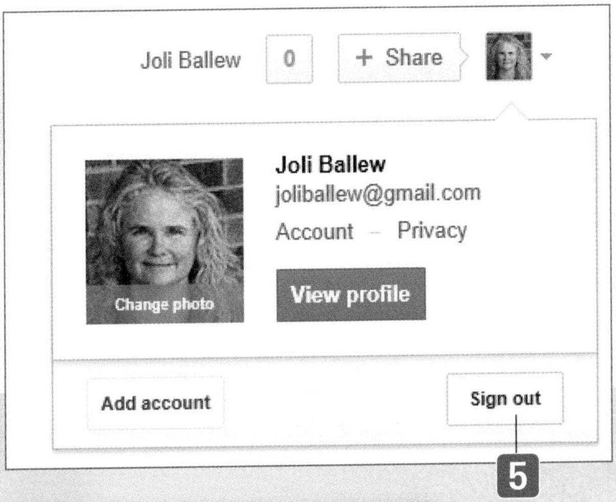

ALERT: Don't put your address and phone number on Facebook or other social networking sites.

DID YOU KNOW?
When you connect to a network you know, such as a network in your home, it's best to opt to share data.

ALERT: You have to purchase and install your own anti-virus software; it does not come with Windows 8. However, Microsoft Security Essentials is free, and provides anti-virus and anti-malware protection (malware stands for malicious software – see p. 190).

Configure the IE desktop app as the default

If you'd prefer that the Internet Explorer desktop app open when you click a link in an email, message, document and so on, instead of the simpler IE app, you can configure it in Internet Explorer's settings. Doing so will make the desktop app the default.

1. Open Internet Explorer on the desktop.
2. Click the Tools icon, then Internet Options.
3. Click the Programs tab.
4. Click the arrow beside Let Internet Explorer decide.
5. Click Always in Internet Explorer on the desktop.
6. Click OK.

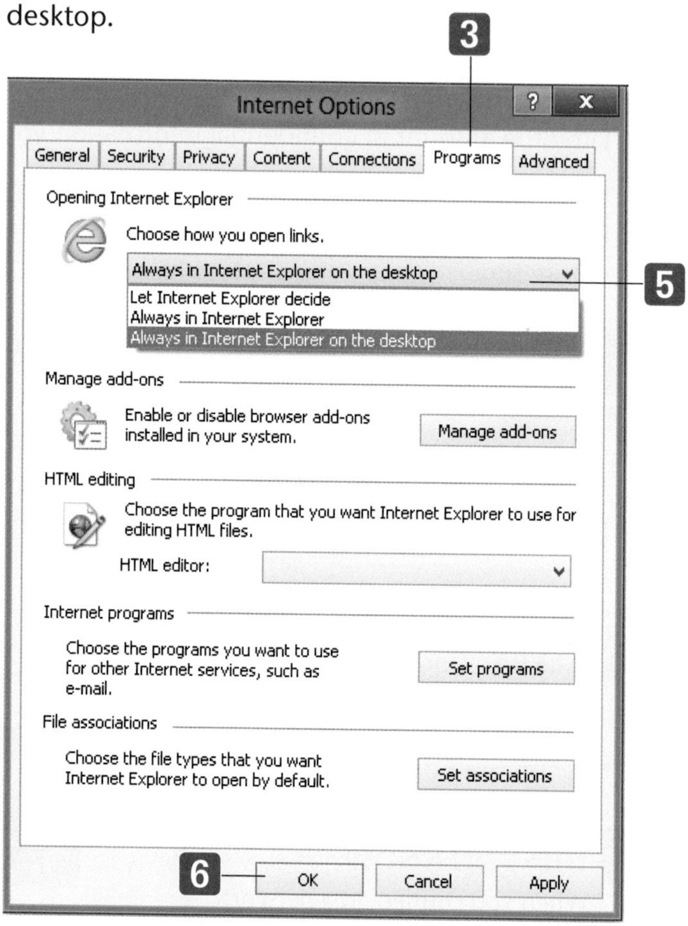

DID YOU KNOW?
You can still use the IE app on the Start screen even if you change the defaults as outlined here.

HOT TIP: While you have the Internet Options dialogue box open, explore the other options available. From the General tab, for instance, you can configure IE to start each time with tabs from the last session instead of your configured home page(s).

8 Set up and use Mail

Introduction

Mail is an app available from the Start screen. Because it's not a fully fledged desktop application, Mail will look and feel more like something you'd see on a smartphone than what you may be used to seeing on a computer. That's okay, and it's exactly what Microsoft wanted to provide, something really easy to use. Even though it is streamlined, it does enable you to view, send and receive email, manage email you've sent, and keep junk mail away, among other things.

If you sign in to your Windows 8 computer or tablet with a compatible Microsoft account like one from Hotmail.com or Live.com, Mail is already set up and ready to use. You can skip the first few sections of this chapter that deal with the set-up process. If you have another email account, you'll have to add that account manually. Once your email accounts are ready, accessing new mail and composing your own are simple processes.

Open Mail and explore the interface

Open Mail and see if the account is configured. You may be in for a surprise!

1. Click the Mail title on the Start screen.
2. If an email account is already configured, you'll see the related Inbox and folders. You may even have email!
3. Click once on an email in the middle pane to read it in the right pane.

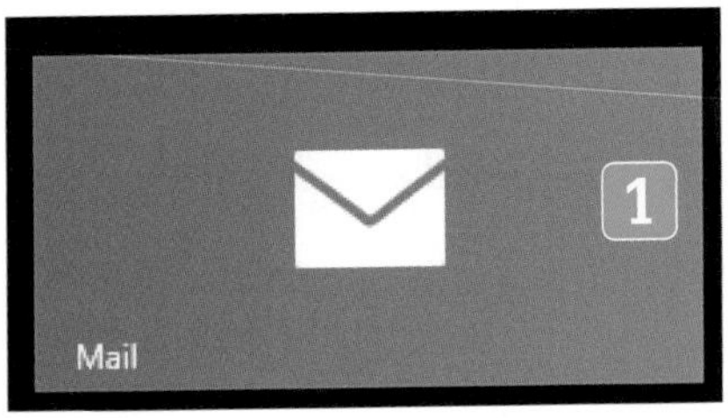
1
Mail

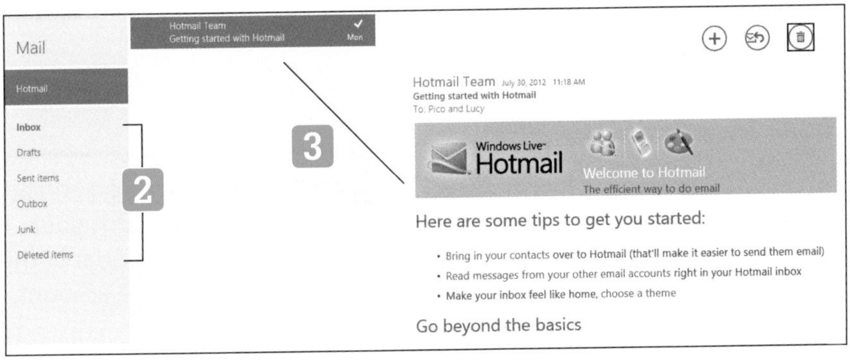
Mail
Hotmail
Inbox
Drafts
Sent items
Outbox
Junk
Deleted items
2
Hotmail Team
Getting started with Hotmail
Mon
3
Hotmail Team July 30, 2012 11:18 AM
Getting started with Hotmail
To: Pico and Lucy
Windows Live
Hotmail
Welcome to Hotmail
The efficient way to do email
Here are some tips to get you started:
Bring in your contacts over to Hotmail (that'll make it easier to send them email)
Read messages from your other email accounts right in your Hotmail inbox
Make your inbox feel like home, choose a theme
Go beyond the basics

HOT TIP: If you have been using a web-based email account from Hotmail or Google and you've created folders to store your mail, you'll see them in Mail when you open it.

HOT TIP: If you need an email account, get one from Microsoft at https://signup.live.com.

Set up a new account

If you need to add your own email account, perhaps one from Google (Gmail), you'll have to set up the account manually.

1. Open Mail and access the charms. Click Settings.
2. From the Settings options, click Accounts.
3. Click Add an account.
4. Choose the type of account to add, or click Other Account.
5. Fill out the information when prompted, including your email account and password.
6. Click Connect.

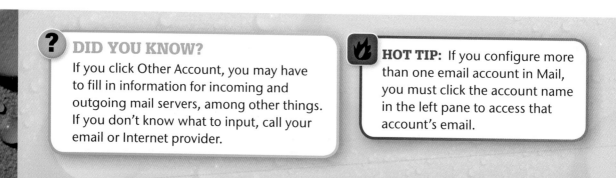

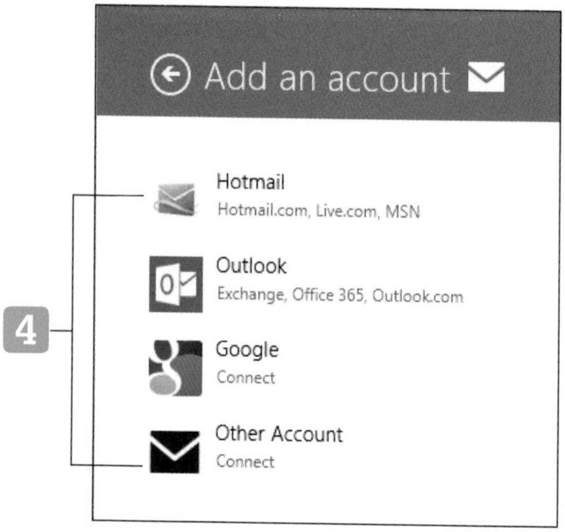

HOT TIP: When you add an email address, it adds your Contacts and Calendar entries associated with the account, if the data exists.

DID YOU KNOW?
If you click Other Account, you may have to fill in information for incoming and outgoing mail servers, among other things. If you don't know what to input, call your email or Internet provider.

HOT TIP: If you configure more than one email account in Mail, you must click the account name in the left pane to access that account's email.

Read email

Mail retrieves email automatically. To read your email you must click the desired account (if you have more than one configured). From there you can read email as desired.

1. If you have more than one email account configured, select the account to use. Here, Hotmail is selected.
2. Click the email to read.

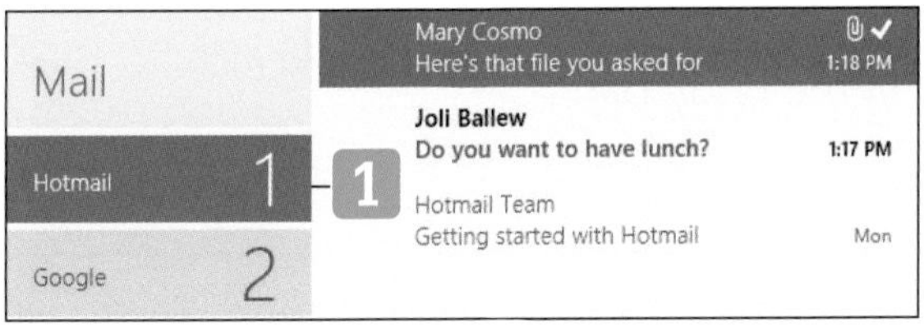

DID YOU KNOW?

If you read email on more than one computer, when you delete an email on one it might also be deleted on the other (or never arrive at all). If this happens you'll have to change the settings so that the email provider leaves the messages on the email server for a period of time, until you can retrieve it from your other computers.

WHAT DOES THIS MEAN?

Deleted items: this folder holds mail you've deleted.

Drafts: this folder holds messages you've started and saved but not completed.

Junk: this folder holds email that is considered junk email. Sometimes valid email gets sent here though, so you'll want to check this folder often to be sure.

Inbox: this folder holds mail you've received.

Outbox: this folder holds mail you've written but have not yet sent.

Sent items: this folder stores copies of messages you've sent.

Compose and send a new email

You compose an email message by clicking the + sign in the upper right-hand corner of the Mail interface. You input to whom the email should be sent and the subject, and then you type the message. If you like, you can click the + sign located just to the right of the To line, and choose your recipient(s) from the People app.

1. Click the + sign from the Mail interface to open a new, blank email.
2. Type the recipient's email address in the To line. You can type multiple addresses.
3. Type a subject in the Subject field.
4. Type the message in the body pane.
5. Click the Send icon.

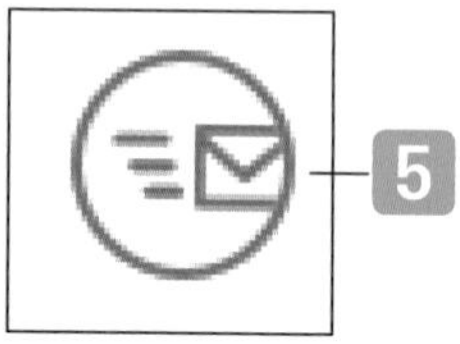

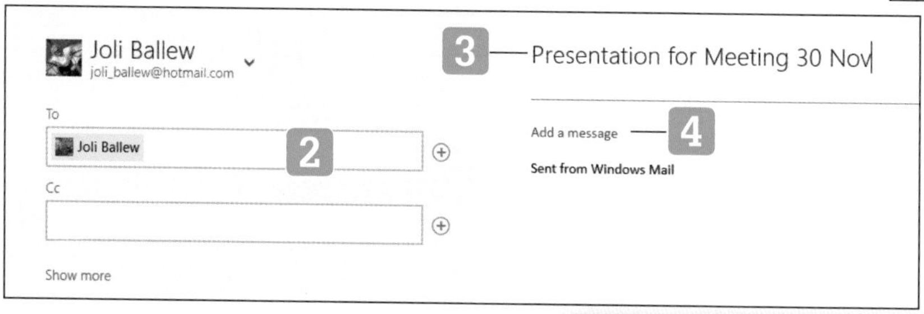

HOT TIP: Make sure the subject adequately describes the body of your email. Your recipients should be able to review the subject line later and recall what the email was regarding.

DID YOU KNOW?

If you want to send the email to someone and you don't need them to respond, you can put them in the Cc line.

If you want to send the email to someone and you don't want other recipients to know you have included them in the email, click Show more, just under the Cc line in the left pane. Then add the address in the resulting Bcc line.

WHAT DOES THIS MEAN?

Cc: stands for carbon copy.

Bcc: stands for blind carbon copy and is a secret copy.

Reply to or forward an email

When someone sends you an email, you may need to send a reply to them. You do that by selecting the email and then clicking the Reply/Reply all/Forward button. You can forward the email to others using the same technique.

1. Select the email you want to reply to or forward.
2. Click the Reply/Reply all/Forward button.
3. If desired, change the subject, and then type the message in the body pane.
4. Right-click in the body of the email to access options to change the font, use bold or italic and more. Make changes as desired.
5. Click the Send icon.

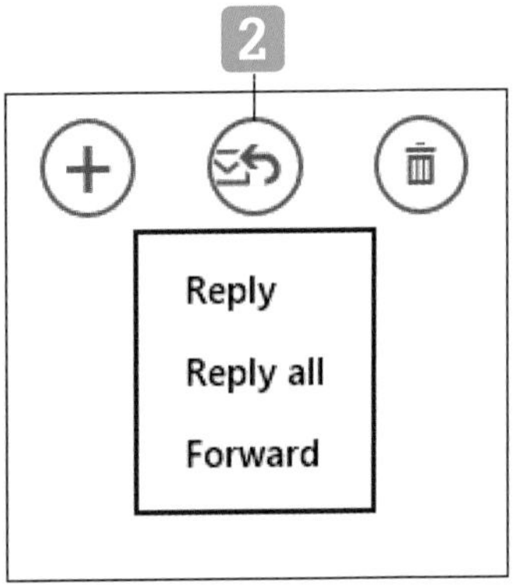

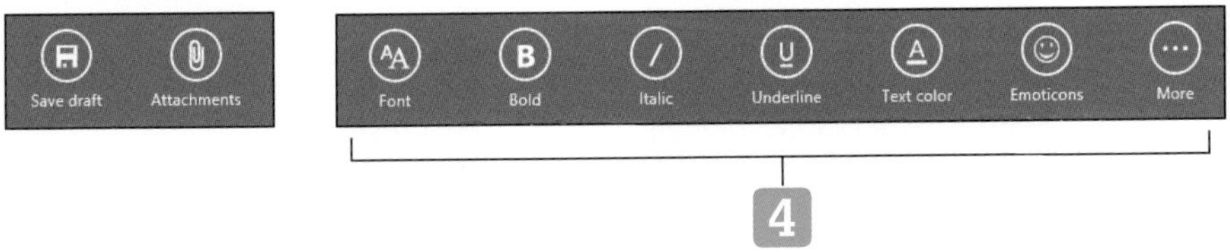

ALERT: If the email you are replying to was sent to you along with additional people, clicking Reply will send a reply to the person who composed the message. Clicking Reply all will send the reply to everyone who received the email as well as the person who sent it.

HOT TIP: When you select text, the formatting options become available automatically. Apply these options with the same technique you'd use in any word processing program.

Print an email

Sometimes you'll need to print an email or its attachment. You access your printer from the Devices charm.

1. Select the email to print.
2. Bring up the default charms (Windows key + C will show these), and click Devices.
3. Select the printer to use.
4. Configure the print options and click Print.

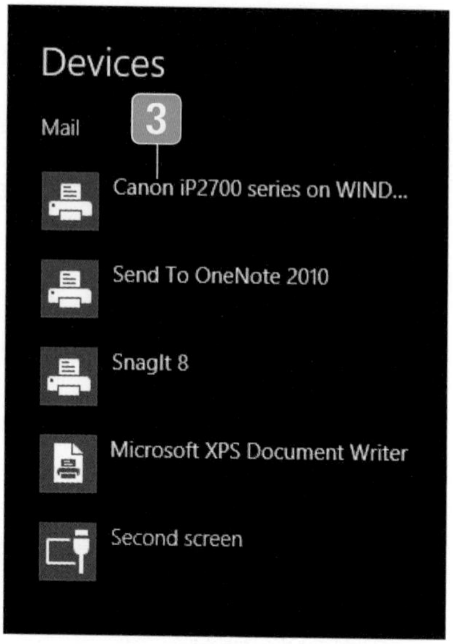

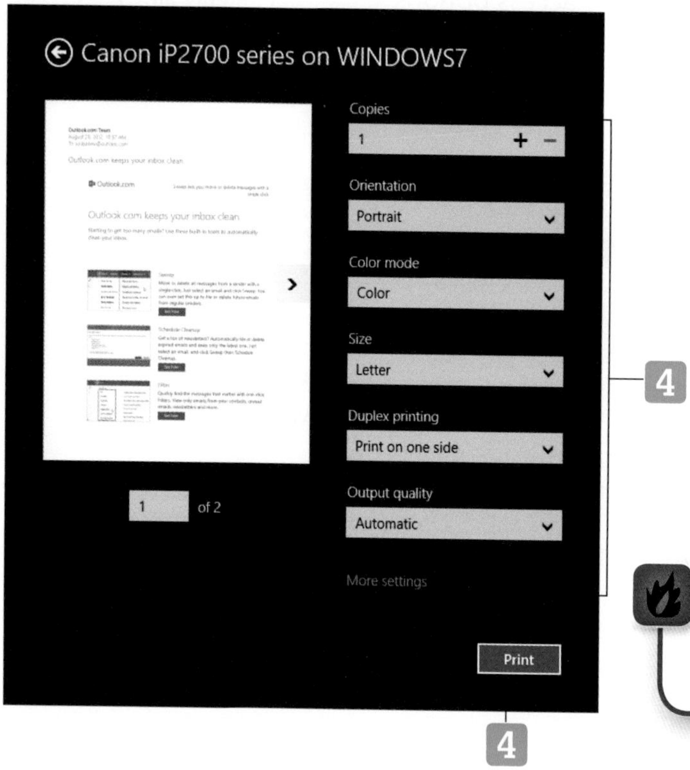

HOT TIP: To bring up the Devices charm, use the Windows key + K shortcut.

DID YOU KNOW?
If you use a keyboard, the shortcut Ctrl + P will open the Print window. From there, select the printer and configure printer options, then print.

Attach something to an email

Although email that contains only a message serves its purpose much of the time, often you'll want to send a photograph, a letter you've written, a presentation or other data. When you want to add something to your message other than text, it's called adding an attachment.

1. Click the + sign to create a new mail message. Select the recipients, type a subject and compose the email.
2. Right click the screen and then click Attachments.
3. Locate the file to attach and click it.
4. Click Attach.

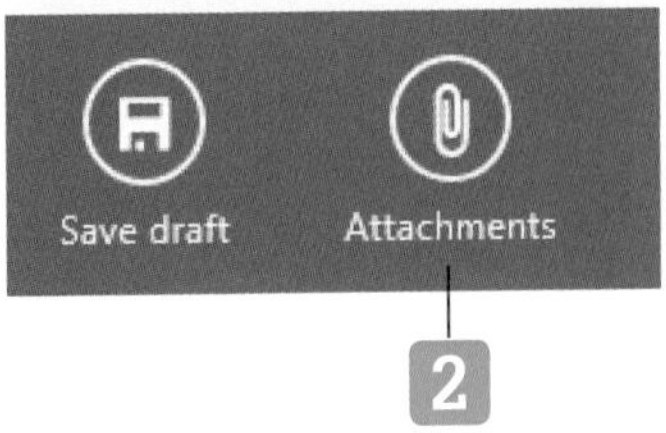

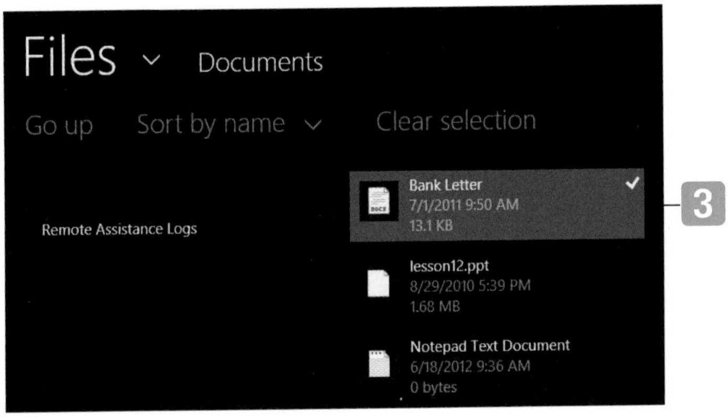

HOT TIP: When attaching files to an email, hold down the Ctrl key to select non-contiguous files, or the Shift key to select contiguous ones.

ALERT: Anything you attach won't be removed from your computer; instead, a copy will be created for the attachment.

View an attachment in an email

If an email you receive contains an attachment, you'll see a Paperclip icon in the middle pane, included with the email. To open the attachment, click it in the right pane.

1. Click the email that contains the attachment.
2. In the email, in the right pane, click the attachment. Generally it needs to be downloaded.
3. Depending on the type of attachment, the data may open in the email itself, or a program may open to show it.

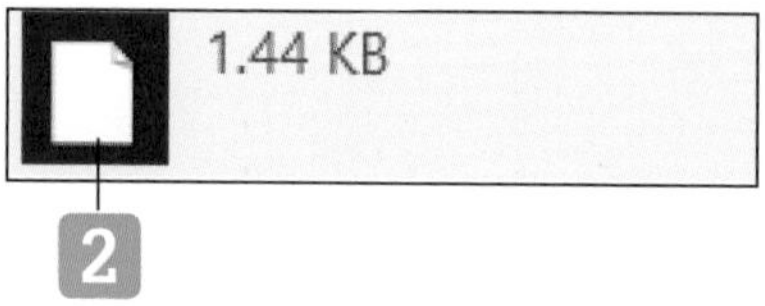

ALERT: Hackers send attachments that look like they are from legitimate companies, banks and online services. Do not open these. Companies rarely send email attachments.

ALERT: Attachments can contain viruses. Never open an attachment from someone you don't know.

HOT TIP: If you get an email from Hotmail Member Services asking you to verify a **new** email account, do so.

View junk email

Email accounts all have junk or spam folders. If an email is suspected to be spam, it gets sent there. (Spam is another word for junk email.) Unfortunately, sometimes email that is actually legitimate gets sent to these folders. Therefore, once a week or so you should look in this folder to see whether any email you want to keep is in there.

1. Click the Junk folder (or the appropriate folder for your email account) once.
2. Use the scroll bars if necessary to browse through the email in the folder.
3. If you see an email that is legitimate, click it once.
4. Right-click to access the charms, and click Move.
5. Click Inbox.

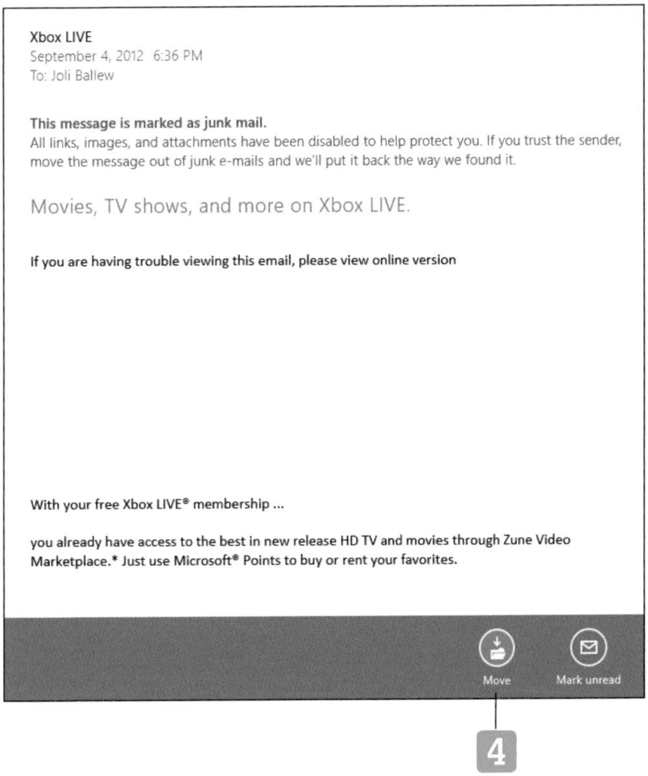

Xbox LIVE
September 4, 2012 6:36 PM
To: Joli Ballew
This message is marked as junk mail.
All links, images, and attachments have been disabled to help protect you. If you trust the sender, move the message out of junk e-mails and we'll put it back the way we found it.
Movies, TV shows, and more on Xbox LIVE.
If you are having trouble viewing this email, please view online version
With your free Xbox LIVE® membership ...
you already have access to the best in new release HD TV and movies through Zune Video Marketplace.* Just use Microsoft® Points to buy or rent your favorites.
Move
Mark unread
4

HOT TIP: Click the sender of an email to add that person to your contacts.

ALERT: Mail requires routine maintenance, including deleting email from the Junk folder. You'll learn how to delete items next.

Delete email

In order to keep Mail from getting bogged down and to stay organised, you'll need to delete email in folders regularly. Depending on how much email you get, this may be as often as once a week.

1 Select a single email to delete.

2 Click the Trash icon.

3 To select a group of emails to delete, hold down the Shift key and select the first and last.

4 Click the Trash icon.

5 To select specific emails, hold down the Ctrl key while selecting.

6 Click the Trash icon.

Hotmail Member Services	✓
Please sign in to your account	1:31 PM
Mary Cosmo	📎 ✓
Here's that file you asked for	1:18 PM
Joli Ballew	✓
Do you want to have lunch?	1:17 PM
Hotmail Team	✓
Getting started with Hotmail	Mon

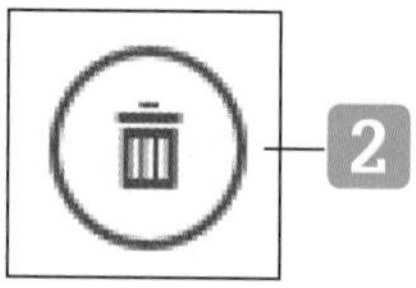

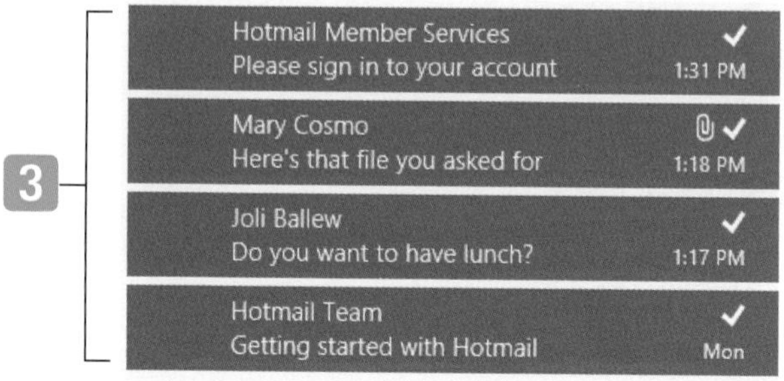

HOT TIP: To deselect emails you've marked for deletion, right-click them.

ALERT: Don't forget to empty your Sent items folders occasionally too.

9 Stay in touch with others

Introduction

Your children and grandchildren would probably prefer to communicate with you via mobile phone text messages, Facebook, Twitter, Windows chat and instant messages, and similar media, over having to answer a phone call. Messaging conversations are shorter, limited in scope, and there's no way they can get stuck on the phone or have to worry about a lull in the conversation. In addition, they can text while at work, at school, or even while at a loud concert or a quiet dinner.

Windows 8 offers two apps to help you keep in touch with others using most of these kinds of message. One is aptly named the Messaging app, the other, the People app. Both are available from the Start screen.

Navigate the Messaging app

The first time you open the Messaging app, you'll be greeted with a message from the Windows Messaging team. You can't reply to this message, but it does give you a sense of how you'll use the app in the future.

1. From the Start screen, click the Messaging tile to open it.
2. Right-click or flick upwards from the bottom with your finger to see the features on the toolbar.

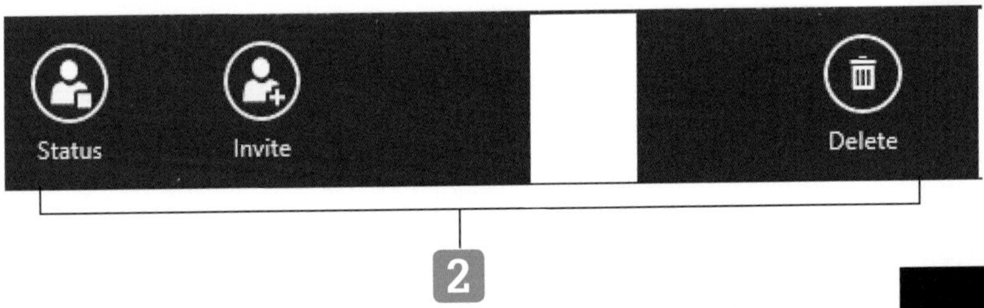

3. Note the options to change your status, invite others and delete a conversation. Use the Windows key + C keyboard shortcut to bring up the charms; click the Settings charm.
4. Note the options. You can add accounts, configure options, view permissions and more.

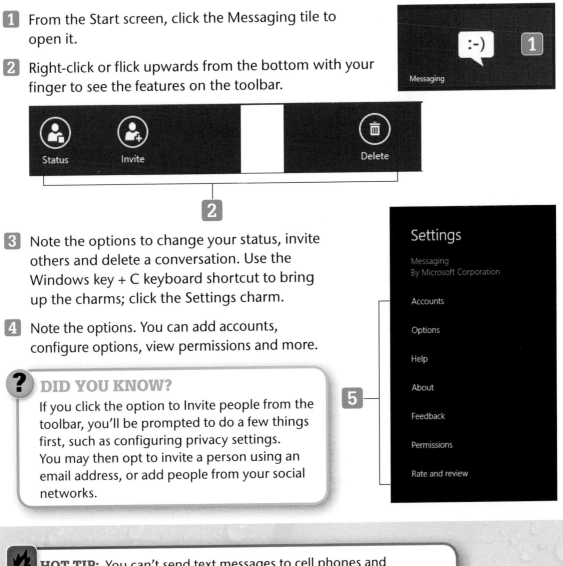

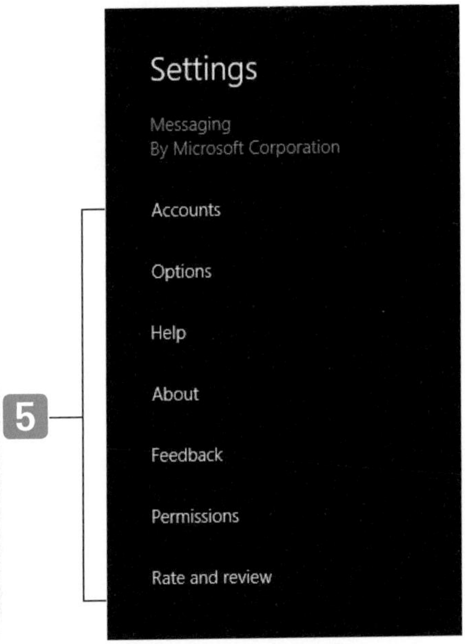

DID YOU KNOW?

If you click the option to Invite people from the toolbar, you'll be prompted to do a few things first, such as configuring privacy settings. You may then opt to invite a person using an email address, or add people from your social networks.

HOT TIP: You can't send text messages to cell phones and smartphones from the Messaging app. You can only send instant messages, which is a different technology. If you want to send a text to a mobile phone, you'll have to use your own to do so. However, if your contact has a compatible app on a smartphone, you may be able to use Messaging to send them an instant message through that app.

Add contacts from social networks

If you intend to send instant messages to people and incorporate specific social networks, such as Facebook, you'll need to associate those accounts with the Messaging app.

1. While inside the Messaging app, access the default charms (Windows key + C or flick inwards from the right side of the screen).
2. Click the Settings charm and then click Accounts.
3. Click Add an account.
4. Choose the account from the resulting list.
5. Click Connect and input the required information. Click Done.

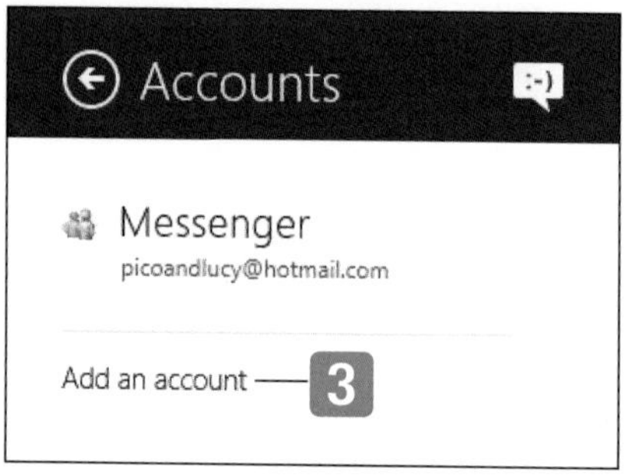
Accounts
Messenger
picoandlucy@hotmail.com
Add an account
3

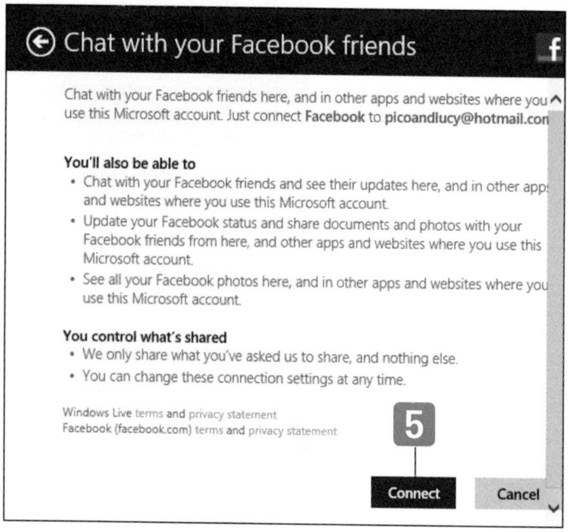
Chat with your Facebook friends
Chat with your Facebook friends here, and in other apps and websites where you use this Microsoft account. Just connect Facebook to picoandlucy@hotmail.com
You'll also be able to
• Chat with your Facebook friends and see their updates here, and in other apps and websites where you use this Microsoft account.
• Update your Facebook status and share documents and photos with your Facebook friends from here, and other apps and websites where you use this Microsoft account.
• See all your Facebook photos here, and in other apps and websites where you use this Microsoft account.
You control what's shared
• We only share what you've asked us to share, and nothing else.
• You can change these connection settings at any time.
Windows Live terms and privacy statement
Facebook (facebook.com) terms and privacy statement
5
Connect
Cancel

DID YOU KNOW?
You can't send a message to a Facebook friend if they aren't online.

DID YOU KNOW?
You add social networking information such as your Facebook user name and password so that you can communicate with others who also use that service and are your contacts there.

HOT TIP: It's possible that in the future additional social networks will be available to add.

Add contacts using an email address

You can invite a friend to chat by inputting their email address. How the contact responds, and when, depends on how they incorporate instant messaging at the present time.

1. In the Messaging app, right-click or flick upwards from the bottom (or down from the top) to access the toolbar.
2. Click Invite.
3. Click Add a new friend.
4. Type the contact's email address and press Enter on the keyboard. Repeat as desired.
5. Click Next.
6. Click Invite.
7. When the contact accepts your invitation, you'll be able to chat with them via Messaging.
8. To return to the Messaging app, use the Alt + Tab keyboard combination.

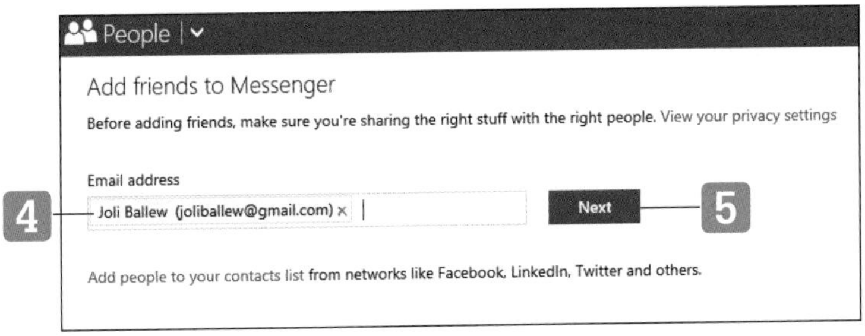
People
Add friends to Messenger
Before adding friends, make sure you're sharing the right stuff with the right people. View your privacy settings
Email address
Joli Ballew (joliballew@gmail.com) ×
Next
4
5
Add people to your contacts list from networks like Facebook, LinkedIn, Twitter and others.

DID YOU KNOW?
If a contact does not respond and accept your invitation it means they opted to reject your invitation, they do not have the proper communication option, or they never received it.

SEE ALSO: To accept an invitation from others, continue to the next task, Accept an invitation.

Accept an invitation

If others send you invitations to connect via the Messaging app, you'll need to accept those invitations to communicate with them.

1. Check your email.
2. If you see an invitation there, click View invitation.
3. If necessary, log in.
4. Click Accept or No, thanks.

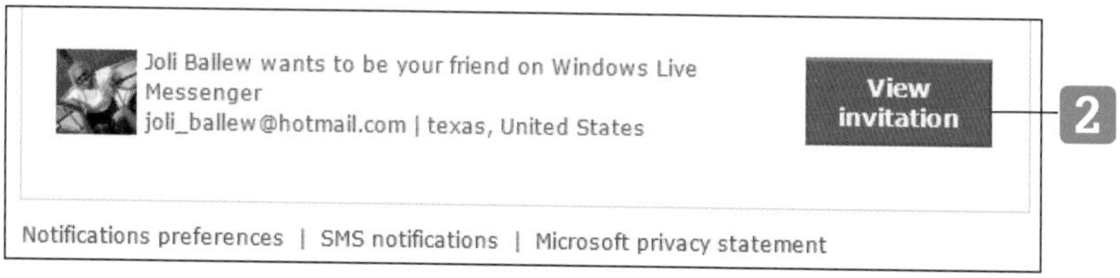

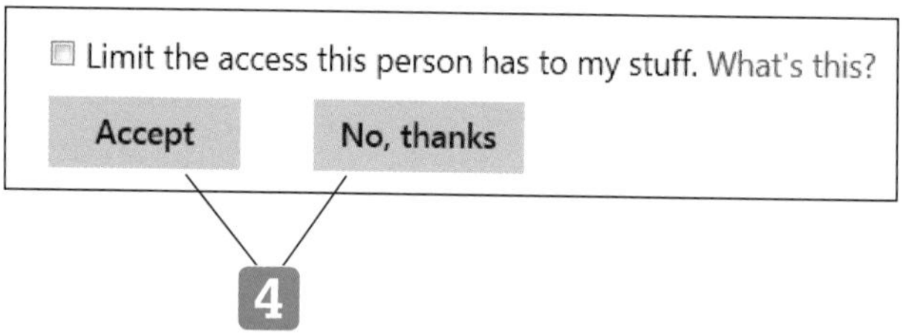

ALERT: You may receive invitations from people you do not know. Do not accept these invitations; they are probably from people you really do not want to communicate with!

DID YOU KNOW?
The Messaging app and the People app go hand in hand. When you accept an invitation to be friends in the Messaging app, that contact will also appear in the People app.

Add contacts from other sources

You can add contacts for the Messaging app by typing a person's email address. You can also add people from services you belong to, such as LinkedIn, Facebook and so on.

1. In the Messaging app, right-click or flick upwards from the bottom (or down from the top) to access the toolbar.
2. Click Invite and then, Add a new friend.
3. Click Add people to your contacts list.

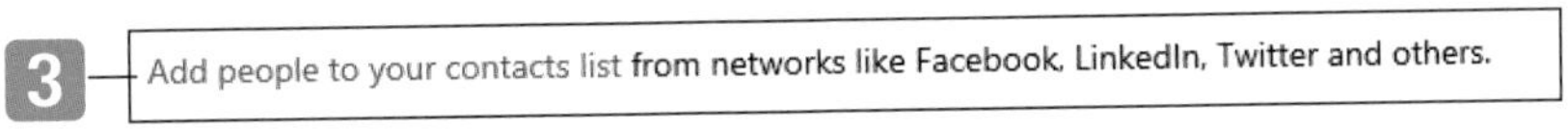

3
Add people to your contacts list from networks like Facebook, LinkedIn, Twitter and others.

4. Choose the network to add. You might choose LinkedIn or Google for instance.

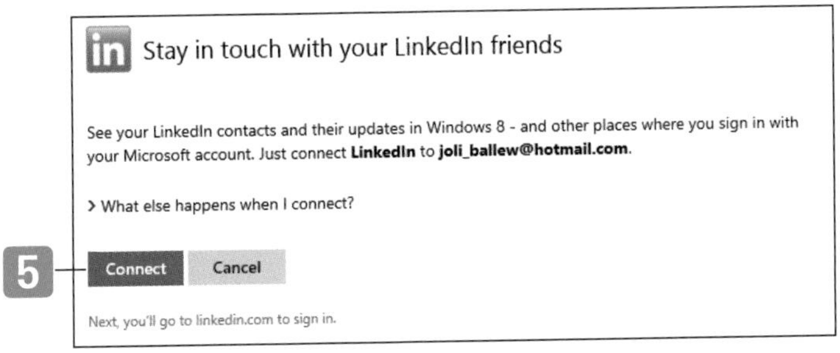

Stay in touch with your LinkedIn friends
See your LinkedIn contacts and their updates in Windows 8 - and other places where you sign in with your Microsoft account. Just connect LinkedIn to joli_ballew@hotmail.com.
What else happens when I connect?
5
Connect
Cancel
Next, you'll go to linkedin.com to sign in.

5. Click Connect, and enter your user name and password, and click OK, I'll Allow it, Sign in or another option as applicable.
6. Click Allow access.
7. Click Done and return to the Messaging app.

ALERT: If you connect with lots of social networks, you'll probably end up with duplicate entries for the same contact in the People app.

DID YOU KNOW?
You may receive an email when your account is connected.

Write a message

To start a new conversation with someone, click New message. This is available from the Messaging interface.

1. Click New message.

2. The People app will open. Choose the desired contact and click Choose.

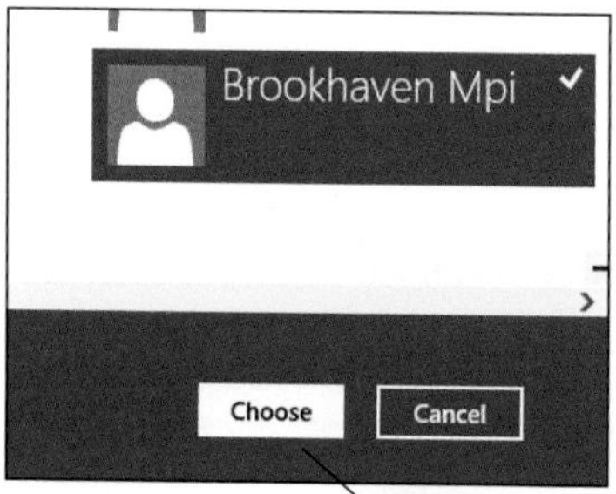

3. Type your message in the text message window and press Enter.
4. Your message will appear at the top of the page.

DID YOU KNOW?
An instant message conversation with a person is called a thread.

HOT TIP: Add all of your contacts to the People app, especially those you communicate with via social networks such as Facebook, and it will be easier to communicate with them.

DID YOU KNOW?
If you close the Messaging app and reopen it later, it will be just as you left it.

Respond to a message

Before you can respond to a message you receive, you must first select the contact in the left pane of the Messaging app. (If you have only one conversation going, you won't have to do this.) Once you've selected who to respond to, you simply type your response and press Enter.

1. In the left pane of the Messaging app, select the thread to respond to. The contact must be online (connected to the Internet and capable of receiving messages).
2. Type your message and press Enter on the keyboard.

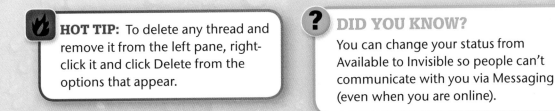

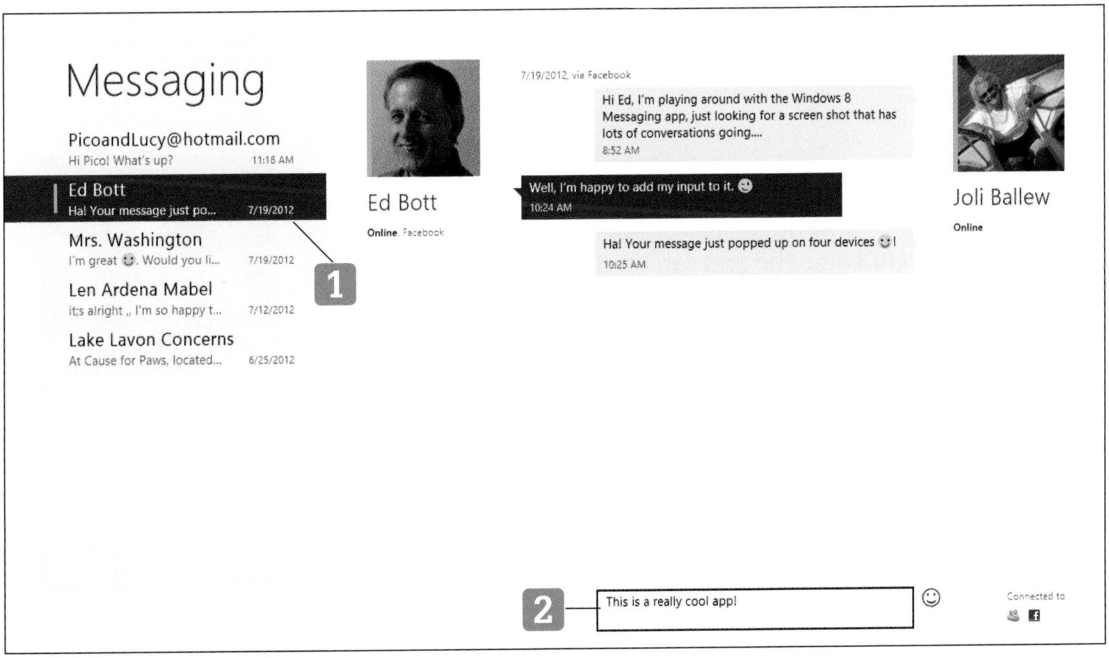
Messaging
PicoandLucy@hotmail.com
Hi Pico! What's up? 11:16 AM
Ed Bott
Ha! Your message just po... 7/19/2012
Mrs. Washington
I'm great. Would you li... 7/19/2012
Len Ardena Mabel
it;s alright ,, I'm so happy t... 7/12/2012
Lake Lavon Concerns
At Cause for Paws, located... 6/25/2012
1
Ed Bott
Online. Facebook
7/19/2012, via Facebook
Hi Ed, I'm playing around with the Windows 8 Messaging app, just looking for a screen shot that has lots of conversations going....
8:52 AM
Well, I'm happy to add my input to it.
10:24 AM
Ha! Your message just popped up on four devices !
10:25 AM
Joli Ballew
Online
2
This is a really cool app!
Connected to

HOT TIP: To delete any thread and remove it from the left pane, right-click it and click Delete from the options that appear.

DID YOU KNOW?

You can change your status from Available to Invisible so people can't communicate with you via Messaging (even when you are online).

Navigate the People app

You use the People app to organise and make available information about your contacts. Contacts will automatically appear when you add social networking sites, connect with Messaging contacts and log on with your own Microsoft account. What you see depends on how you've used your Windows 8 computer so far.

1. Open the People app from the Start screen.
2. Note the options, including Social, Favorites and All. You can scroll to view these three tabs.
3. Under Social, click What's new.
4. If you have connected with social networks, you can view data from those networks now.

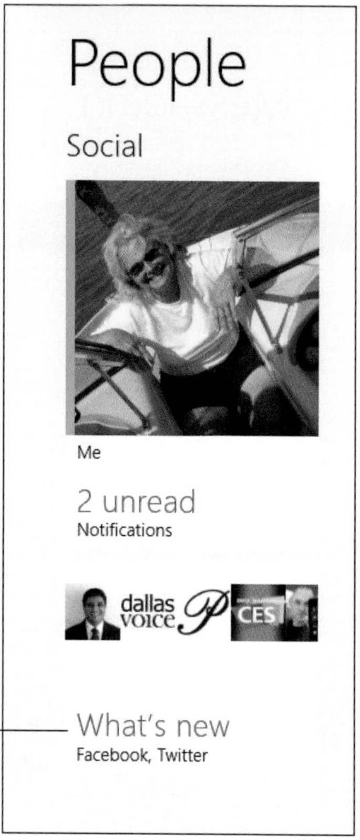

HOT TIP: If you navigate away from the People landing page and can't get back, right-click or flick upwards and click Home to return to it.

DID YOU KNOW?
You can add a contact from the People app from scratch; right-click or flick upwards and click New to get started.

HOT TIP: While in the People app, in What's new, right-click or flick upwards to access the option to filter contacts to show only those from a single social network if you're connected to more than one. Likewise, while viewing all of your contacts, right-click to switch to 'Online only'. You may be able to send those online contacts messages using the Messaging app.

Add social networking accounts

Like the Messaging app, you can add information about the social networks you belong to while inside the People app. When you do, you can see their status updates, access their contact information, send them email and messages and more.

1. While inside the People app, access the default charms and click Settings.
2. Click Accounts.
3. Click Add an account.
4. Choose the account from the resulting list.
5. Input the required information and click Connect.

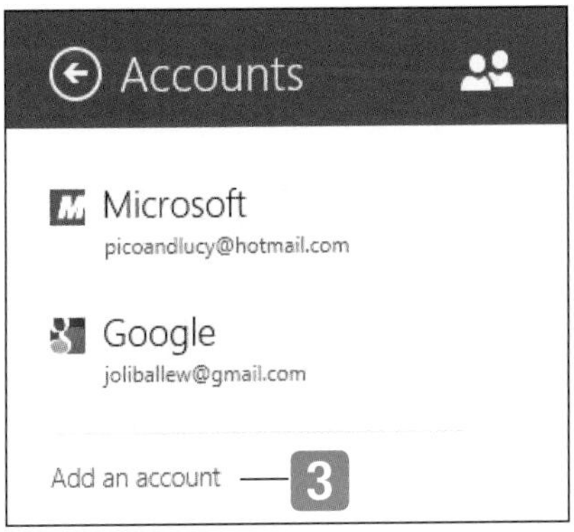

HOT TIP: If you see duplicate entries for a single contact, delete all but one (open the contact card and then right-click) and edit the one you keep so that it contains all of the information about the person.

DID YOU KNOW?

If you position your mouse in the bottom right corner of the People app and click the – sign that appears, the screen will change from the large tiles you currently see for your contacts to small alphabetic tiles you can use to go directly to that group of contacts. (Click any tile to change it back.)

View others' updates

You view others' updates, posts and tweets from What's new. You can click any option available under an entry to reply, like, retweet or respond to it, as applicable. If you have signed in with multiple social networks, you can filter what you see from the toolbar.

1. Open the People app and click What's new.
2. Use your finger to flick left and right, or use the scroll wheel on your mouse to move through the posts. (There's a scroll bar at the bottom of the screen as well.)
3. Notice the options under each post or tweet. Click to respond as desired.
4. Right-click or flick upwards and click Filter.
5. Choose which social network(s) you'd like to view.

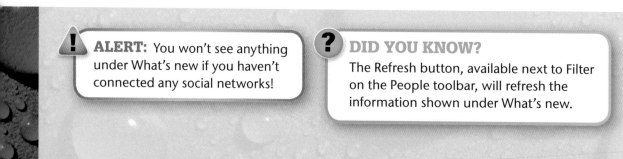

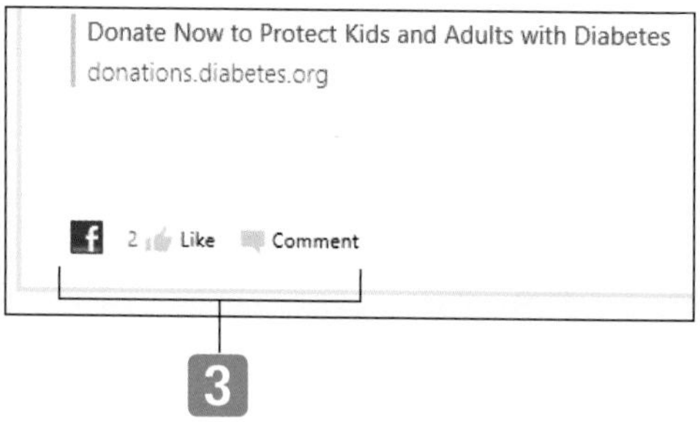

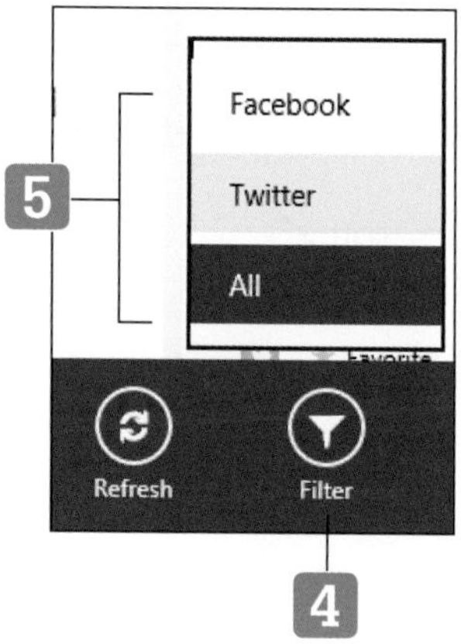

ALERT: You won't see anything under What's new if you haven't connected any social networks!

DID YOU KNOW?

The Refresh button, available next to Filter on the People toolbar, will refresh the information shown under What's new.

Add shortcuts on the Start screen

If the People app doesn't meet your needs, you can create a shortcut on the Start screen for your favourite social networking websites. You might create shortcuts for Facebook.com, Twitter.com, Live.com, AOL.com, Wordpress.com and so on.

1. From the Start screen, open the Internet Explorer app.
2. Navigate to the website you'd like to create a shortcut for.
3. On the address bar at the bottom of the page, click Pin to Start.
4. Type the desired name and click Pin to Start again.
5. Return to the Start screen and scroll right. You'll see the new tile there.

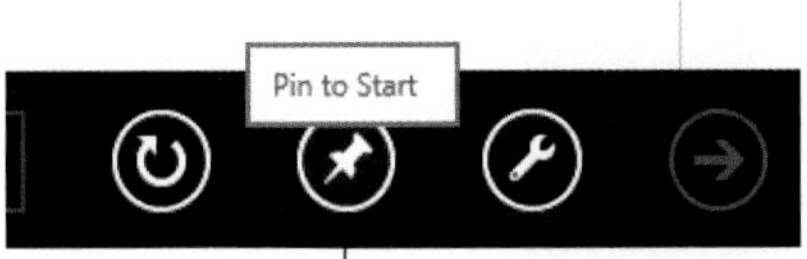

3

5

DID YOU KNOW?

When you create a shortcut to a website, when you click the tile the full website opens. You might prefer the full website to the What's new section of the People app; if so, add tiles for all of the social networks you use.

Get more social networking apps

You can get more social networking apps from the Store, available from the Start screen. Most are free. You might prefer these apps over those that come with Windows 8, specifically the Messaging app and the People app.

1. From the Start screen, click Store.
2. Scroll to locate the Social apps.
3. Locate an app you think you might like and click it.
4. If you like the app after reading the reviews and other information, click Install.
5. Open the app, log in and repeat!

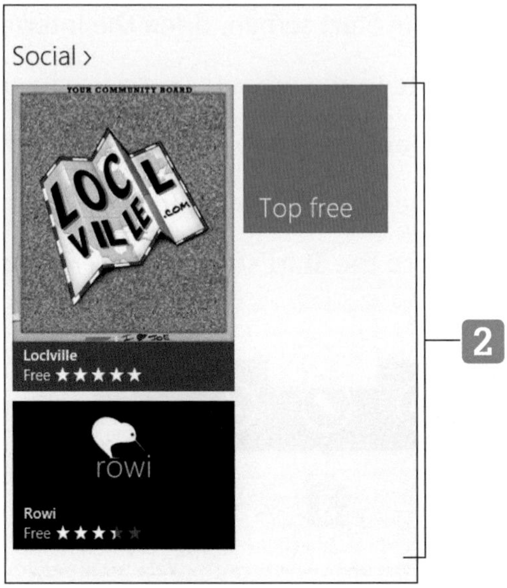

HOT TIP: Once you own an app you can review and rate it. You'll see that option on the app page in the Store.

DID YOU KNOW?
You can uninstall any app you don't like from the Start screen's toolbar.

10 View, navigate and share photos

Introduction

Windows 8 comes with several ways to view and share photos. One is the Photos app available from the Start screen. From there you can access all of your pictures in a single place, and you can view, print and share them easily. You can also access pictures you've made available online such as those stored on Facebook, Flickr and SkyDrive.

If you'd like to do something a bit more complex, perhaps create folders to organise your photos, rotate them or open them in an editing program, you'll want to do so from the desktop, specifically, using File Explorer. There you can access your Pictures library, move and organise pictures easily, and use the File Explorer interface to share photos in lots of different ways (including burning them to a CD or DVD). You can even sort photos by date, rating, when the pictures were taken and more.

Navigate the Photos app

The Photos app, available from the Start screen, is the easiest place to view your photos. The app separates your photos by what's stored on your computer, and what is stored in various places on the Internet. If you've created subfolders to organise your photos, those subfolders will appear too.

1. From the Start screen, click Photos.
2. Note the folders that already appear. This is the landing page. (If you see something else, locate and click the applicable Back arrows to navigate to this page.)
3. Click the Pictures library.
4. If you see subfolders, click them to access the pictures stored there.

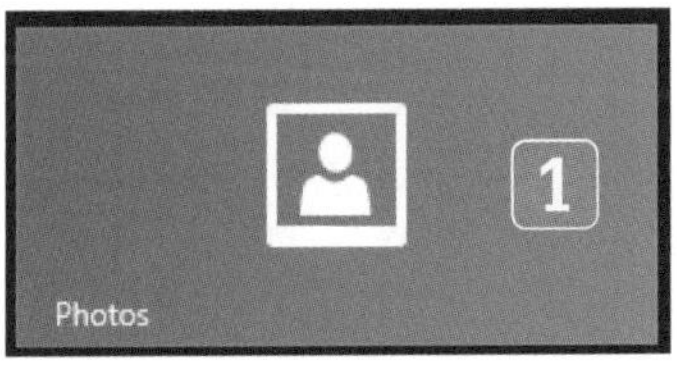

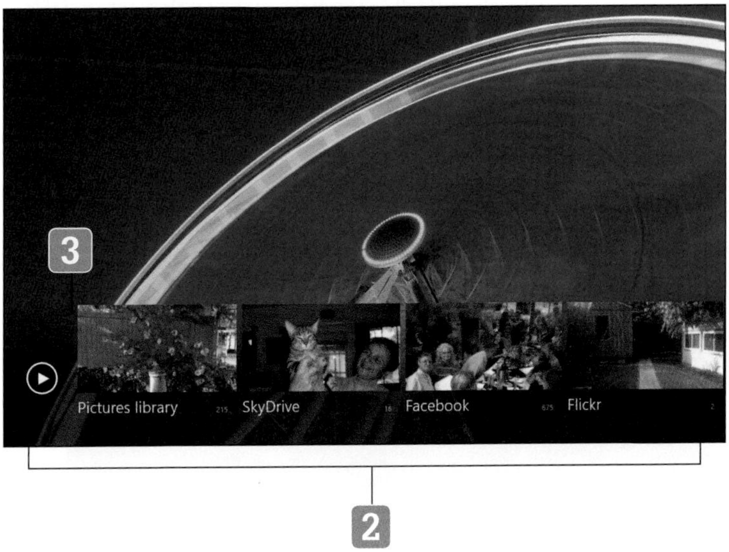

HOT TIP: You may not have any photos on your computer yet. If this is the case, skip forward two sections to learn how to import pictures from an external source and then return here to view them.

ALERT: When you save pictures to your computer, make sure to save them to the Pictures library. You can save them specifically to the My Pictures or the Public Pictures folders if you'd rather. Saving to the Pictures library or a specific pictures folder will make the pictures easy to find in the Photos app.

View a photo

While navigating the folders and subfolders in the Photos app, you'll see the photos you've stored on your computer and other places. While in folders in subfolders, the photos are in preview mode. You can view them this way or click them to view them in full screen mode. We'll explore both here.

1. Open the Photos app from the Start screen.
2. Click the Pictures library.
3. If applicable, click any subfolder. The photos you'll see after doing so are in preview mode.
4. Click any photo to view it in full screen mode.
5. Use the Back arrow that appears near the middle of the left side of the screen or the one that appears in the top left corner to return to the previous screen.

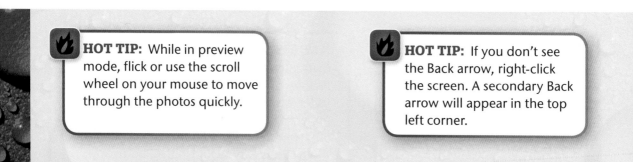

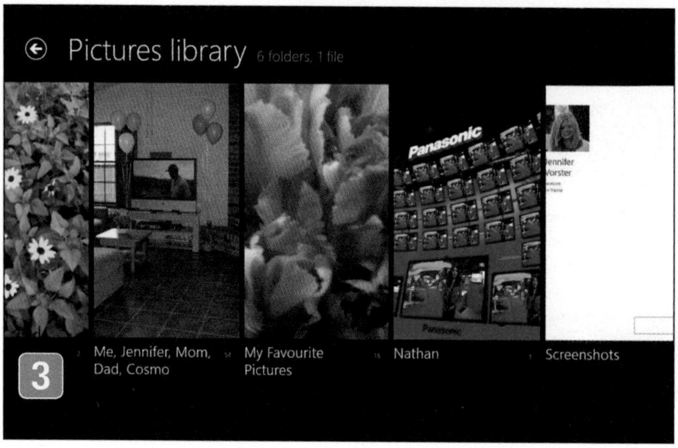

HOT TIP: While in preview mode, flick or use the scroll wheel on your mouse to move through the photos quickly.

HOT TIP: If you don't see the Back arrow, right-click the screen. A secondary Back arrow will appear in the top left corner.

Import pictures from an external source

You can put photos on your computer in lots of ways, but the easiest way is to use the Photos app. The landing page offers an option to add a device to *see* photos that are on that device, but if you right-click while on that page, the option to *Import* those photos appears.

1. Open the Photos app and click any Back buttons as necessary to access the landing page.
2. Connect your camera, insert a memory card, or connect an external hard drive that contains photos.
3. Select the pictures to import.
4. Click Import.
5. Click Open folder (not shown) to view the photos.

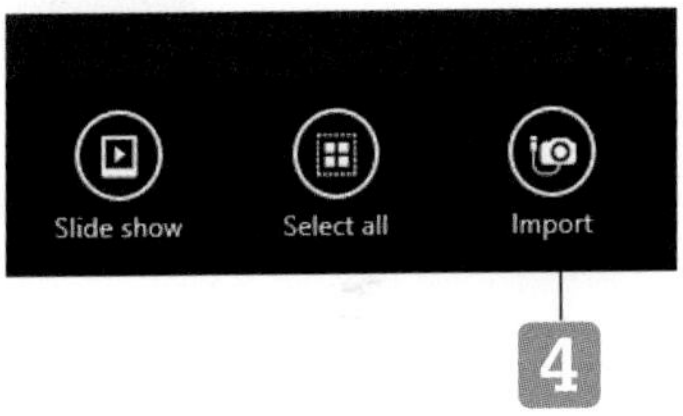

WHAT DOES THIS MEAN?

Import: when you import photos, you copy them to your computer.

HOT TIP: Create a descriptive name for the folder that will hold the imported photos; don't just accept the default name offered.

Play a slide show of photos

You can play a slide show of pictures in any folder. Once it starts to play, you can stop it in many ways. You can click Esc on the keyboard, right-click with a mouse, touch the screen and more.

1. Open the Photos app from the Start screen.
2. Navigate to any folder that contains photos.
3. Right-click and choose Slide show. (Remember, on a tablet you can swipe up.)
4. Stop the show using any method desired.

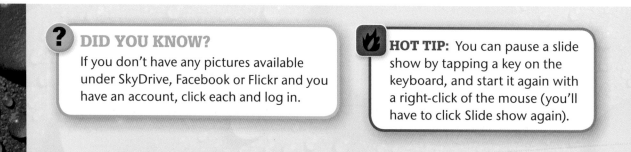

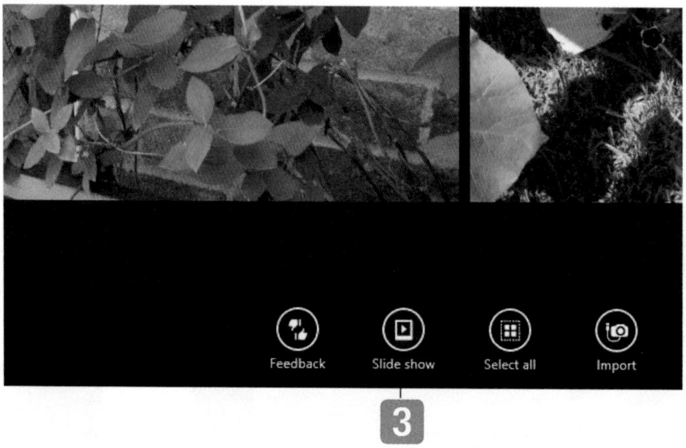

DID YOU KNOW?
If you don't have any pictures available under SkyDrive, Facebook or Flickr and you have an account, click each and log in.

HOT TIP: You can pause a slide show by tapping a key on the keyboard, and start it again with a right-click of the mouse (you'll have to click Slide show again).

Delete photos

You can delete photos that are stored on your own computer from the Photos app. You cannot delete photos that are stored on Facebook and the like. You have to access that website to delete photos stored there.

1. In the Photos app, navigate to a picture stored in your Pictures library folder.
2. Right-click the photo to delete (it can be in preview or full screen mode). In preview mode, a tick will appear on the picture.
3. If desired, and if you are in preview mode, right-click additional photos.
4. Click Delete.

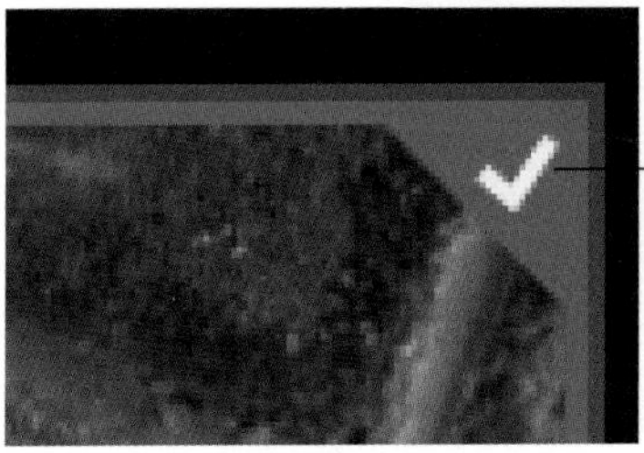

2

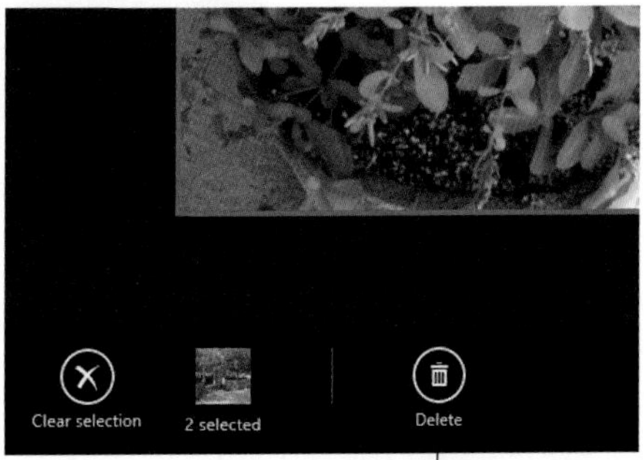

4

HOT TIP: If you change your mind about the photos you've selected for deletion, either right-click a single photo to remove the tick (and deselect it), or click Clear selection to clear all selections.

DID YOU KNOW?
It's best to delete photos you don't want. Unwanted photos not only make the Photos app harder to navigate, the photos also take up valuable hard drive space on your computer.

Use a photo on the Lock screen

You can set a photo to be the background on the Lock screen, the image for an app tile or even serve as an app background.

1. Open the Photos app from the Start screen.
2. Navigate to a photo and open it in full screen.
3. Right-click to access the toolbar, and then click Set as and then Lock screen.

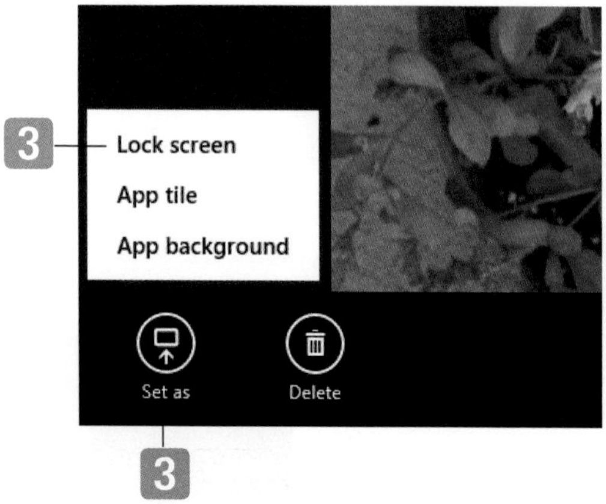

HOT TIP: To change the picture that appears on the landing page of the Photos app, choose Set as App background.

DID YOU KNOW?
The Photos tile is a live tile, and by default it will flip through photos. Right-click the tile on the Start screen to access the option to disable the live feature.

HOT TIP: To change the picture that appears on the Photos tile on the Start screen, choose Set as App tile.

Connect social accounts

You can view the pictures stored on SkyDrive, Facebook or Flickr from the Photos app. These are all free online storage spaces. You'll have to click their respective tiles and log in with your account first (if prompted) in order to use those areas though.

1. From the Photos app, on the landing page, click Facebook or Flickr.
2. Click Connect.
3. If prompted, type your email or user name, and your password.

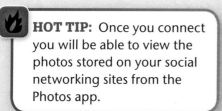

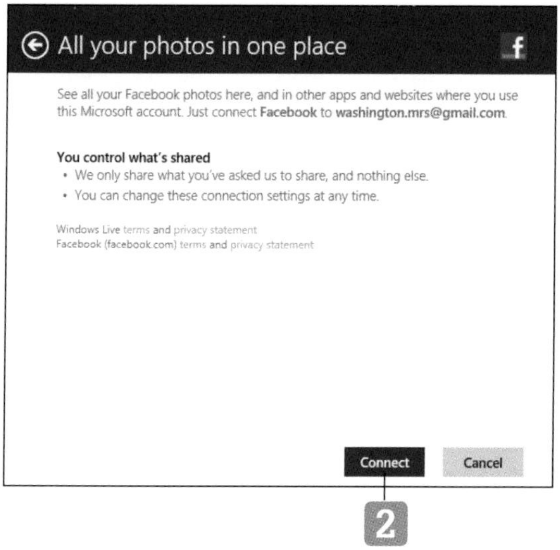

All your photos in one place
See all your Facebook photos here, and in other apps and websites where you use this Microsoft account. Just connect Facebook to washington.mrs@gmail.com.
You control what's shared
• We only share what you've asked us to share, and nothing else.
• You can change these connection settings at any time.
Windows Live terms and privacy statement
Facebook (facebook.com) terms and privacy statement
Connect
Cancel
2

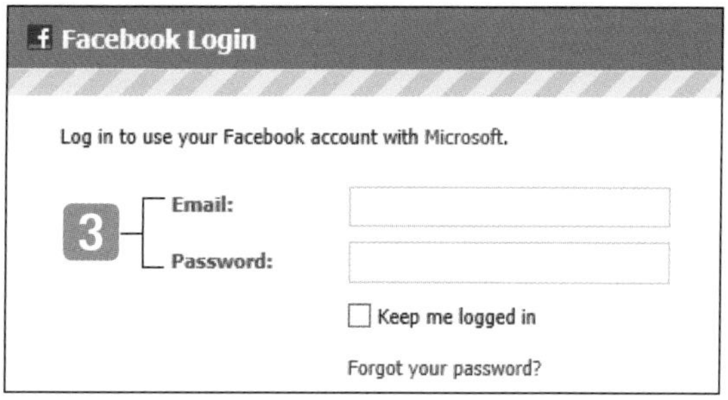

Facebook Login
Log in to use your Facebook account with Microsoft.
3
Email:
Password:
Keep me logged in
Forgot your password?

HOT TIP: Once you connect you will be able to view the photos stored on your social networking sites from the Photos app.

DID YOU KNOW?

If you decide later you don't want to connect to a specific social network from Photos, from the Settings charm, click Options. From there you can disable any previously connected site. (Use the Windows key + C to access the default charms.)

Access your Pictures library on the desktop

Music, pictures, documents, videos and other data are stored on your computer's hard drive, and are organised in folders and libraries. You can navigate to that data with File Explorer. You will want to do this when you want to perform tasks you can't achieve in the Photos app, such as burning a group of photos to a CD or DVD, among other things.

1. From the Start screen, click Desktop.
2. On the taskbar, click the Folder icon.
3. Click Pictures in the left pane, under Libraries.
4. What you see in the resulting window are the pictures available to you from your Pictures library. You may see subfolders you've already created.

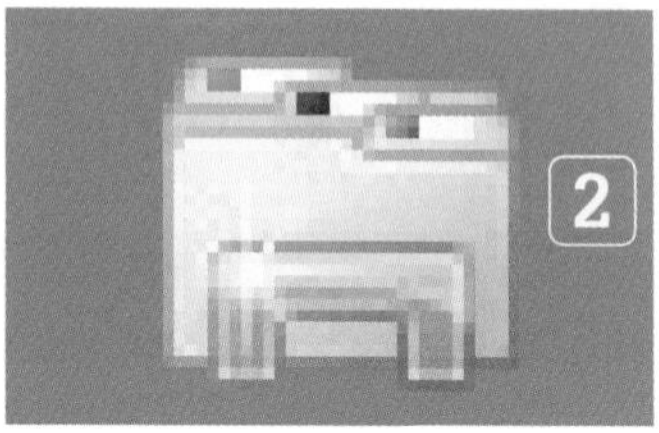

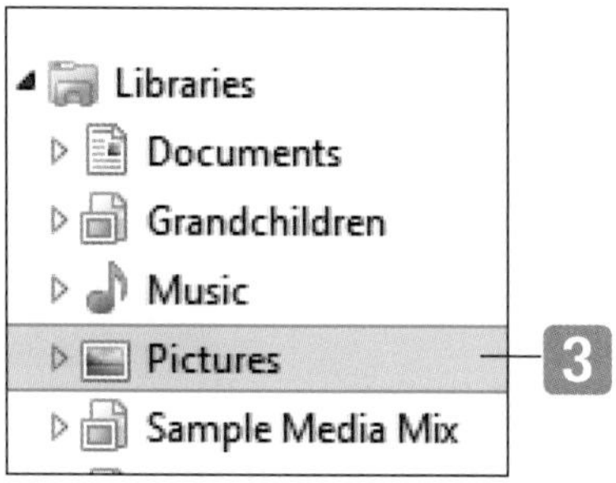

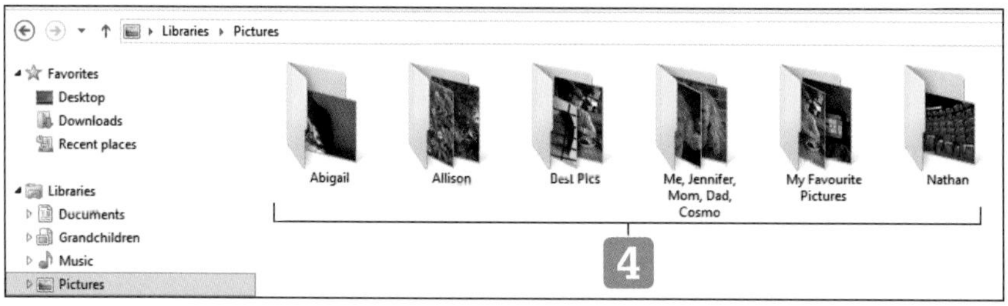

WHAT DOES THIS MEAN?

Library: a library offers access to data stored in two related folders. As an example, the Pictures library offers access to the My Pictures folder and the Public Pictures folder.

DID YOU KNOW?

From the View tab you can choose how to show the items in a folder. We prefer Large icons, but you can also choose Extra large icons, Medium icons, List, Small icons and others.

Explore the File Explorer ribbon

File Explorer has three main features. The Navigation pane is the vertical pane on the left, the Content pane is the larger area on the right, and the ribbon is the area just above both, near the top of the screen. When you select a folder in the Navigation pane and/or content in the Content pane, what appears on the ribbon changes.

1. In File Explorer, click Pictures in the Navigation pane. That's the pane that appears on the left side and contains Favorites, Libraries, Computer, Network and so on.
2. In the Content pane, navigate to a photo and click it once.
3. From the ribbon, click the Share tab. Note a few of the options:
   - Email – To email a photo. (You'll need to have a compatible email client configured for this to be available.)
   - Burn to disc – To copy selected photos to a CD or DVD.
   - Print – To print a photo.

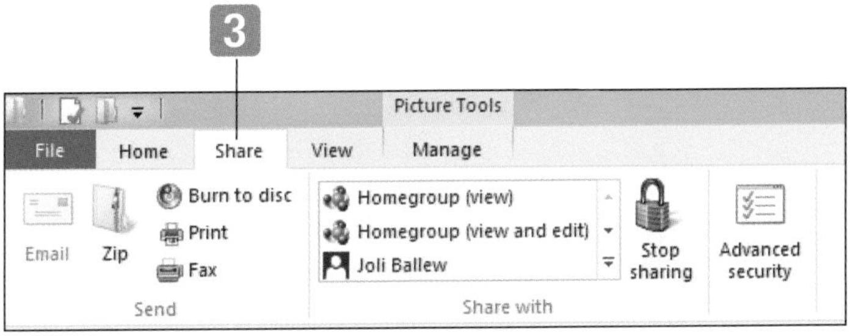

ALERT: If you can't see the Navigation pane, click the View tab. Then click Navigation pane and click Navigation pane from the drop-down list.

ALERT: If the ribbon appears only when you click a tab title, but does not appear all of the time, click the down-facing arrow located in the top right corner of the File Explorer window.

HOT TIP: To select multiple items, hold down the Ctrl key.

4 From the ribbon, click the Home tab. Note a few of the options:

- Copy – To copy the photo for pasting elsewhere.
- Move to – To move the photo to a different folder.
- Delete – To delete the photo.
- Rename – To rename the photo.

5 From the ribbon, click the Manage tab. Note a few of the options:

- Rotate left or Rotate right – To rotate the image.
- Slide show – To play a slide show using the images in the folder (or the selected images).
- Set as background – To use the selected image(s) as background on the desktop.

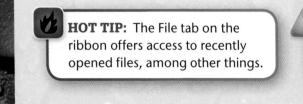

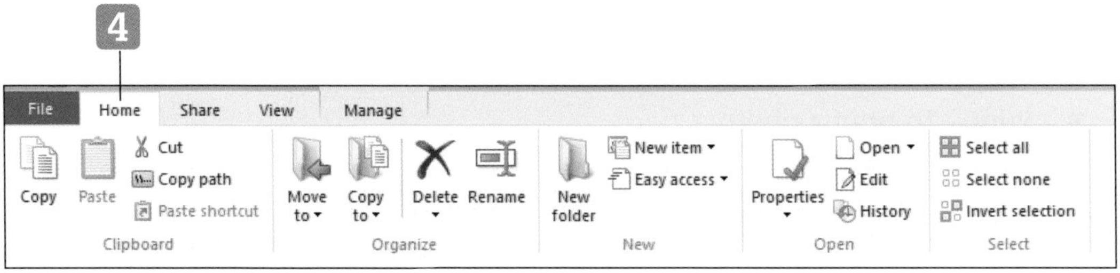

HOT TIP: The File tab on the ribbon offers access to recently opened files, among other things.

ALERT: From the View tab, select Large or Extra Large icon. You'll be able to see what's in the Content area much better.

Rotate a photo

If you worked through the last exercise, you can probably figure out how to rotate a photo. For the sake of completeness though, and because photos often need to be rotated, we'll detail it here.

1. Open File Explorer and navigate to a photo that needs to be rotated.
2. Click the photo once.
3. Click the Manage tab.
4. Click the desired rotate option.

DID YOU KNOW?
You can right-click any picture to access its contextual menu. You'll see familiar options there, including Rotate right and Rotate left, Delete, Rename and Share with, among others.

HOT TIP: To move multiple photos from one folder to another, select the photos and, from the Home tab, select Move to. Then you can select the desired folder.

View pictures with the Windows Photo Viewer

By default, if you double-click a picture while in File Explorer (in order to view it in full screen mode), the Photos app opens to show it. If you don't want to use the app and would rather view the picture on the desktop instead, you'll want to opt for Windows Photo Viewer.

1. While in File Explorer, right-click the photo to view.
2. Position your mouse over Open with, and click Windows Photo Viewer.

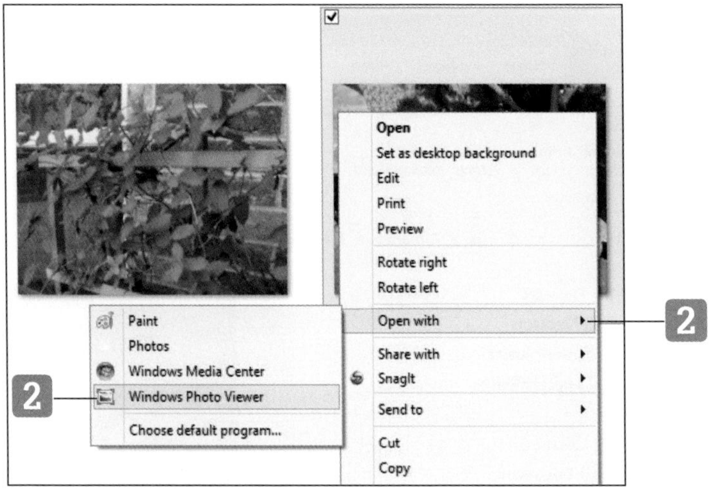

HOT TIP: Choose to view a photo in Photo Viewer when you want to make a copy of, print, email, burn to a disc, or perform some other compatible task.

HOT TIP: If you see an additional pane to the right of the Content pane, you can make it disappear using the View tab. Click either Preview pane or Details pane to hide it. (Alternatively, you can opt to show it!)

Note the available options:

3 File – To delete, make a copy, view the image properties, or exit the program.

4 Print – To print using your own printer or to order prints online.

5 E-mail – To email the photo.

6 Burn – To burn the image to a data disc.

7 Open – To open the image in another program.

8 Zoom options – To zoom in and then out of an image.

9 Previous – To view the previous image in the folder.

10 Slide Show – To start a slide show of the images in the folder (click Esc to exit).

11 Next – To view the next image in the folder.

12 Rotate options – To rotate the photo.

13 Delete – To delete the photo.

Print a photo

If you've explored Windows Photo Viewer, you know you can print a photo from there. You can also access the Print command from inside File Explorer.

1. Navigate to a single photo to print.
2. Click the photo and then click the Share tab on the ribbon.
3. Click Print.
4. Use the drop-down lists to choose a printer, a paper size, quality settings and paper type.
5. Depending on your selections in Step 4, you may also be able to choose how many prints to include on a single page.
6. Configure additional options if applicable and click Print.

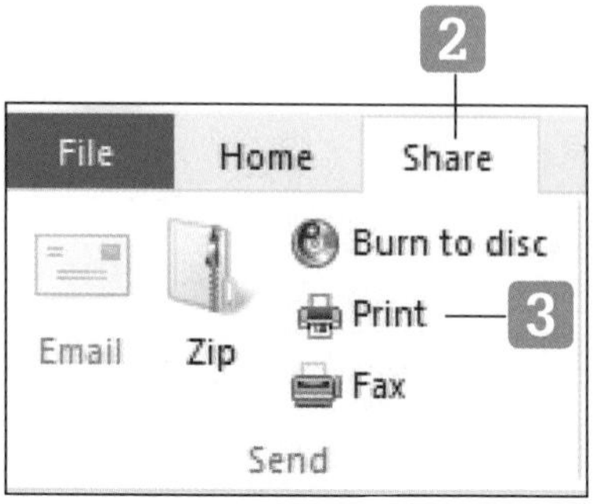

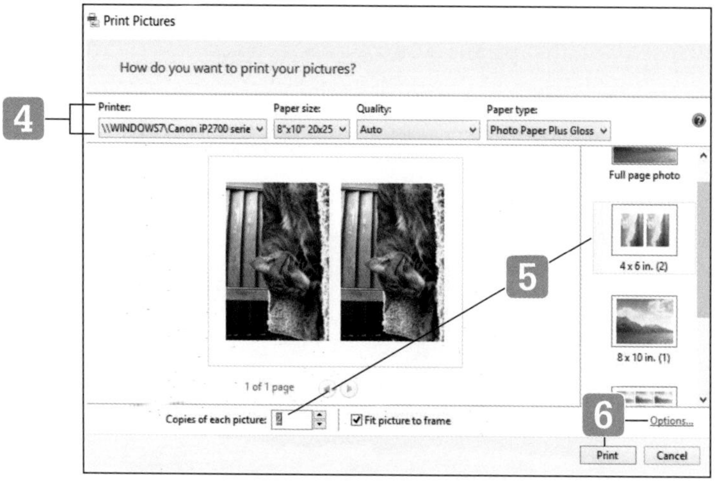

HOT TIP: To get the best results, print pictures using glossy photo paper.

HOT TIP: You can print from the Photos app, but the interface looks quite a bit different from what you see here.

Email a photo

You can use the Mail app to attach photos to an email you've already started, or you can start an email using File Explorer. When you select photos to email from File Explorer, you're prompted to choose what size to configure the photos. This is a great feature because it enables you to easily resize the photos however you desire. You'll need a dedicated email client configured for this to work.

1. In File Explorer, select the photos to email. (Remember, you can hold down the Ctrl key to select multiple photos.)
2. From the Share tab, click Email. Alternatively, you can right-click any selected photo, and choose Send to > Mail recipient.
3. Use the drop-down list to choose the desired photo size. When sending multiple photos, it's best to keep the total size below 2 MB.
4. Click Attach and complete the email as desired.

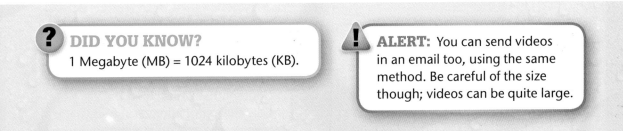

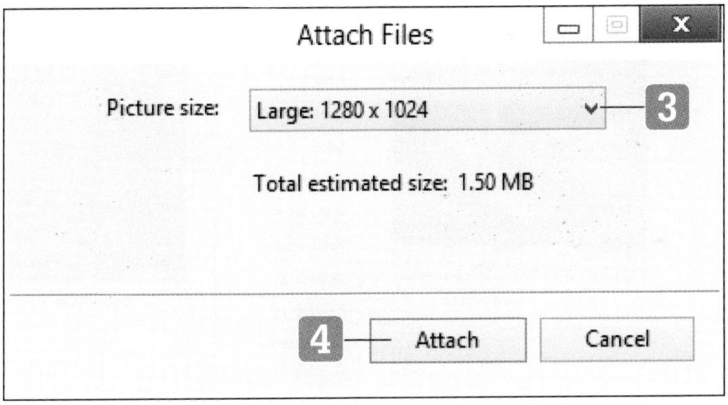

DID YOU KNOW?
1 Megabyte (MB) = 1024 kilobytes (KB).

ALERT: You can send videos in an email too, using the same method. Be careful of the size though; videos can be quite large.

Sort photos

The photos that appear in any File Explorer window are sorted automatically by their name. You can sort them differently though, perhaps by size, by the date they were taken and more.

1. Navigate to any folder that contains photos.
2. Click the View tab.
3. Click Sort by and select a new option.

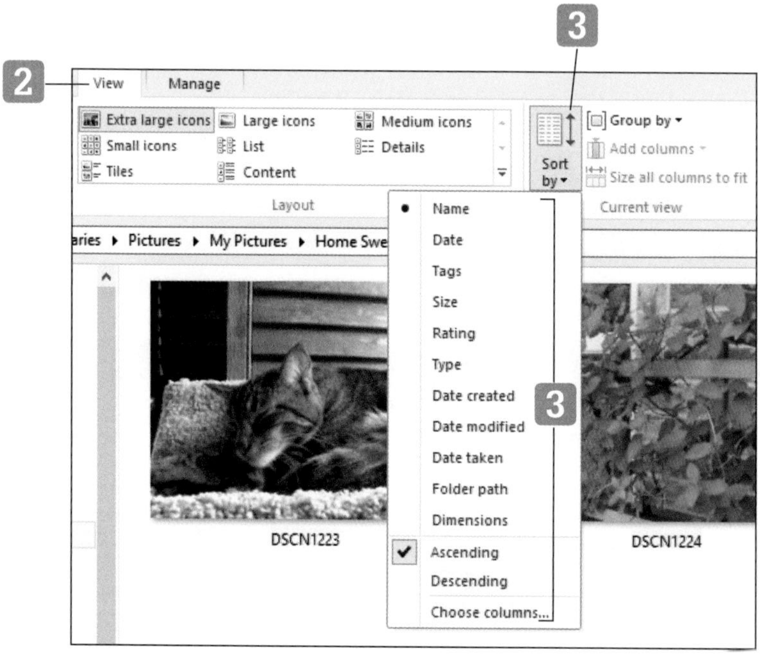

HOT TIP: If you choose to sort, say, by date taken, and the images appear from newest to oldest, you can reverse the order (oldest to newest) by clicking the same option again in the Sort by drop-down list.

HOT TIP: If you haven't tried the various View options on the ribbon yet, do so now. From the View tab click Content, then Tiles, then Details. Note how the information changes.

Explore editing options

You can edit photos, but you'll need to use an editing program. To find out what your editing options are, right-click any photo while inside File Explorer and choose Edit. Paint may open. Paint is a desktop application included with Windows 8. Paint isn't a very good editing tool though. Consider the following instead.

1. Windows Live Photo Gallery – This is part of the free Windows Live Essentials suite. Like most editing programs, it enables you to fix red-eye, crop, adjust exposure and sharpness and more. There are lots of automatic fixes to make it easy.
2. Picasa – This is a free digital photo *organiser*, so it might complicate locating and managing photos, but the editing tools that come with the program enable you to edit photos quickly and easily. Picasa offers the usual editing tools, including crop and various auto adjustments.
3. Photoshop Elements – You'll have to pay for this program but, for what you get, it's well worth the cost if you want to do some serious editing. The interface is user friendly and enables you to edit your photos in ways you never imagined.

3

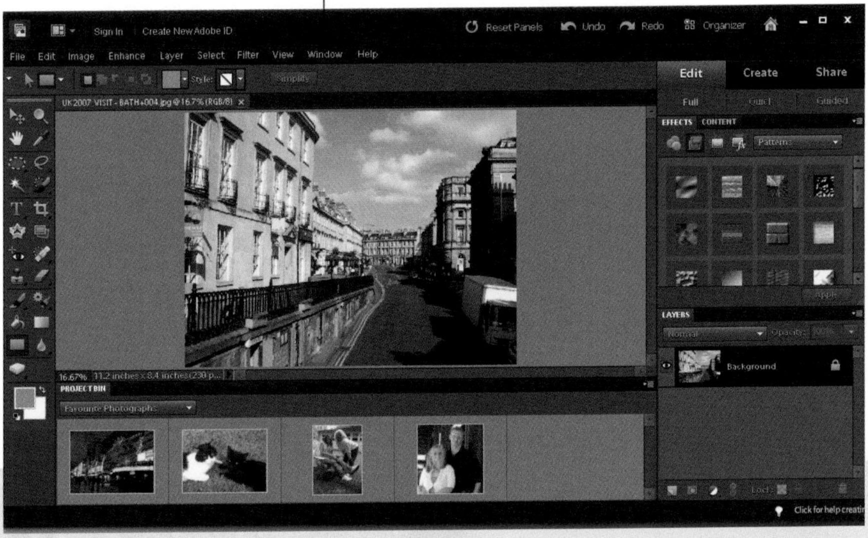

HOT TIP: Almost all editing programs have an Undo or Revert command. Apply it before you save the file to undo any changes you don't like.

HOT TIP: Try Windows Live Photo Gallery first. It's made by Microsoft so you know it will work well with Windows 8.

11 View, manage and listen to music and media

Play a song in Media Player

To play any song, navigate to it and double-click it. Once the song is playing you can manage the media using the playback controls located at the bottom of the Media Player interface.

1. Open Windows Media Player, and click Music in the Navigation pane. (Note you can also click Artist, Album or Genre to locate a song.)
2. Double-click any song to play it.

Use the following media controls located at the bottom of the Media Player interface:

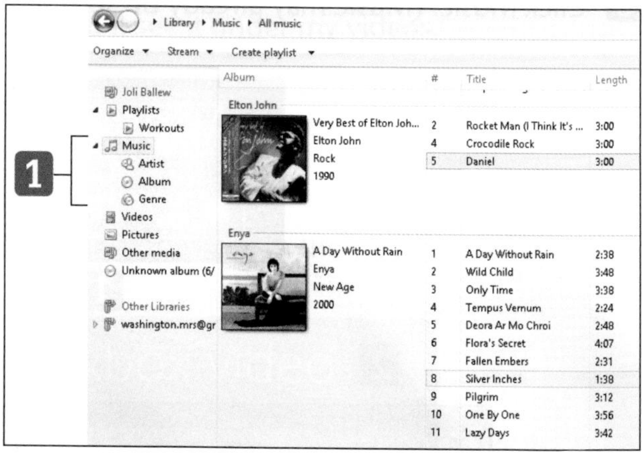

3. Shuffle – To let Media Player choose the order in which to play the selected songs.
4. Repeat – To play the current song again.
5. Stop – To stop playback.
6. Previous – To play the previous song in the list, on the album and so on.
7. Play/Pause – To play and pause the song (and playlist).
8. Next – To play the next song in the list, on the album and so on.
9. Mute – To quickly mute the song.
10. Volume – To change the volume of the song.

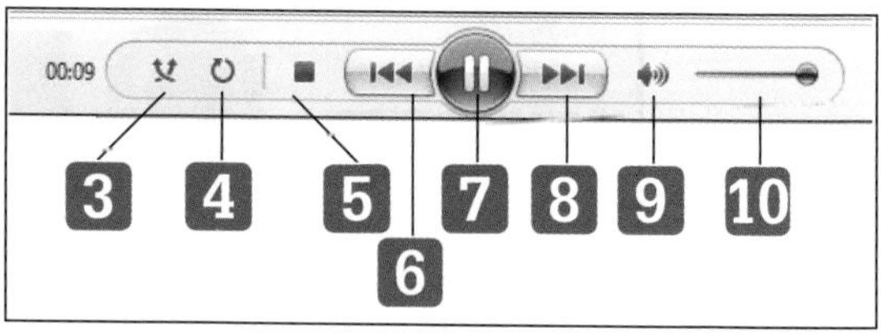

HOT TIP: While a song is playing, right-click any other song and choose Play Next, Play All or Play, as desired.

DID YOU KNOW?
Media Player has Back and Forward buttons you can use to navigate Media Player.

Copy a CD to your computer

You can copy your own music CDs to your hard drive. This is called 'ripping'. To rip means to copy in media-speak. Once music is on your PC, you can listen to it in the Music app and in Media Player, burn compilations of music to other CDs, and sync the music to a portable music player.

1. Insert the CD to copy into the CD drive.
2. Deselect any songs you do not want to copy to your PC.
3. In Windows Media Player, click the Rip CD button.

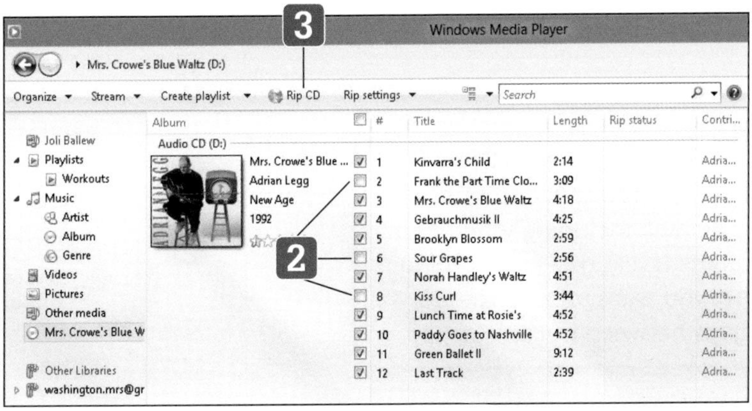

HOT TIP: Click the arrow beside Organize, and click Options to change the settings configured by default, such as what format you use when you rip a CD. (You'll want to choose MP3 if you plan to copy the music to a portable player, for instance.)

DID YOU KNOW?
You have the right to rip any CD you own to your PC for no extra cost and without breaking any laws.

HOT TIP: Right-click any album cover and click Find Album Info, and Windows Media Player will look online for the album cover, track list and other information.

Copy music files to a CD

There are two ways to take music with you when you are on the road or on the go. You can copy the music to a portable device (music player, tablet or phone), or you can create your own CDs, choosing the songs to copy and placing them on the CD in the desired order.

1. Open Media Player.
2. Insert a blank CD and click the Burn tab.
3. Click any song or album to add and drag it to the List pane, shown here. You can drag any song to move it to a new position in the Burn list.
4. When you've added the songs you want, click Start burn.

HOT TIP: Click the arrow beside Organize, and click Options to change the settings configured by default, including whether or not to use 'volume leveling' when burning CDs or whether you want to burn the CD without any gaps between tracks.

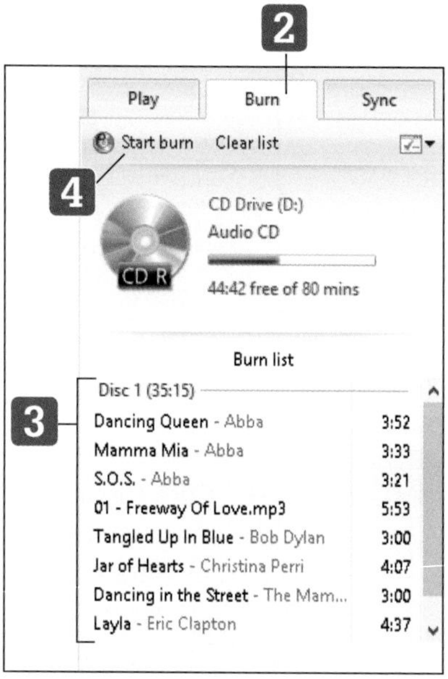

DID YOU KNOW?

Look at the slider in the List pane to see how much room is left on the CD. A typical CD can hold about 80 minutes of music.

WHAT DOES THIS MEAN?

Burn: a term used to describe the process of copying music from a computer to a CD.

12 Install hardware and software

Introduction

You probably have a printer, scanner, phone, music player or other gadget you want to connect to your Windows 8 computer. This hardware, as it's referred to, must be installed before it can be accessed and used from the computer. Most of the time this is as easy as connecting the device and turning it on.

As well as hardware devices you may also have software applications you want to install, such as Microsoft Office or Photoshop Elements, or something you downloaded from the Internet, such as iTunes. In this chapter you'll learn how to install both.

Install a digital camera, webcam or smartphone

Most of the time, installing hardware is easy. You simply plug in the device and wait for it to be installed automatically. Once it's installed, you can set what you'd like to happen by default. Before you start, make sure the device is charged, plugged into a wall socket or has fresh batteries.

1. Read the directions that came with the device. If there are specific instructions for installing it, follow them. If not, continue here.
2. Connect the device.
3. If applicable, turn on the device. (You may have to set an older digital camera or camcorder to its playback position.)
4. Wait while the installation completes. When prompted, click or tap to choose what happens when you connect the device next time.

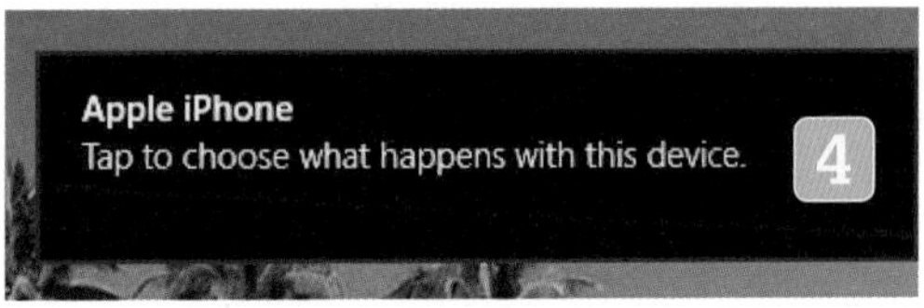

5. Choose what to do when you connect the device.

HOT TIP: If you missed the prompt to configure what to do when you connect the device and it's no longer available, don't worry. Just disconnect and reconnect it. It will appear again (at least until you set what you'd like to do all the time).

DID YOU KNOW?

Sometimes you'll receive a CD with a device. The hardware may work fine without it. If you want to keep unnecessary data and programs off your PC, see if the hardware will work without it first. You can always install the CD later if you need to.

Install a printer

Printers, fax machines and scanners often come with a CD, and sometimes, features won't be available until you install the software on it. Therefore, it's generally best to insert the CD and see what happens.

1. Connect the device to a wall socket and turn it on, if applicable.
2. Connect the device to the PC using the applicable cable.
3. Insert the CD for the device if you have it.
4. If you see a prompt to run the installation file, click it and work through the set-up process.
5. If you do not see any prompt and the device installs on its own, simply wait.
6. From the Start screen, type Devices, then Settings. Look for Devices in the results.
7. Click Devices and view the newly installed printer.

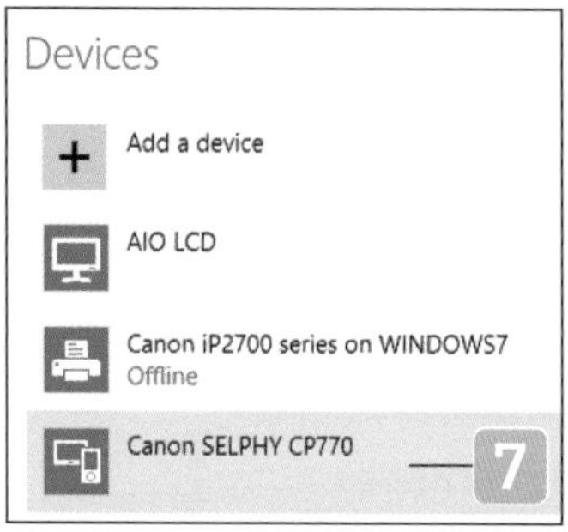

SEE ALSO: Install software, later in this chapter.

ALERT: Read the directions that come with each new device you acquire. If there are specific instructions for installation, follow those directions, not the generic directions offered here.

ALERT: Scanners often require specialised software to function. Printers often require specialised software to offer advanced features, such as printing envelopes or both sides of a page.

Troubleshoot hardware installations

If, when you connect and turn on a device, nothing happens, you'll have to install the device manually. Although there is more than one way to add a device in Windows 8, the most comprehensive is to use the Devices and Printers window. (Before you start, though, insert the CD if the device came with one, and see if you are prompted to install it without working through these steps.)

1. Open Control Panel (you can type Control Panel at the Start screen to locate it).
2. Under Hardware and Sound, click Add a device. (Note the option View devices and printers. You'll access this later.)
3. Click the device in the resulting list, select it and click Next.
4. Return to the Control Panel, and click View devices and printers. Verify the device has installed.

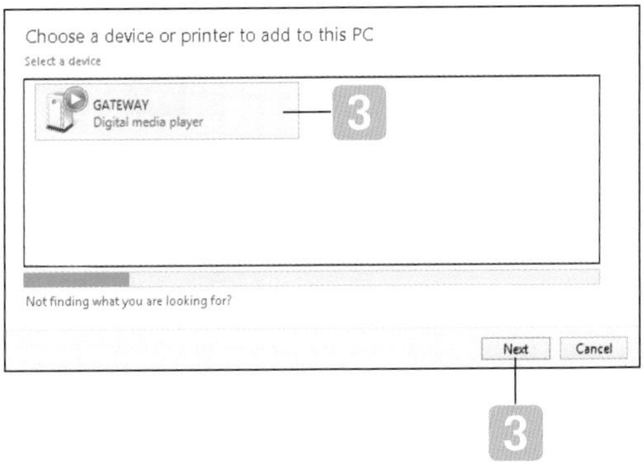

ALERT: A device needs a driver to communicate with the computer, and vice versa. If a piece of hardware still doesn't install or work properly, visit the manufacturer's website for help.

DID YOU KNOW?
If you see the device in the Devices and Printers window but it has an exclamation mark beside it, right-click the device and click Troubleshoot.

Improve performance with ReadyBoost

ReadyBoost is a technology that enables you to use a USB flash drive or a secure digital memory card as a cache (a place where data is stored temporarily and accessed when needed) to increase computer performance.

1. Insert a USB flash drive, thumb drive or memory card into an available slot on the outside of your PC.
2. When prompted in the upper right corner, click to view your options.
3. Choose Speed up my system, Windows ReadyBoost.
4. Choose to dedicate the device to ReadyBoost and click OK.

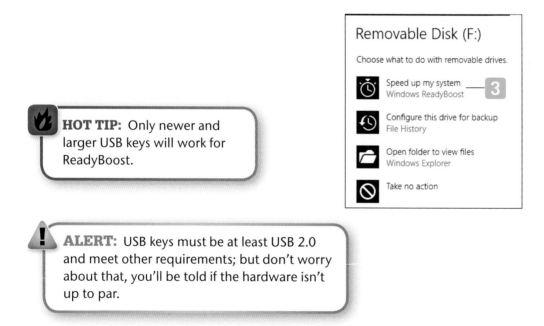

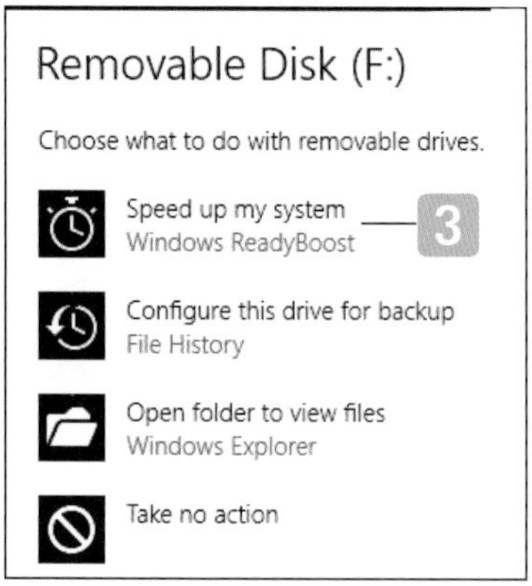

HOT TIP: Only newer and larger USB keys will work for ReadyBoost.

ALERT: USB keys must be at least USB 2.0 and meet other requirements; but don't worry about that, you'll be told if the hardware isn't up to par.

WHAT DOES THIS MEAN?

Cache: a temporary storage area similar to RAM.

RAM: random access memory is where information is stored temporarily so the operating system has quick access to it. The more RAM you have, the better your PC should perform.

Install a software program

As with installing hardware, software installation goes smoothly almost every time. Just make sure you get your software from a reliable source, like Amazon, Microsoft's website, Apple's website (think iTunes, not software for Macs only), or a retail store.

1. Download the installation file from the Internet and skip to Step 4, or, insert the CD or DVD into the appropriate drive and proceed to Step 2.
2. Click the prompt that appears in the top right corner to see your options.

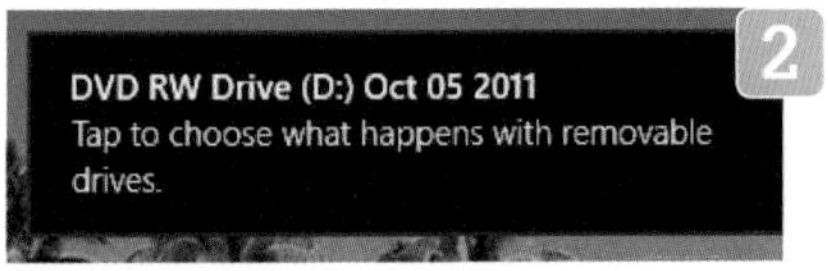
DVD RW Drive (D:) Oct 05 2011
Tap to choose what happens with removable drives.
2

3. If you are not prompted or you miss the prompt, you can eject and reinsert the CD or:
   - Open the Computer window. (You can type Computer at the Start screen.)
   - Double-click the CD or DVD drive.
4. Double-click the application file or do whatever else is necessary to start the installation.
5. Work through the installation wizard.

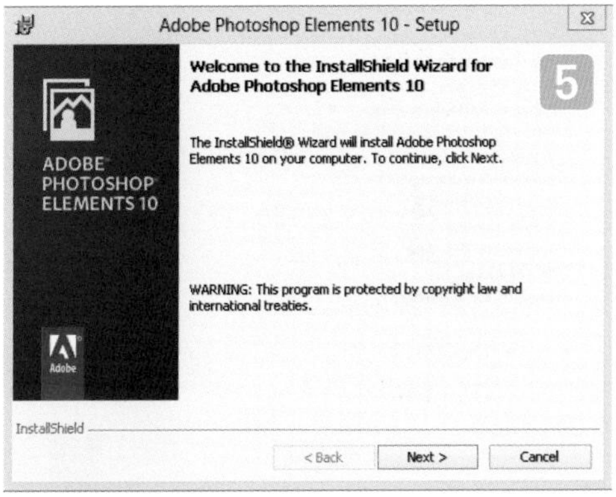
Adobe Photoshop Elements 10 - Setup
Welcome to the InstallShield Wizard for Adobe Photoshop Elements 10
5
The InstallShield® Wizard will install Adobe Photoshop Elements 10 on your computer. To continue, click Next.
ADOBE PHOTOSHOP ELEMENTS 10
WARNING: This program is protected by copyright law and international treaties.
Adobe
InstallShield
< Back
Next >
Cancel

ALERT: To install software you must locate the application file or the executable file. Often this is named Setup, Install or something similar. If you receive a message that the file you are trying to open can't be opened, you've chosen the wrong file.

HOT TIP: If you download software from the Internet, copy the installation files to a CD or DVD for safekeeping and write the product ID or key on it.

Use Program Compatibility Mode

If you install a software program but it doesn't work properly, you can run it in Program Compatibility Mode. This lets you run programs made for previous versions of Windows. Often this resolves software problems.

1. From the Start screen, type Program Compatibility.
2. Click Settings.
3. Click Run programs made for previous versions of Windows.
4. Click Next to begin.
5. Choose the problematic program. Click Next.
6. Click Troubleshoot problems.
7. Answer the questions as prompted.

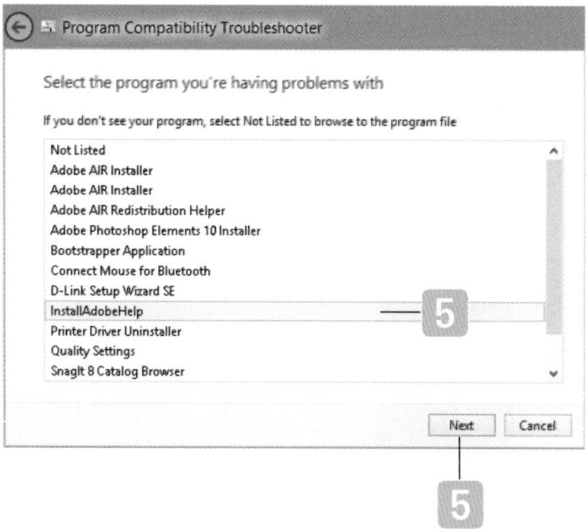

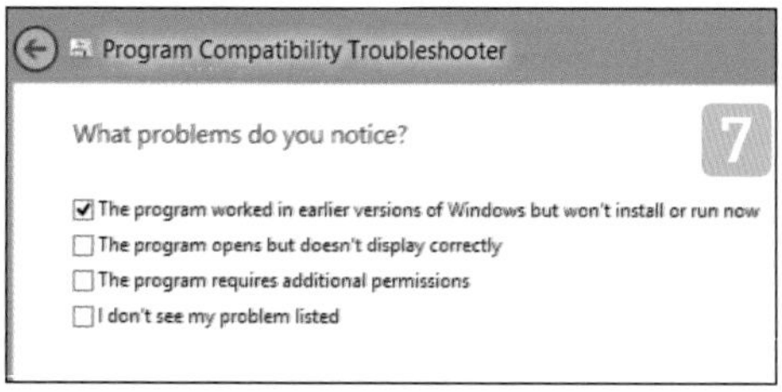

HOT TIP: Even programs made for Windows XP can be run in Program Compatibility Mode.

HOT TIP: Don't run anti-virus software in Program Compatibility Mode.

Resolve problems with the Action Center

If you've encountered problems that you can't resolve, have no fear. Windows 8 is working in the background to find solutions for you. You can check to see if any suitable solutions have been found in the Action Center.

1. Access the Desktop.
2. On the taskbar in the Notification area, click the flag icon.
3. Click Open Action Center.
4. If you see issues in the Action Center, such as not having anti-virus software installed, resolve those issues.
5. Click the arrow beside Maintenance.
6. Click Check for solutions.
7. If solutions are found, follow the prompts to resolve them.

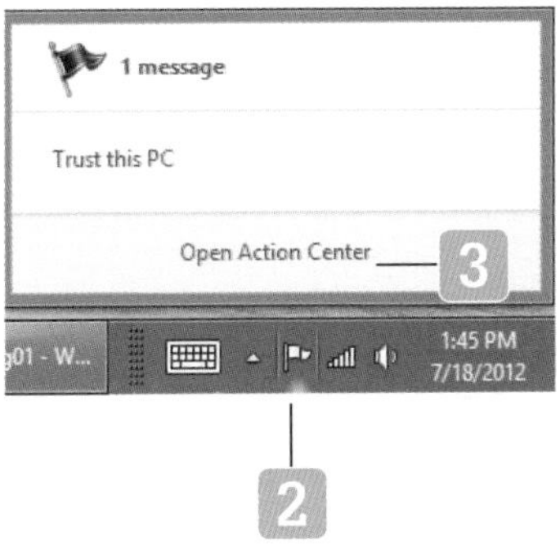

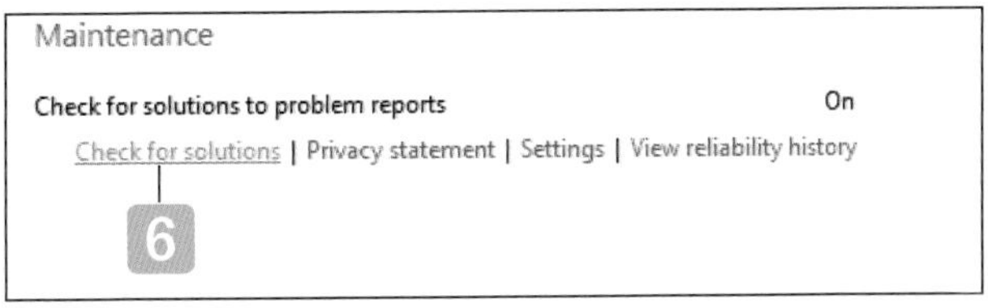

ALERT: You have to submit problem reports when prompted in order for Windows 8 to look for solutions!

DID YOU KNOW?
The Action Center offers troubleshooting wizards to help you resolve problems related to program installation, hardware, connecting to your network or the Internet, and system and security.

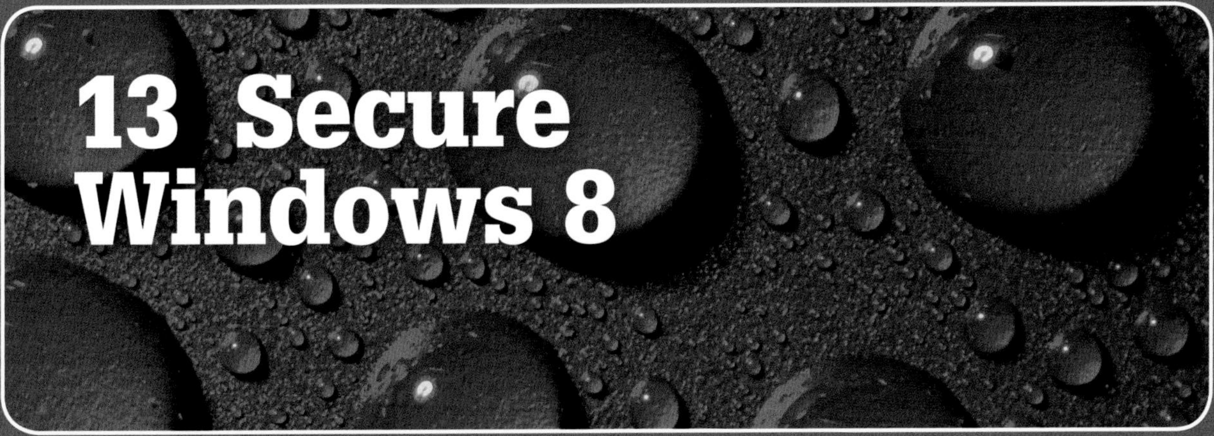

13 Secure Windows 8

Introduction

Windows 8 comes with a lot of built-in features to keep you and your data safe. The security tools and features help you avoid email scams, harmful websites and hackers, and also help you protect your data and your computer from unscrupulous co-workers or nosy family members. If you know how to take advantage of the available safeguards, you'll be protected in almost all cases. You just need to be aware of the dangers, heed security warnings when they are given (and resolve them), and use all of the available features in Windows 8 to protect yourself and your PC.

Install anti-virus software

Windows 8 does not come with anti-virus software. You have to obtain and install this yourself. It's extremely important to do this if you haven't already; it will protect your computer from known threats, viruses, malware and so on.

1. You can purchase popular anti-virus software from well-known companies such as Kaspersky, Symantec, AVG and McAfee.
2. You can obtain free and reliable anti-virus software from Microsoft: Microsoft Security Essentials. Visit www.microsoft.com to learn more.
3. Once you've installed the software, configure the software to check for updates and install them daily.

HOT TIP: Consider purchasing a book to help you learn more about staying safe, such as *Staying Safe Online*, an *In Simple Steps* guide from Pearson Education.

DID YOU KNOW?

If a threat does get by your anti-virus software, theoretically it can do less damage if you're logged on with a standard user account than if you are logged on with an administrator account. Consider creating a standard user account for yourself if you often access websites that aren't 'mainstream', where these threats are more prolific.

Verify security settings in Internet Explorer

Although you can configure a few security settings in the Internet Explorer app available from the Start screen, the full set of settings is only available from the Internet Explorer desktop app, available from the desktop.

1. From the desktop, open Internet Explorer.
2. Click the Tools icon and click Internet options.
3. From the General tab, note that you can delete your browsing history.
4. From the Security tab, note that you can configure security zones. Medium-high is best.
5. From the Privacy tab, note that you can turn on the Pop-up Blocker.
6. If desired, make changes and click OK.

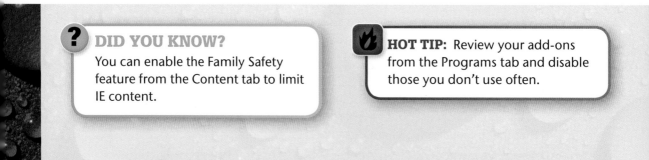

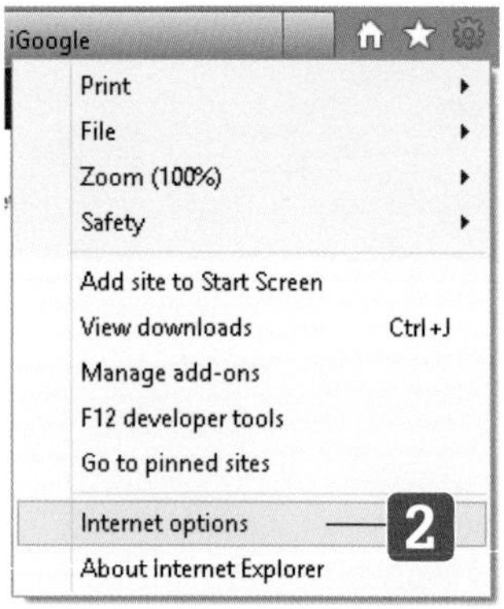

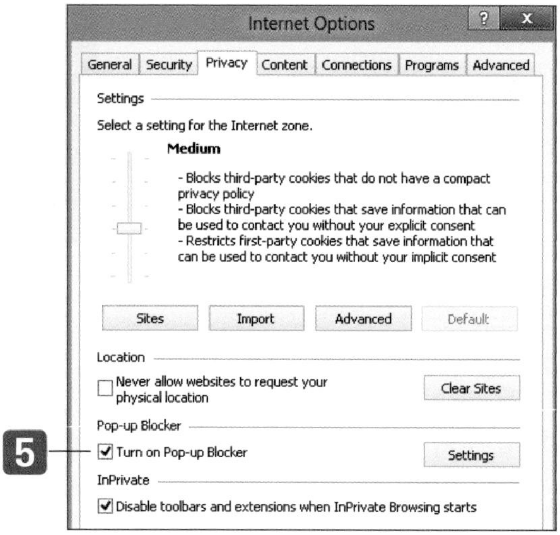

DID YOU KNOW?
You can enable the Family Safety feature from the Content tab to limit IE content.

HOT TIP: Review your add-ons from the Programs tab and disable those you don't use often.

Configure Windows Update

It's very important to configure Windows Update to get and install updates automatically. This is the easiest way to ensure your computer is as up to date as possible, at least as far as patching security flaws that Microsoft uncovers, having access to the latest features and obtaining updates to the operating system itself are concerned. I propose you verify that the recommended settings are enabled as detailed here and occasionally check for optional updates manually.

1. From the Start screen, type Update.
2. Click Settings; click Windows Update.
3. Verify that your computer is set to automatically install updates. If it is not, open the Action Center to remedy this.

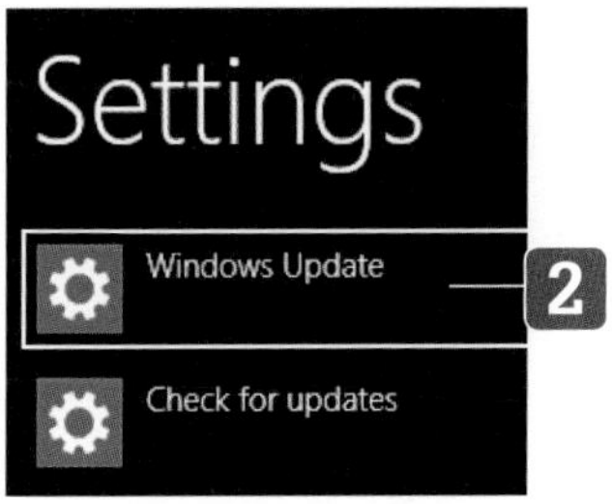
Settings
Windows Update
2
Check for updates

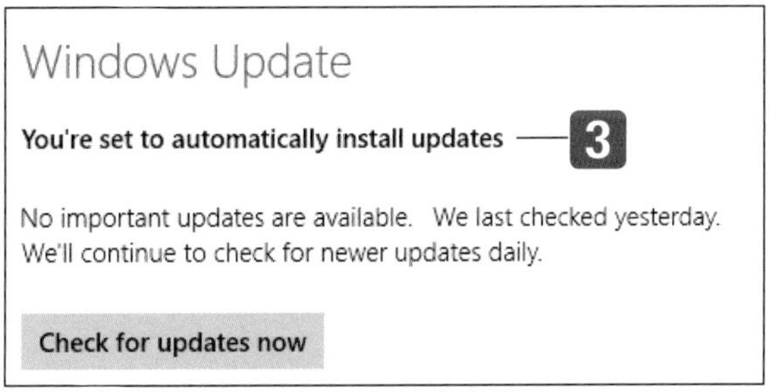
Windows Update
You're set to automatically install updates
3
No important updates are available. We last checked yesterday.
We'll continue to check for newer updates daily.
Check for updates now

SEE ALSO: Heed Action Center warnings, later in this chapter.

WHAT DOES THIS MEAN?

Windows Update: if enabled and configured properly, when you are online Windows 8 will check for security updates automatically and install them. You don't have to do anything and your PC is always updated with the latest security patches and features.

Use Windows Defender

You don't have to do much with Windows Defender except understand that it offers protection against some of the more common Internet threats. It's enabled by default and it runs in the background. However, if you ever think your computer has been attacked by an Internet threat or malware (adware, worm, spyware, etc.), you can run a manual scan here. Windows Defender or malware may be able to get rid of it.

1. Open Windows Defender. (You can search for it from the Start screen.)
2. Verify that Windows Defender is enabled and note the option to run a scan if desired.
3. Click the X in the top right corner to close the Windows Defender window.

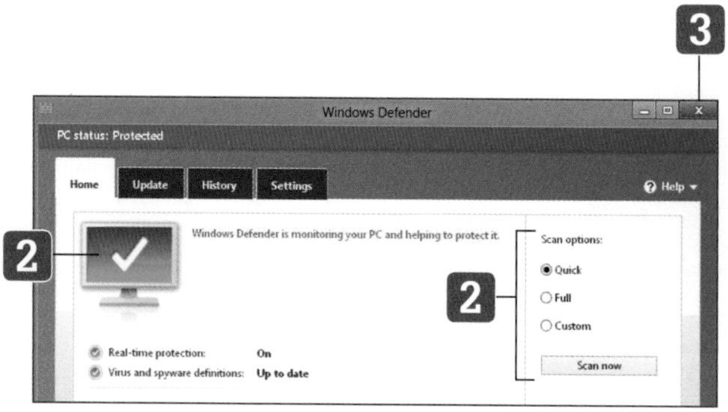

WHAT DOES THIS MEAN?

Malware: stands for malicious software. Malware includes such things as adware, worms and spyware, among others.

ALERT: Windows Defender and Windows Firewall will likely be disabled if you've purchased and installed a third-party anti-virus, anti-malware tool. Do not enable it if this is the case.

HOT TIP: Click each tab available from Windows Defender to explore all of the options.

Enable the firewall

Windows Firewall is a software program that checks the data that comes in from the Internet (or a local network) and then decides whether it's good data or bad. If it deems the data harmless, it will allow it to come though the firewall; if not, it's blocked.

1. Open Windows Firewall. (Type Firewall at the Start screen and click Settings to find it.)
2. Verify that the firewall is on. If not, select Turn Windows Firewall on or off, enable it, and click OK.
3. Review the other settings.

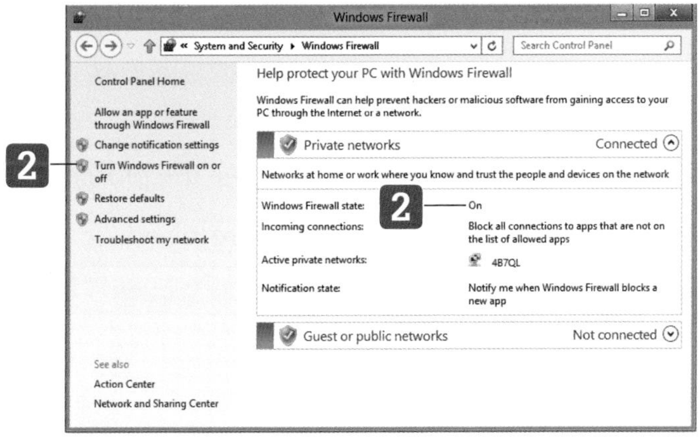

ALERT: You have to have a firewall (either Windows Firewall or a third-party firewall) to keep hackers from getting access to your PC and to help prevent your computer from sending out malicious code if it is ever attacked by a virus or worm.

DID YOU KNOW?

The first time you use a program that is blocked by Windows Firewall by default, you'll be prompted to 'unblock' the program. This is a safety feature to protect rogue programs from gaining unwanted access to your computer.

Heed Action Center warnings

Windows 8 tries hard to take care of your PC and your data. You'll be informed if your anti-virus software is out of date (or not installed), if you don't have the proper security settings configured or if Windows Update or the firewall is disabled. You can resolve these issues in the Action Center, a desktop application.

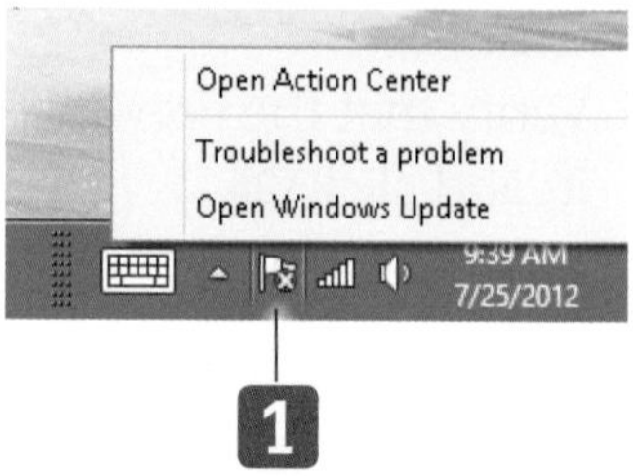

1. From the desktop, on the taskbar, locate the Action Center flag.
2. Right-click the flag icon and then click Open Action Center.
3. If there's anything in red, click the down-arrow (if necessary) to see the problem.
4. Click the button that offers the resolution suggestion to view the resolution option.
5. If there's anything in yellow, click the down-arrow to see the problem and solution.
6. Close the Action Center when all problems have been resolved.

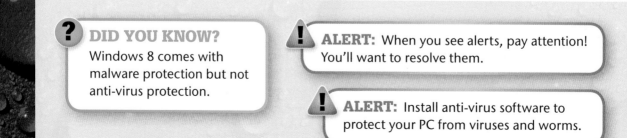

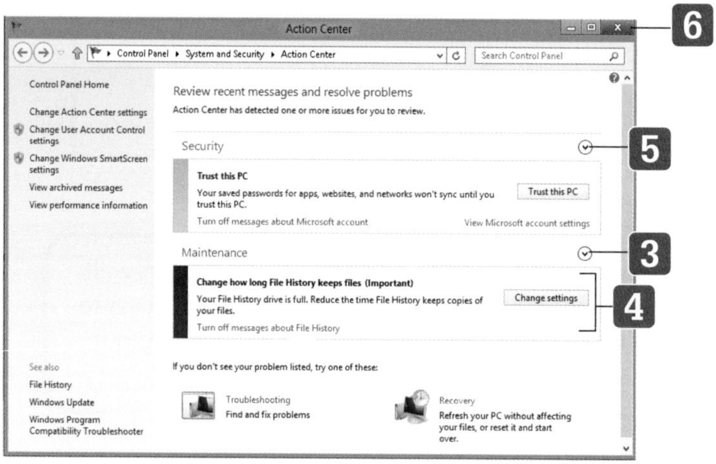

DID YOU KNOW?
Windows 8 comes with malware protection but not anti-virus protection.

ALERT: When you see alerts, pay attention! You'll want to resolve them.

ALERT: Install anti-virus software to protect your PC from viruses and worms.

Use File History

Most of the security features in Windows 8 are enabled by default. File History is not. File History saves copies of your files so you can get them back if they're lost or damaged. You'll need an external drive for File History for it to be effective.

1. Connect an external drive or make sure a network drive is available.
2. From the Start screen, type File History.
3. Click Settings, and then click File History.
4. In the File History window, click Turn on.
5. Wait while File History copies your files for the first time.

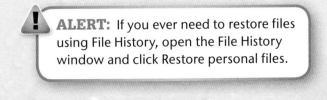

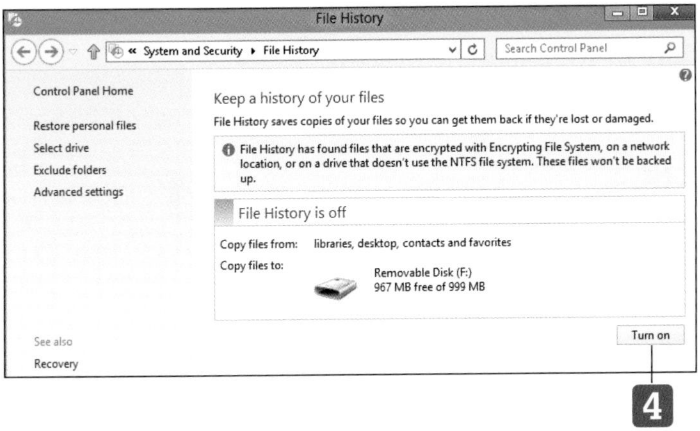
File History
« System and Security ▸ File History
Search Control Panel
Control Panel Home
Restore personal files
Select drive
Exclude folders
Advanced settings
See also
Recovery
Keep a history of your files
File History saves copies of your files so you can get them back if they're lost or damaged.
File History has found files that are encrypted with Encrypting File System, on a network location, or on a drive that doesn't use the NTFS file system. These files won't be backed up.
File History is off
Copy files from: libraries, desktop, contacts and favorites
Copy files to:
Removable Disk (F:)
967 MB free of 999 MB
Turn on
4

ALERT: If you ever need to restore files using File History, open the File History window and click Restore personal files.

HOT TIP: Click Advanced settings to change how often File History makes copies of files. Every hour is the default.

Verify user accounts

You learned earlier (see Chapter 6) that each user account on your computer should be protected with a password. You also learned how to verify that this is the case. Now you want to double-check this and remove unwanted user accounts.

1. Open Control Panel. If you need to, click the Back button to get to the main Control Panel window.
2. Click User Accounts and Family Safety, then click Remove user accounts.
3. First, verify that each user name has a password applied. Second, click any account to remove.
4. Click Delete the account.
5. Click Delete Files or Keep Files, as desired.
6. Do what is necessary to complete the process.

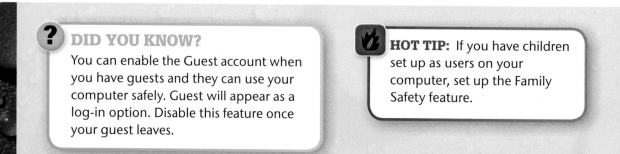

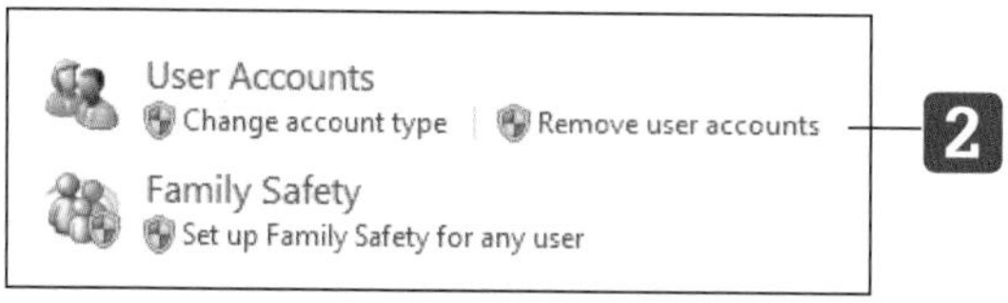

DID YOU KNOW?
You can enable the Guest account when you have guests and they can use your computer safely. Guest will appear as a log-in option. Disable this feature once your guest leaves.

HOT TIP: If you have children set up as users on your computer, set up the Family Safety feature.

Configure a password-protected screen saver

Your computer will automatically sleep after a specific amount of idle time (requiring you to input your password when you're ready to use the computer again), but you can configure a screen saver to engage after as little as one minute of inactivity. You can also configure your computer to display the log-on screen when you are ready to access the computer again.

1. Open Control Panel.
2. Click Appearance and Personalization.
3. Click Change screen saver.
4. Select a screen saver, choose how long to wait, and place a tick in On resume, display logon screen.
5. Click OK.

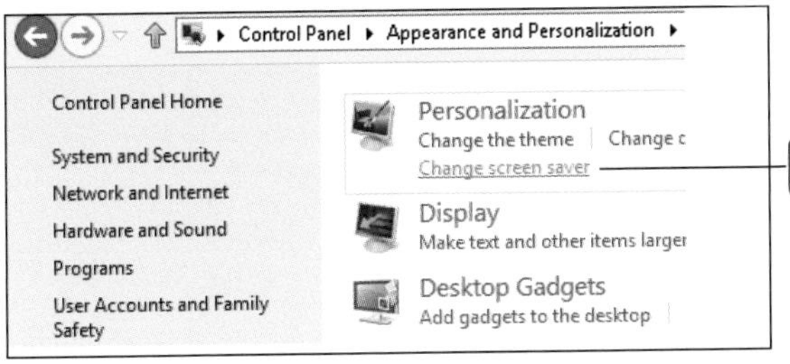

3

4

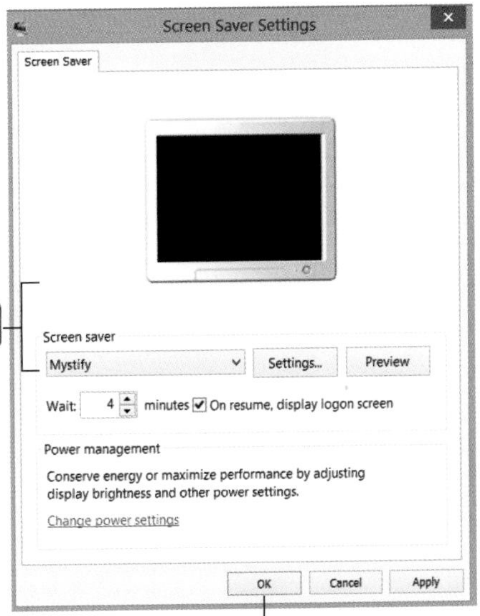

5

HOT TIP: If you work on sensitive data regularly that you don't want anyone else to see, make sure you set a screen saver to engage after a very short amount of idle time.

ALERT: The Bubble screen saver is see-through. Even when it's engaged you can still see what's on the screen. Select something else if you're looking for privacy.

Top 10 Windows 8 Problems Solved

Problem 1: I want to change what happens when I connect something or insert a CD or DVD

When you connect a USB drive, a smartphone, a memory card, or insert a blank CD or DVD into the appropriate drive (among other things), Windows 8 might ask you what you'd like to do. It might not. You can configure exactly what you want to happen so that you aren't prompted every time, and so that the desired action happens by default.

1. Insert or connect media.
2. When you see the prompt, click it. (If you miss the prompt, disconnect and reconnect the media.)

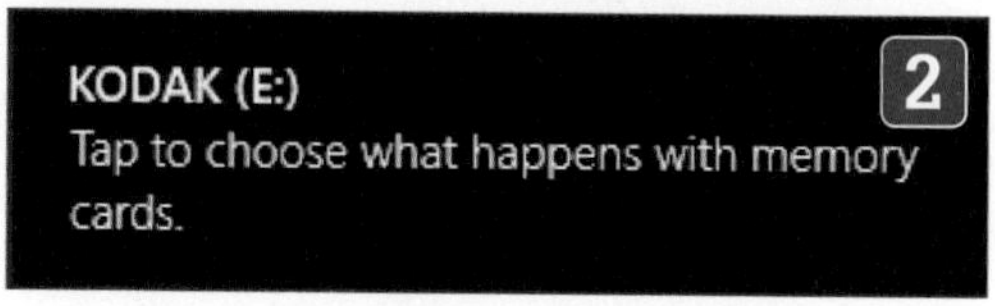

3. Click the desired action. The next time you insert this same media, the default action will occur automatically, and you will not be prompted.
4. If you decide later to change the default action, open the AutoPlay settings. You can search for AutoPlay from the Start screen.
5. From the AutoPlay window, you can change the default action you've already set, or set new ones.

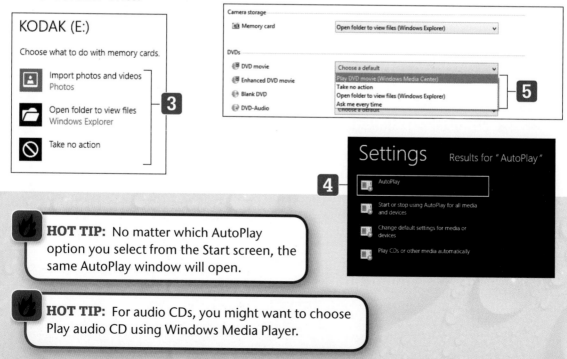

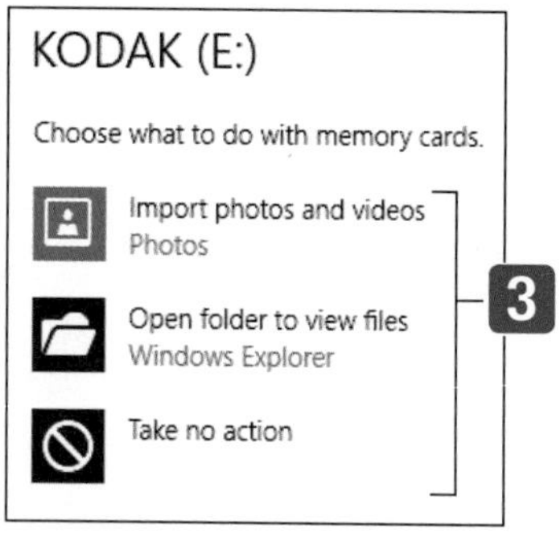

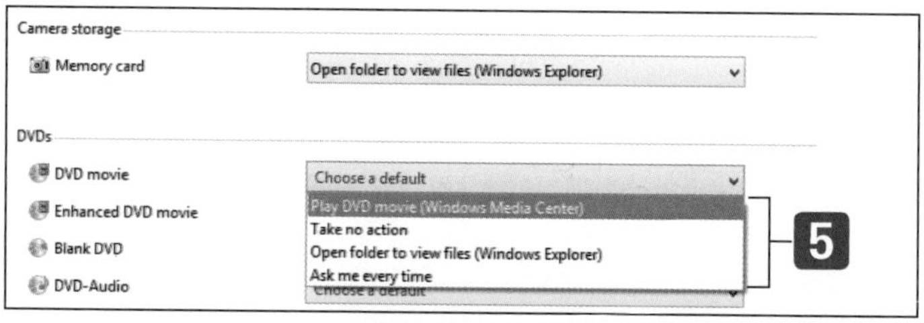

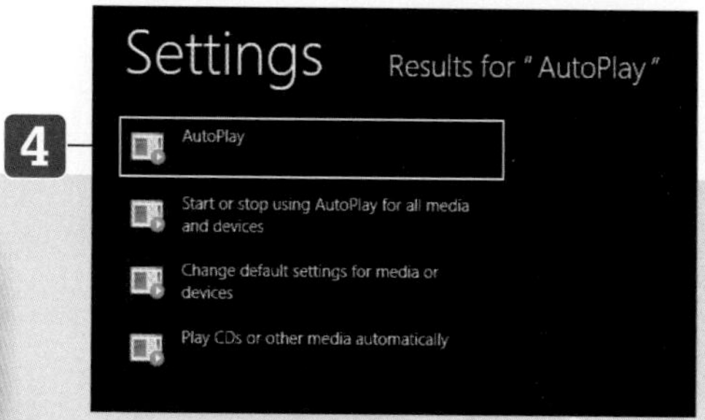

HOT TIP: No matter which AutoPlay option you select from the Start screen, the same AutoPlay window will open.

HOT TIP: For audio CDs, you might want to choose Play audio CD using Windows Media Player.

Problem 2: My computer keeps going to sleep and I don't want it to

Your computer is configured to go to sleep after a specific period of idle time. In addition, the display will turn off after a time too. If you aren't happy with the current configuration, you can change this behaviour.

1. From the Start screen, type Power.
2. Click Settings, and click Power Options.
3. Next to the selected plan, Balanced, click Change plan settings.
4. Use the drop-down lists to make changes as desired.
5. Click Save changes.

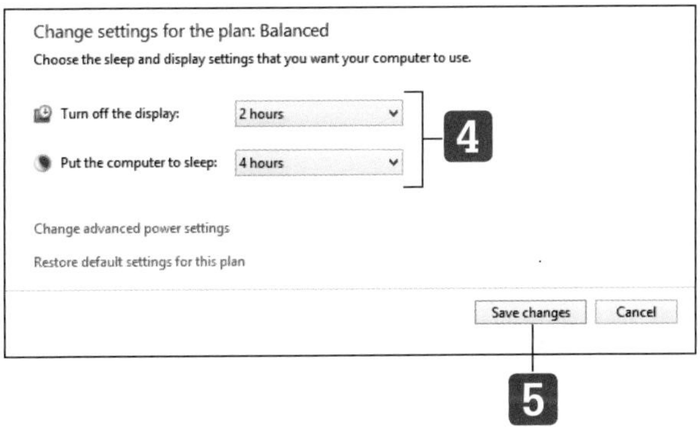

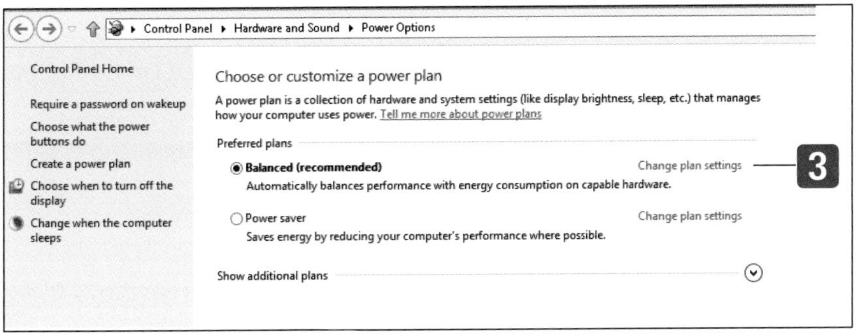

DID YOU KNOW?
You can restore any power plan's defaults by clicking Restore default settings for this plan.

HOT TIP: If you have a laptop or tablet, you'll see two sets of settings, one for when the computer is running on batteries and one for when it's plugged in.

Problem 3: I can't get my new hardware device to install

If hardware isn't working as it should be, you can search for a new driver. The driver is what facilitates the exchange of information between the device and the computer. If you download and install a new driver for a piece of hardware and it doesn't work properly, you can use Device Driver Rollback to return to the previously installed driver.

1 From the Start screen, type device manager.

2 Click Settings, and click Device Manager.

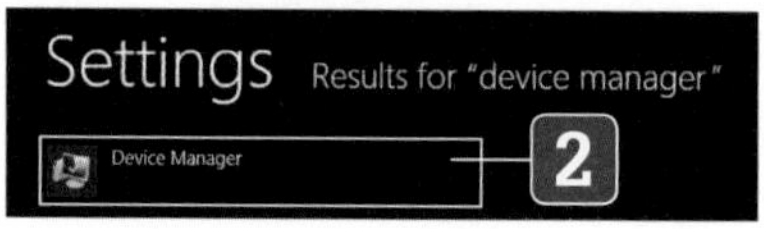

3 Click the right-facing arrow next to the problematic hardware (if applicable). It will change to a down-facing arrow.

4 Double-click the device name.

ALERT: You can roll back only to the previous driver. This means that if you have a driver (D) and then install a new driver (D1) and it doesn't work, and then you install another driver (D2) and it doesn't work, using Device Driver Rollback will revert to D1, not the driver (D) before it.

DID YOU KNOW?
Many items of hardware have multiple connections and connection types. If one type of connection doesn't work, like USB, try FireWire.

5 Click the Driver tab.

6 To search for a new driver, click Update Driver. To reinstall the previous driver, click Roll Back Driver.

7 Follow the prompts to complete the selected task.

8 Click OK.

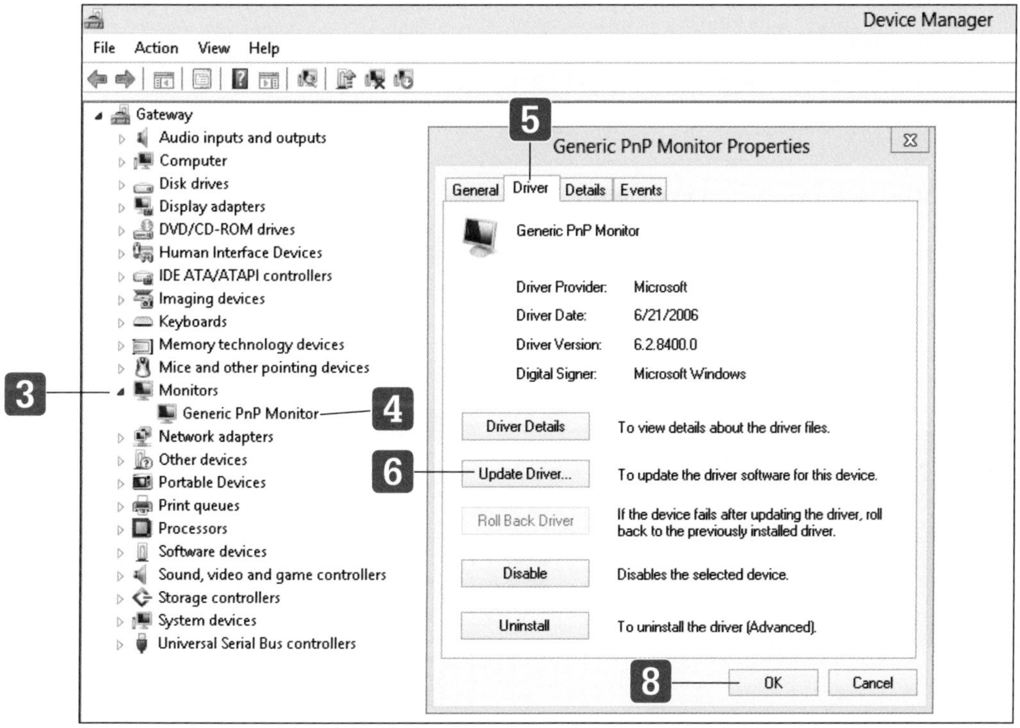

ALERT: If you see a red X or a yellow exclamation mark when you open Device Manager, that device isn't working properly or is working under limited capacity.

ALERT: The Roll Back Driver option will be available only if a new driver has been installed.

Problem 4: My computer seems to be running slowly, or, I've seen a message that I'm running out of disk space

Disk Cleanup is a maintenance tool that can help you rid your computer of unnecessary files. This should improve performance and keep your computer running in tip-top shape.

1. From the Start screen, type Disk Clean.
2. Click Settings and then click Free up disk space by deleting unnecessary files.
3. Choose the files to delete.
4. Click OK.

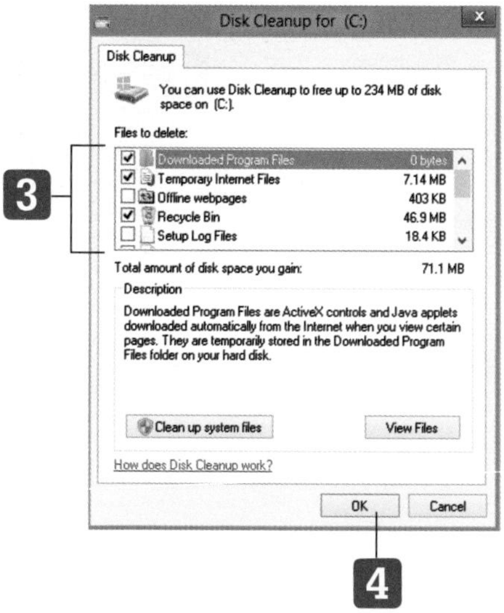

HOT TIP: Run Disk Cleanup monthly.

DID YOU KNOW?
It's okay to select all of the options listed in Disk Cleanup and delete them all. However, you may want to keep items in the Recycle Bin until you're sure you don't need them.

Problem 5: I've installed an app that I don't want any more (or doesn't work)

It's unlikely that apps will be troublesome; they simply may not work as well as you'd like. You may decide you don't need or want them too. You can uninstall apps you no longer want from the Start screen.

1. From the Start screen, right-click the app to uninstall. (You can also tap and drag downwards to make the selection.)
2. From the toolbar, click Uninstall.
3. Click Uninstall again when prompted.

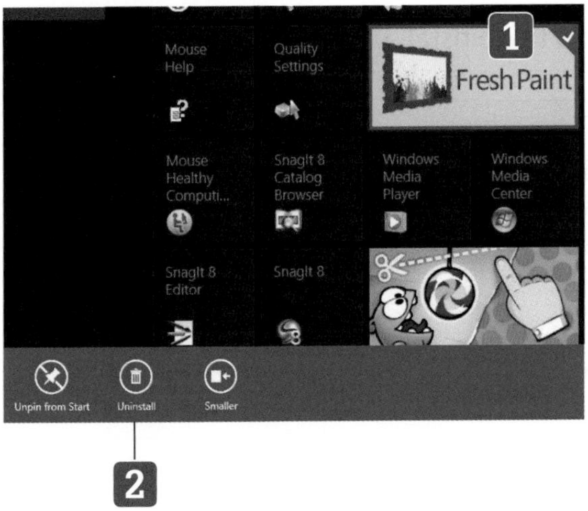

HOT TIP: If you think you might want to use an app later and simply want to remove it from the Start screen, right-click it and select Unpin from Start.

DID YOU KNOW?
If you uninstall an app and decide you want it back, you can probably get it from the Store.

Problem 6: I have desktop programs I never use or that don't work

If you haven't used a desktop application in more than a year, you probably never will. You can uninstall unwanted programs from the Control Panel. You should also uninstall programs that don't work, or consider running them in Program Compatibility Mode (Chapter 12).

1. Open Control Panel.
2. In Control Panel, click Uninstall a program.
3. Scroll through the list. Click the program to uninstall.
4. Click Uninstall.
5. Follow the prompts to uninstall the program.

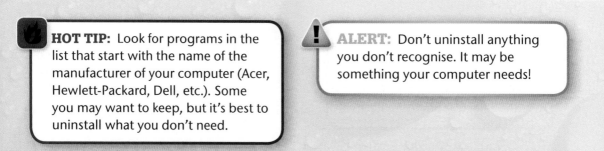

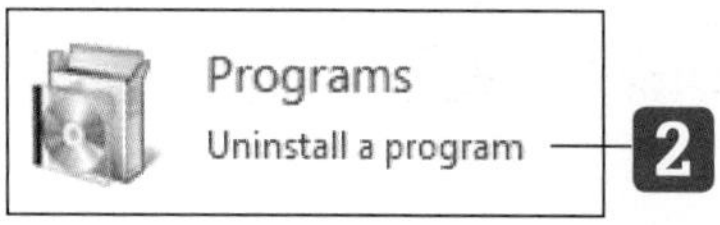

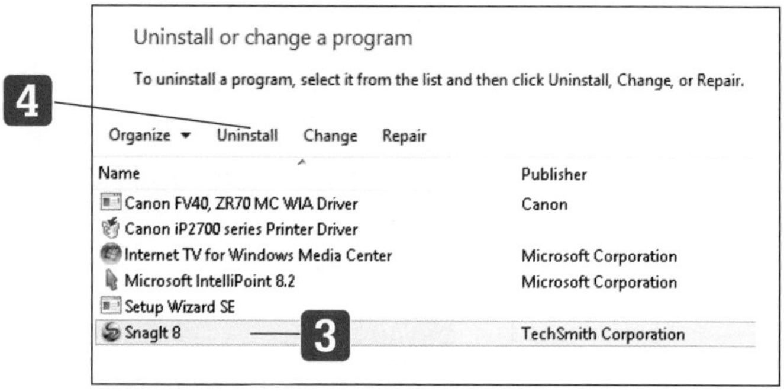

HOT TIP: Look for programs in the list that start with the name of the manufacturer of your computer (Acer, Hewlett-Packard, Dell, etc.). Some you may want to keep, but it's best to uninstall what you don't need.

ALERT: Don't uninstall anything you don't recognise. It may be something your computer needs!

Problem 7: My computer takes a long time to boot up, or, it seems to run slower than it should

Lots of programs and applications start when you turn on your computer. This can cause the start-up process to take longer than it needs to. Additionally, desktop applications that start with Windows also run in the background, and can hamper computer performance. You should disable unwanted start-up items to improve all-around performance.

1. At the Start screen, type Task Manager. (You can also click Ctrl + Alt + Del.)
2. Click Task Manager in the results.
3. Click the Startup tab.
4. Select a third-party program you recognise but do not use daily.
5. Click Disable.

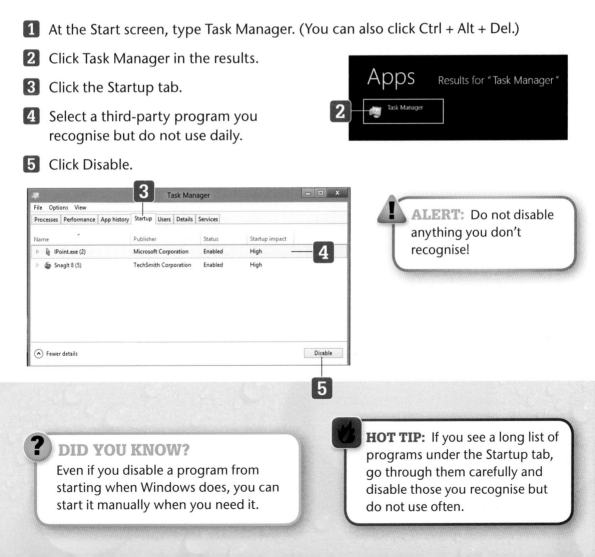

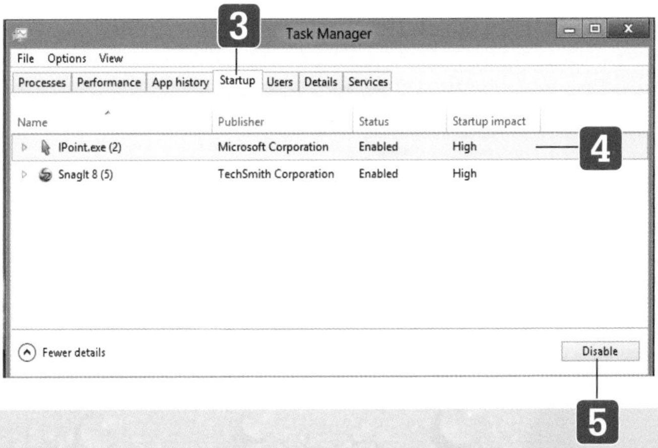

ALERT: Do not disable anything you don't recognise!

DID YOU KNOW?
Even if you disable a program from starting when Windows does, you can start it manually when you need it.

HOT TIP: If you see a long list of programs under the Startup tab, go through them carefully and disable those you recognise but do not use often.

Problem 8: My computer is in a real mess and I think I should reinstall it; what are my options?

If your computer isn't running well, you can refresh it. When you do, all third-party programs you've installed from discs or websites are removed and your computer settings are returned to their defaults. This resolves almost all problems most users will encounter. Apps from the Windows Store will remain, as will your photos, music, videos and other personal files, so you won't have to start from scratch once the restore is complete.

1. Access the Settings charm.
2. Click Change PC settings.
3. Click the General tab.
4. Scroll to locate Refresh your PC without affecting your files.
5. Click Get started.
6. Read the information offered, click Next, and work through the refresh process.

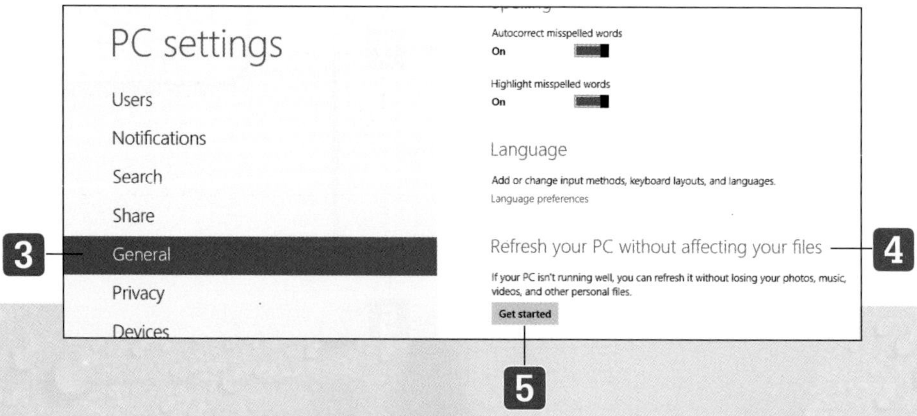

HOT TIP: Only refresh your PC if other options have failed to fix the problem.

ALERT: Before you refresh your PC, locate the product codes you'll need to reinstall third-party programs.

Problem 9: I need to return my computer to factory settings, or, refreshing the PC did not resolve my problem

If refreshing your PC doesn't resolve your existing problem, then you'll have to reset your PC and start again from scratch. When you do, everything will be deleted, including all of your personal files. You'll need to back up these files before continuing here. This is a drastic step, so be sure this is what you want to do before you do it.

1. Access the Settings charm.
2. Click Change PC settings.
3. Click the General tab.
4. Scroll to locate Remove everything and reinstall Windows.
5. Click Get started.

ALERT: Reset your PC before you sell it or give it away.

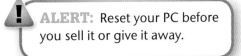

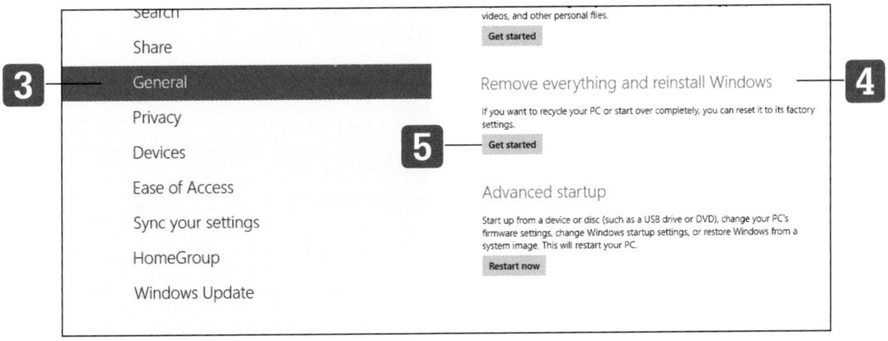
Search
Share
General
Privacy
Devices
Ease of Access
Sync your settings
HomeGroup
Windows Update
videos, and other personal files.
Get started
Remove everything and reinstall Windows
If you want to recycle your PC or start over completely, you can reset it to its factory settings.
Get started
Advanced startup
Start up from a device or disc (such as a USB drive or DVD), change your PC's firmware settings, change Windows startup settings, or restore Windows from a system image. This will restart your PC.
Restart now
3
4
5

HOT TIP: The option under Remove everything and reinstall Windows is Advanced startup. Choose this option to boot from a USB or DVD, change Windows startup settings, restore from a system image and more.

ALERT: If you reset your PC, when it starts again it'll perform, act and look just like it did the day you brought it home!

Problem 10: I need to fix a minor problem, how do I use System Restore?

System Restore lets you undo system changes and return your computer to the state it was in at a previous time. You do this by selecting a 'restore point', which is a point in time when the computer last worked properly.

1. From the Start screen, type System. In the results, click System.
2. In the System window, click System protection.
3. Click System Restore.
4. Work through the wizard to select point of return, and wait while the process completes.

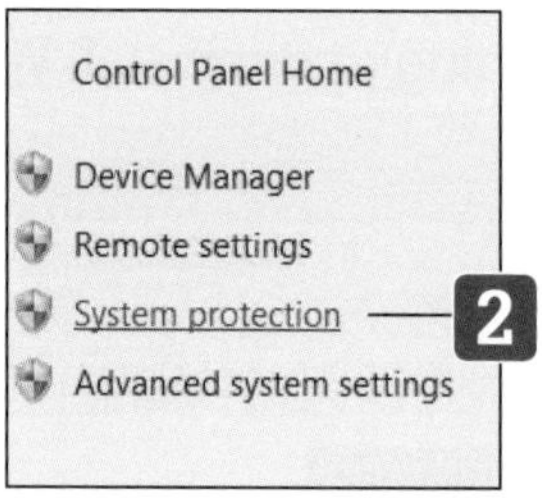

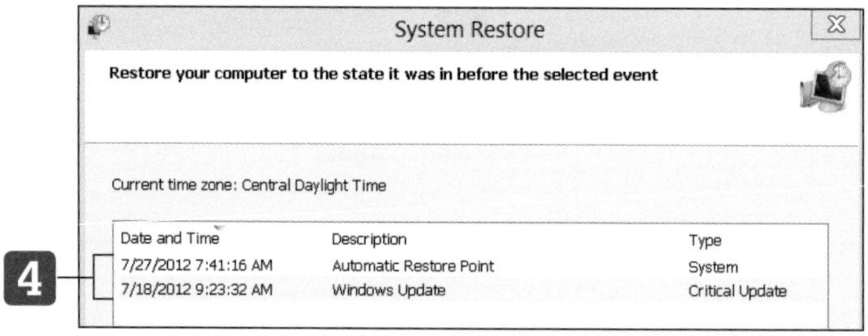

HOT TIP: Your computer will restart during the System Restore process.